Revenue Management and Pricing:
Case Studies and Applications

REVENUE MANAGEMENT AND PRICING:
Case Studies and Applications

Edited by

IAN YEOMAN AND
UNA McMAHON-BEATTIE

THOMSON

Australia • Canada • Mexico • Singapore • Spain • United Kingdom • United States

Revenue management and pricing: Case studies and applications

Copyright © Ian Yeoman and Una McMahon-Beattie 2004

The Thomson logo is a registered trademark used herein under licence.

For more information, contact Thomson Learning, High Holborn House, 50-51 Bedford Row, London WC1R 4LR or visit us on the World Wide Web at:
http://www.thomsonlearning.co.uk

British Library Cataloguing-in-Publication Data
A catalogue record for this book is available from the British Library

ISBN-13: 978-1-84480-062-9
ISBN-10: 1-84480-062-8

Published by Thomson Learning 2004
Reprinted 2005 by Thomson Learning

Typeset by YHT Ltd, London
Printed in the UK by TJ International, Padstow Cornwall

To Dad

Ian Yeoman

To my mother, Ellen

Una McMahon-Beattie

Contents

Contents

Editors and Contributors

Ian Yeoman is an established champion and expert in the field of revenue management, over 60 works having been published in journals, books and conferences. Ian is the founding editor of the *Journal of Revenue and Pricing Management* and contributing editor to *Yield Management: Strategies for the Service Industries.*

Una McMahon-Beattie is a lecturer, researcher and consultant at the University of Ulster. She graduated with an MSc in international hotel management from the University of Surrey. Her research interests focus on the areas of revenue management, variable pricing and consumer trust. She has published widely in the UK and internationally in these areas. Una is co-editor of *Yield Management: Strategies for the Service Industries* and the Practice Editor for the *Journal of Revenue and Pricing Management.*

Gerald Barlow is Lecturer in Operations Management and Management Science at Canterbury Business School, University of Kent at Canterbury. His current research area involves work with the NHS on problems around queuing and queuing psychology, and in issues related to capacity and capacity management.

Raul Bermudez is currently the Director of Global Charter Sales and Revenue Management for The Moorings, the world's premier yacht charter organization. Bermudez is responsible for the worldwide charter sales organization, pricing and fleet planning. Prior to joining The Moorings, Raul spent ten years at Ryder where he served in a variety of roles, from pricing consultant to computer systems designer.

Montgomery Blair has worked both on the client and vendor side of revenue management systems for the past five years. He is currently the Director of Science for Dollar Thrifty Automotive Group, Inc., where he is most passionate about the pricing, business strategy, price elasticity, performance measurement and training aspects of revenue management application. He is past President and Chair and currently sits on the Board of Directors for the INFORMS (Institute for Operations Research and Management Science) Revenue Management and Pricing Section and is on the editorial board of the *Journal of Revenue and Pricing Management*. He holds a BS and MS in economics from the Colorado School of Mines.

Mike Boella is Honorary Faculty Fellow at the University of Brighton. He is co-author of *Principles of Hospitality Law* together with barrister Alan Pannett. Mike worked for Forte and Co., Bass and PriceWaterhouse before joining the University of Brighton. Mike also teaches at the University of Applied Sciences in Bad Honnef, Germany, at the Ecole Hoteliere de Lausanne, and he is also a visiting professor at the University of Perpignan. He is editor of a number of Croner CCH Catering publications.

Elizabeth Carnegie lectures in tourism at Napier University. A graduate of Edinburgh University and Museum Studies, Leicester, she worked at Glasgow Museums, becoming Deputy Director of North East Lincolnshire Museums prior to entering academia. She is working towards a PhD in feminist geography at Edinburgh University, has published on museums and oral history and is reviews editor of *Oral History Journal*.

Dietrich Chen is a member of senior management at Grupo Financiero Uno – a Central American financial services group. He received an MA in mathematics from the Claremont Graduate University in 1995 and a PhD in operations research from Cornell University in 2000. Before joining Grupo Financiero Uno, he was a senior consultant at McKinsey & Company.

Tamara Dieck is a vice president at Veritec Solutions, a revenue management and pricing consulting firm. Ms Dieck specializes in the application of management science and statistical tools to design customized solutions. She enjoys variety and has worked on revenue management assignments in the airline, boat charter, car rental, cruise line, e-commerce, hotel, passenger rail, self-storage, timeshare, tour operator and trucking industries.

Catherine Drudy is a research student at Napier University, interested in the revenue and health issues of sex tourism in Edinburgh.

Michael Freimer is an assistant professor in management science and information systems at the Smeal College of Business Administration at the Pennsylvania State University. He received a PhD in operations research from Cornell University in 2001, and afterwards spent a year as a visiting assistant professor at Cornell's School of Hotel Administration.

Douglas Harvey is currently a forecast analyst at The Goodyear Tire & Rubber Company, working at their world headquarters offices in Akron, Ohio. He received his BS in mathematics from Rensselaer Polytechnic Institute (Troy, NY) and his MS in statistics from the University of Illinois at Urbana-Champaign. Prior to joining Goodyear, Doug served as a research scientist for PROS Revenue Management in Houston, Texas.

Thriné Hely worked in the travel industry for 28 years prior to entering higher education. The majority of that time she worked for scheduled and charter airlines. From 1996–9 she served as a member of the Air Transport Users Council (AUC). During this time she was a member of the Economic Policy Committee for the Council and represented them on the Gatwick Airport Consultative Committee (Passenger Services Sub-Committee). Having studied for a part-time MBA from 1990–2, Thriné is now studying for a PhD.

Julian Hoseason is the Academic Dean at the Bulle Campus of the Glion Institute for Higher Education based in Switzerland. His professional background started in tour operations and his teaching has focused on tourism, operations management, the heritage and attractions sector, gravity modelling and the development of e-learning in higher education. His research interests focus on capacity and revenue management across the tourism industry. He is also the editor of a specialist web site, polandinexile.com, that has recorded the testimonies and archive material of WWII veterans.

Nick Johns is Honorary Professor of Service Sector Management at Queen Margaret College, Edinburgh, and Senior Visiting Fellow at the Centre for Regional and Tourism Research, Bornholm, Denmark. He is well known for his work on the quality and productivity of hospitality operations and has published widely in these areas.

Sheryl E. Kimes is Professor of Operations Management in the School of Hotel Administration at Cornell University. She holds a PhD in operations management from the University of Texas–Austin and specializes in the teaching, research and practice of revenue management in a wide variety of industries.

Boet Kreiken is Senior Vice President, Pricing & Revenue Management. His responsibilities include NWA/KLM joint venture RM activities as well as responsibilities with other partners such as Kenya Airways. During 1999–2000 he was responsible for international pricing and revenue management of the KLM/Alitalia joint venture based in Rome. Boet is a member of the editorial board of the *Journal of Revenue and Pricing Management*.

Kenneth D. Lawrence is Professor of Management and Marketing Science in the School of Management at the New Jersey Institute of Technology. He has 227 published works in the areas of management science, statistics and forecasting. His publications can be found in 24 journals and he has been cited a great number of times in over 50 journals.

Warren Lieberman is President of Veritec Solutions, a consulting and software development firm specializing in custom revenue management and pricing solutions. He holds a PhD in operations research from Yale University. Dr Lieberman began his career in revenue management in 1984 with American Airlines. He has served as Chairman of the Yield Management Study Group of the Airline Group of the International Federation of Operations Research Societies (AGIFORS). Warren is a recognized authority on non-traditional implementations of revenue management, with his experience spanning many industries. He is a member of the editorial board of the *Journal of Revenue and Pricing Management*.

Patrick Liu is a senior consultant in operations research and revenue/pricing optimization. He holds a PhD from the University of Toronto. He has successfully completed systems such as the optimal natural gas trading/pricing/transportation for Williams Energy, pricing/revenue optimization and demand forecasting systems for major hotels (including Starwood Hotels & Resorts chains, MGM Grand in Las Vegas, and Swissôtels), optimal pricing/bandwidth trading/product portfolio/traffic routing for telecom providers, and a production planning/workforce scheduling system for the US postal service.

Adrian Palmer is Professor of Services Marketing at the University of Gloucestershire Business School, Cheltenham, UK. After holding marketing management positions within the travel industry, he joined academia where he has researched buyer–seller relationships within the services sector. Recent research has been published in the

European Journal of Marketing, Journal of Marketing Management, Journal of Strategic Marketing and *Journal of Services Marketing.*

Charlotte Rassing is employed as a tourism researcher at the Centre for Regional and Tourism Research in Bornholm. At the same time she works as a project manager at IFKA in Copenhagen where she is responsible for the publication *Quarterly Economic Outlook* and the preparation of forecasting models.

Ruth Robertson studied tourism management at Napier University, Edinburgh, with a special interest in the social and political issues of sex tourism in Scotland.

Nicola Secomandi earned a PhD in operations research and statistics in 1998 and an MS in computer science in 1993, both from the University of Houston, Houston, TX. After joining PROS Revenue Management in 1998, he spent part of 2001 as a research associate in the Department of Civil and Environmental Engineering at Cornell University, Ithaca, NY. His research interests include decision support to the energy industry, dynamic pricing/revenue management, and investment science. He is a member of The Institute of Operations Research and the Management Sciences.

Julie Swann is an assistant professor in the School of Industrial and Systems Engineering at the Georgia Institute of Technology. She is currently focused on the modelling and analysis of problems and algorithms in logistics, and supply chain management, with particular interest in pricing and revenue management. Recent awards include the Council of Logistics Management Doctoral Dissertation Award (2002) for her thesis in dynamic pricing for manufacturing.

Theodore Valkov is Director of Product Development at PROS Revenue Management, where he is pursuing his long-time interest in the creation of enterprise software that uses fact and science-based analysis to help companies improve and automate commercial decision-making. Pricing optimization is one such application that has enjoyed substantial business interest in the recent year. Theodore holds a ScD in computer modelling and management of technology from MIT, and served as Business Development Advisor for Shell International prior to joining PROS.

Richard H. Zeni is Director of Revenue Management Optimization for US Airways. He has over twenty years of airline industry experience that includes working in all areas of airport operations. He holds a PhD in management science from Rutgers University. His recent work includes research into unconstraining demand and developing best practices for implementing and operating an O&D revenue management system.

Foreword

Companies that are better at fulfilling customer needs make better returns. In the current state of the world economy and cut-throat competition, the essence for survival is to create more customer value as perceived by your customers relative to your competitors. Low inflation and global competition are fierce barriers to price increases. Many companies have already jumped through hoops to cut costs and productivity. So now they need to create new products, additional value and other ways to generate more revenues from their customers.

Apart from world-class product development, pricing and revenue management are key to success. Pricing is vital in attracting and capturing demand. Pricing is also fundamental in optimizing your product's true worth out there in the real market-place, while revenue management is managing and controlling displacements (do not sell now, if you can get more later or vice versa). Pricing is more concerned with dilution. Without having the right segmentation and distribution and terms and conditions in place, a customer could be willing to pay more but you yourself could unintentionally be offering the same product at a lower price, basically destroying value.

In the age of internet transparency, sometimes distressed inventories and, for example, low-cost product offerings, the balancing act of managing customer value, pricing and revenue management practices should be managed as a whole and not as independent entities.

This new book delivers a wealth of new cases, best practices and a broad range of experiences covering many industries and service sectors. It also complements Una and Ian's other book *Yield Management: Strategies for the Services Industries*, as it shows how revenue management really works in practice. The book is both aimed at practitioners and MBA students mastering the growing profession of pricing and revenue management worldwide. It covers a wide diversity of case studies and applications.

Within KLM, pricing, revenue management and forecasting are considered core competencies. We invest heavily in systems as well as in the 'intellectual human capital' of our staff, in order to stay ahead of competition. It is strategic to continuously invest in these areas, and it pays off well.

I am sure that this state-of-the-art book will contribute further to the effective application and growing understanding of revenue management and pricing tactics and strategies.

E.J. Kreiken
KLM Royal Dutch Airlines
Senior Vice President Pricing & Revenue Management

Introduction: Using the Book

Revenue Management and Pricing is an extension of our previous book *Yield Management: Strategies for the Service Industries*. This first book provided readers with the necessary underpinning theory, knowledge and application of yield management. This new, case study book, treats revenue management and pricing as a practical subject that is more than a management science algorithm. It is certainly an area that deserves wider reading and dissemination. One of the best ways to learn is to benchmark best practice through telling a story of 'how in fact, revenue management is practised': hence the purpose of this book. Opening this case book will help the reader gain an insight into revenue management and pricing. It will allow the practitioner and student to develop a useful understanding of the complexities of this often misunderstood scientific subject. More importantly, the book will give you the opportunity to know how Revenue Managers work, how they face the issues and how they work with problems. The book is an opportunity for readers to assess, experiment and learn from leading academics, researchers and practitioners. Essentially, the book will allow you to:

- Search for best practice examples of revenue management and pricing.
- Give you a chance to evaluate real situations faced by Revenue Managers.
- Gain useful insight into Revenue Managers' thinking.
- Assess a problem, without the pressures of operational time.
- Reflect upon suggested solutions from the case studies.
- Debate, discuss and interpret revenue management scenarios, that could improve your business performance.
- Understand revenue management and pricing in a wider context of business.

All the cases in this book are designed to provoke debate and thinking within the realms of revenue and pricing decisions. The cases have been selected in order that the practitioner can understand a specific application in different industries or evoke issues and implications. Its purpose is to promote discussion as how the Revenue Managers might improve the business and contribute to organizational objectives, through a range of skills and techniques needed to understand and practise revenue management and pricing. Analysis of the cases allows you the opportunity to apply and test out many of the ideas and examples of best practice from industry and academia.

The book asks you a number of things: either to understand a situation and its implications or provide a solution to a specific problem. Reading the case studies is the equivalent of observing the practices of revenue management and pricing, in order to understand the context of the situation. You will be able to:

- Draw upon the facts, whether hard or soft, in order to form a precise account of the problem situation.
- Infer facts, in order that a problem can be reconstructed in such a manner that draws logic to a chaotic or unstructured account.
- Find out what the purpose of the case study is all about, which will allow you to conclude possible aims and objectives of the case study.

Many of the cases are subjective, and they include hearsay statements or opinions which are not factual. But they are a reliable source of information that can shape debate in order to understand the practices of revenue management and pricing. Also, the nature of case studies is often based upon assumptions that require an interpretation and subjectivity when analysing the cases.

The next stage involves analysing the situation in order to determine the elements of the case studies. It is a process of breaking down the issues and bringing to the surface assumptions that determine the component parts of the case studies. A good idea is for the reader to use mind maps in order to map out the most important issues and related components. This will help you summarize your findings in a graphic format, which assists thinking and makes it easier. Many students use cause and effect diagrams as a means to identify root causes and show logical connections in the case studies. This simple process of identification forms the basis of an analysis of the case studies, in which solutions or options can be developed.

Having spent time analysing a case study, the reader needs to move forward to identify possible options in order to take a course of action. Readers will find a range of questions in each case study, which will have multiple answers. The purpose of the questions is to shape debate rather than provide a final solution. As revenue management and pricing solutions are never a final answer but rather a purposeful answer, the searching of solutions involves the reader in developing and evaluating options. The process of evaluation means determining the value or worth of solutions, through using criteria such as feasibility, acceptance and risk. But once this decision is taken, the reader then turns to the issues of implementation. Implementation is concerned with questions of when, speed, cost, times and order that leads to the implementation of revenue management and pricing decisions.

Therefore, the aim of this book is to provide readers with a practical insight into the workings of revenue management and pricing which will cross the diversity of industries and provide meaningful knowledge of application. So enjoy your journey of discovery and learning.

Ian Yeoman and Una McMahon-Beattie

1

Revenue Management Basics in the Charter Boat Industry

Raul Bermudez, Tamara Dieck and Warren Lieberman

INTRODUCTION

Picture yourself on a 45 foot yacht exploring the tropical islands and warm waters of the Caribbean as you enjoy a first-class sailing vacation. With a product like that to offer, what could a boat charter company want with revenue management? The Moorings is well known for its quality boat charters, enjoying excellent customer satisfaction and strong product demand, especially from repeat customers. But, having heard about the revenue management benefits other industries were claiming, its senior management wondered if revenue management could benefit the company.

Although many travel-related companies, including cruise lines, car rental companies, hotels, tour operators and even some golf resorts use revenue management, its principles had not been applied to the boat charter industry. The question in this case is to consider how The Moorings could make use of revenue management tools and principles to enjoy even more success. Boat charter companies do have similar issues with industries that employ revenue management techniques. For example, they have perishable products, seasonal demand and price competition. But they also have customer service and operational needs that are significantly different than do firms in these other industries. This case focuses on key revenue management principles that helped The Moorings improve on its success.

AIMS AND OBJECTIVES

At the core of revenue management is the maximization of profits from the sale of perishable assets by controlling price and inventory. Revenue management in the airline

1

industry has its roots in availability controls of different fares. For the hotel industry, the greatest benefits often arise from controlling availability by length of stay. And in the cruise line and car rental industries, revenue management typically involves offering the right price and promotions. Although the same principles of revenue management might apply to each of these industries, the applications of revenue management techniques differ.

In essence, The Moorings has a unique opportunity to define what revenue management should mean for its industry. The objective of this case is to think about what techniques and decision support capabilities can be used by The Moorings to better control its inventory and prices.

BACKGROUND

The Moorings offers both bareboat (i.e., self-skippered) and crewed (professional captain and cook are provided) yacht vacations on monohulls and catamarans that can accommodate from two to ten persons. You can sail away to exotic waters in the South Pacific, Caribbean, Mediterranean, or North America. They have 24 bases to sail from including Tortola, St Lucia, Grenada, St Martin, Tahiti, Tonga, Palma, Nice, Athens, Bahamas and Baja.

Boat Types

Each base has from eight to 30 different boat types and from one to 40 boats in a given boat type. The larger bases have more than 150 boats and smaller bases may have only a dozen boats. Boats are mainly classified based on overall length and passenger capacity.

In addition, the fleet is segmented into two lines, generally according to age. Both lines comprise monohulls and catamarans and include such amenities as linens, towels, dishes, pots and pans, and housekeeping supplies. The Exclusive Line yachts are brand new yachts that spend approximately two years in charter before moving into the Club Line, where they are available from their second through fifth anniversaries. The Exclusive Line yachts generally produce higher prices than the Club Line yachts.

Vacations

Vacations are typically booked for one or two week durations. For sailors, it is a great way to experience sailing waters far from home. For those new to sailing, a crewed charter can be the ultimate luxury, with a captain who will sail you where you want to go and a cook to delight your taste buds.

Services

The company is well known for its outstanding service and personal attention. Prior to each charter, the yachts are given a comprehensive review that takes approximately eight hours. In addition, yachts are subject to a set of scheduled preventative maintenance procedures. In the unlikely event of mechanical difficulties while on charter, The Moorings will get to the yacht with the parts necessary to fix the problem.

In addition to the boat charter, The Moorings offers trip cancellation insurance, hotel and air bookings (often discounted from publicly available fares), provisions and special services. Provisioning plans for bareboat charters range from a Charter-Starter Kit with the basic supplies and staples (napkins, garbage bags, coffee, salt and pepper, etc.) to a Split Provisioning Plan that includes the Starter Kit, breakfasts, lunches, dinners, and snacks. Other offerings include the rentals of kayaks and windsurfers and the services of a skipper or cook.

Yacht Ownership and Management

The company offers a yacht ownership and management programme. Most private yacht owners sail an average of 25 to 30 days a year while having to pay the year-round costs of maintenance, insurance and dockage. With The Moorings ownership programme, however, you own the yacht and earn a charter income stream, while receiving up to six weeks of sailing time. Owners may also vacation aboard other Moorings yachts at bases around the world. The Moorings charters and maintains the yacht and pays all operating expenses. The Moorings can make owning a boat within the financial reach of more people, while still allowing boat owners to sail.

In order to keep the wear and tear equal across a given type of yacht at a base, the company seeks to balance the usage of each boat. Boat owners receive an income stream based on the revenue received by The Moorings for chartering their specific boat. Because the owners receive an income stream based on the boat's charters, The Moorings aims to equalize the revenue produced by each boat.

The Moorings also offers flotillas, regattas and group events. Learn-to-sail and live-aboard cruising courses prepare sailors with some experience for taking the next step to bareboat cruises.

Booking Charters

Charters are booked with The Moorings' charter agents. While these staff members provide a service similar to that provided by reservation agents at many travel companies, many of these reservations agents are experienced sailors themselves. Consequently, they often provide useful product and regional information to the customers. The largest percentage of clients book directly with charter agents in response to sailing and luxury magazine advertisements. Many bookings come from repeat clients. Indirect bookings are also received from brokers that specialize in yacht charter vacations and from travel agents who primarily bring the product to the non-sailors of the world. More and more interest is also being generated over the Internet.

Pricing of boat charters is fairly simple. The year is split into four seasons with different prices by base, season and yacht type. Sample rates for two bases in the Caribbean, St Lucia and Grenada, are shown in Table 1.1.

Table 1.1   Sample charter rates for St Lucia and Grenada (Daily Yacht Rates, US$)

	Season A Dec 18–Jan 3 Jan 30–Apr 11	Season B Jan 4–Jan 29 Apr 12–May 2	Season C May 3–July 11 Oct 30–Dec 17	Season D Jul 12–Oct 29
Exclusive Line – Newest Model Yachts				
Moorings 362	530	430	350	280
Moorings 413	640	530	430	350
Moorings 505	970	800	680	530
Moorings 3800 Catamaran	825	700	600	485
Club Line				
Moorings 405	525	435	375	305
Moorings 505/503	880	740	640	495
Moorings 3700 Catamaran	720	590	520	420

Rates

The Moorings develops and publishes its rates once a year. This is the industry standard for pricing. These rates are effective until the next year's rates are established. The rate sheets claim that all prices are subject to change without notice. Despite this disclaimer, changing rates is labour intensive and is rarely done. The effective rate sheets are good for charters being booked up to five years in the future.

Discounting

Price competition has been fierce among the largest charter vacation providers and has led to frequent discounting. The Moorings is worried that this hurts their leadership position in the market. They do not want to be known as the discounting brand, but as the sailing vacation industry leader that provides first-class sailing vacations. Relative to other firms that charter yachts, The Moorings is known throughout the industry as providing a higher level of service.

Available discounts include 10 per cent-off coupons distributed at boat shows, Holiday Escape special rates for 30 November to 17 December, three days free when you buy ten days in the Caribbean, and two days free when you buy five in the Bahamas. Special deals to generate demand are also sent in direct mailings to previous clients.

There has been a shift recently to put less emphasis on discounts. Where charter agents used to offer some form of discount to many prospective clients, revenue management controls now limit the use of discounts. Where before there were pages of approximately 40 available discounts, there is now one page of approximately ten valid discounts that the charter agent may utilize.

The difficulty for revenue management is in knowing when and where discounts are needed to stimulate demand. The Moorings does not have formal demand forecasts. A typical booking curve is shown in Figure 1.1, but the booking curve does vary by base, charter month and yacht type.

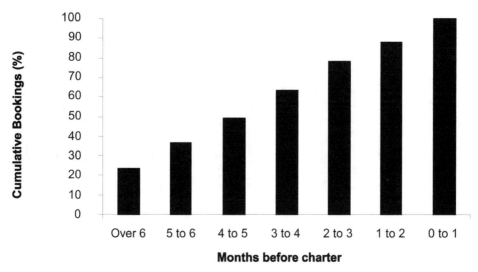

Figure 1.1 Sample charter booking curve

Demand and Boat Utilization

Demand for the newest yacht or catamaran is always strong. Also, certain bases and seasons typically enjoy demand that is greater than capacity. For example, the President's Day holiday in February is a popular travel week for American customers. However, there are certain base, boat and season combinations where The Moorings wants to stimulate additional demand.

While profits have been increasing steadily the past few years, boat utilization levels have been less than the company's goals. During the past few years, monthly utilization levels have never been greater than 70 per cent. Figure 1.2 depicts typical monthly utilization levels in the Caribbean.

As illustrated by Figure 1.2, The Moorings experiences a seasonal drop in utilization levels from August through October. This has been attributed to the less desirable weather in the Caribbean during this time period. August through October corresponds to the middle of hurricane season, with September weather being the most problematic. Utilization levels greater than 90 per cent are generally not achievable because of the time needed to clean and turn boats around in-between charters; senior management has noted that this still leaves a 20 per cent gap for improvement.

The Moorings has noticed dips in utilization at shoulder seasons (i.e., just before the start of a lower-rate season). Customers seemingly wait for the price break to book their charters, although charter rates are prorated. So, customers booking a seven-day charter, that has two days in Season B and the remaining five days in Season C, only pay the higher Season B rate for those first two days.

Customers are assigned to a specific boat at the time of booking, although this information is not conveyed to the customer. For example, when a customer calls and requests a Moorings 413 (a three-cabin, six to eight passenger monohull) for 14–21 March in Tortola the charter agent checks the availability of each boat. An availability screen provides the information shown in Table 1.2. Each letter represents a different contract for a boat charter. Boat and date combinations that do not contain a letter are dates on which that boat is available for charter.

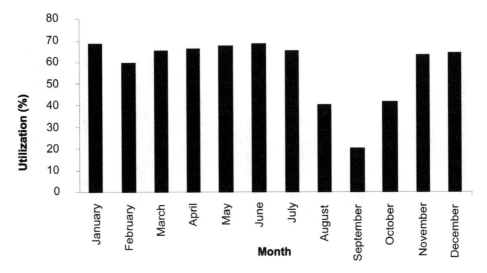

Figure 1.2   Monthly boat utilization

The screen shows, for each date, the contracts assigned to each boat. For example, Boat 413–1 has two contracts assigned to it: Contract 'a' from the 11th to the 17th and Contract 'b' from the 19th to the 24th. The agent must search the list of boats on the screen to determine if there is a boat available for the requested dates; if none are available, the agent should then determine whether the current contracts could be moved so as to create an available boat. As you might imagine, contracts cannot be split between boats.

Table 1.2   Current March bookings for Moorings 413 in Tortola

Boat	11th	12th	13th	14th	15th	16th	17th	18th	19th	20th	21st	22nd	23rd	24th
413–1	a	a	a	a	a	a	a		b	b	b	b	b	b
413–2		c	c	c	c	c	c	c			d	d	d	d
413–3			e	e	e	e	e	e	e	e			f	f
413–4	g	g	g	g				h	h	h	h	h	h	h
413–5		i	i	i	i	i	i	i	i		j	j	j	j
413–6	k	k	l	l	l	l	l	l	l	l				
413–7						m	m	m	m	m	m	m	m	
413–8		n	n	n	n	n	n	n	n	n	n			
413–9	o	o	o	o			p	p	p	p	p	p	p	

In this example we have nine boats and there is a way to reassign the contracts to boats so that the request received for chartering a boat from 14–21 March can be accepted. Whether or not this actually occurs, however, depends on how long it takes to do so and whether the agent who is handling the call is willing to take the time to do so (and, can figure out how to do so). When a boat class only has two or three boats the problem is not too difficult, but for boat classes with nine boats and certainly if there are 20 or 30 boats, the problem quickly becomes complex. The Moorings is convinced there must be a better way to manage their inventory, but no one has yet figured out a practical way to do so.

While the majority of bareboat charters begin and end at the same base, approximately 5 per cent of these charters end at a different base from where the charter began. At some bases, this can be as high as 20 per cent. One route that has a high percentage of these 'one-way' charters is in the Caribbean, between St Lucia and Grenada. Due to wind and current directions, customer demand is heaviest in the route going north to south. Customers start their sailing trip in St Lucia and end in Grenada. Sailing in this direction is much easier than sailing in the reverse direction. Consequently, excess inventory can end up in Grenada. Indeed, because customers are given the option of returning to the same base or sailing to a different base at the time of booking, all of the St Lucia fleet would ultimately end up in Grenada if the one-way boats were not brought back to St Lucia. To alleviate the over-fleeting issue, the company hires individuals to sail its yachts back to St Lucia. The trip from Grenada to St Lucia usually takes two days. Although customers are charged a drop-off fee for the redelivery, the fee does not cover all the incremental costs incurred by The Moorings to reposition the yacht.

The Moorings staff has considered increasing the repositioning fee that is paid by customers. But, they do not believe that customers will be willing to pay the full charge, so the company has accepted this incremental expense as a 'cost of doing business'.

The time required to deliver boats back to St Lucia reduces the time that a boat can be generating revenue for The Moorings. The amount of time spent in shuttling boats back to St Lucia can be quite significant. For example, if a yacht is rented for fifteen one-way trips during the year, this results in 30 days in which the boat cannot be rented. In this case, the maximum possible utilization for a boat would be just under 92 per cent. Because an additional day has to be spent cleaning and maintaining a boat after each rental, the maximum time a boat can be rented decreases even more.

In addition, it is a manual process to track the boat movements from base to base. Each boat has a home base in the system, and only one home base. If a boat has its home base in St Lucia, but has just arrived in Grenada at the end of a one-way charter, the reservation system still shows the boat to be at its home base. The agents do not see where a boat is physically located; they only see the home base. When the boat is being redelivered back to St Lucia, the redelivery time looks like charter utilization because the system does not allow for the tracking of delivery time. The delivery days are added to the customer contract and discounted out. Not only does this procedure confuse the customer, it overstates utilization and discount percentages. This manual procedure of accounting for delivery days makes it difficult for agents to select and assign a St Lucia home base boat to a customer who wants to reserve a boat in Grenada for a Grenada to St Lucia one-way.

The pricing and inventory management for one-way transactions between the islands of St Lucia and Grenada can be summarized as follows:

- The same price is charged for a one-way charter from either base (as shown earlier in Table 1.1).
- An additional drop-off fee is charged to redeliver the boat to its starting base.
- One-way transaction flow is approximately 90 per cent from St Lucia to Grenada.
- Yachts are automatically redelivered back to their starting base.
- Reservation agents manually assign specific yachts to reservations.

The company is considering making some changes to improve the profitability and boat utilization for St Lucia and Grenada charters.

The Moorings is already moving forward on its revenue management path. Some progress has been made, as evidenced by the reduced number of discounts that charter agents can offer. As part of its efforts, The Moorings has engaged a revenue management firm to provide a strategic plan to enhance revenue management capabilities.

DISCUSSION QUESTIONS

1. How could The Moorings provide a more flexible charter to boat assignment (rather than assigning charters to boats as requests come in)? Try to find the best matching of charter contracts to boats for a given base and boat type. The best matching comes closest to equalizing revenue across boats.
2. Develop a pricing strategy to improve the utilization of boats in St Lucia and Grenada.
3. What recommendations would you give The Moorings to improve its pricing?

2

easyJet: An Airline that Changed our Flying Habits

Gerald Barlow

The objectives of this case are to identify how a successful low-cost airline has used yield management. Why it is a vital tool in the operations of this industry and the problems that face a new entrant to the industry.

THE HISTORY OF A BRAND

Stelios Haji-Ioannou, an LSE graduate, started his successful entrepreneurial life at 25 when he launched what was to become a successful shipping company, Stelmar Tankers, not too much of a surprise when you realize that his family were already considerably successful in the shipping industry.

November 1995 saw the arrival and take-off of the 'no-frills' airline easyJet, which has become a generic term for this sector of the industry and is loved by many in the UK, for its low-cost, easy access service. But back then, all of seven and a half years ago, easyJet was the first UK airline to operate a direct sales only approach using no agents, no tickets, no meals, snacks or drinks, within the UK and then Europe.

Stelios, as he prefers to be addressed and referred to, developed his ideas after flying with and then researching into America's most successful low-cost airline, Southwest Airlines. This approach, which skilfully employs Michael Porter's (1985) low cost strategy, led him to develop the plans for a European low-cost airline. The first step was a £5 million loan/investment from his father Lukas Haji-Ioannou which provided basic financial support.

THE EARLY DAYS

The aim was to manage the business at the lowest possible cost base, but also to provide the best possible no frills service. His first decision was to arrange a base and routes. The obvious UK base had to be London, but the two main airports, Heathrow and Gatwick, were certainly not low cost, and Stanstead, was still not that well known or popular. However, Luton, well known for cheap budget holiday flights going as far back as the 1960's with operator like Clarksons, offered the appropriate base, easy access from London, low cost, and was well suited to the airline's first destination, Glasgow. The first adverts were for a one-way exceptionally low cost flight of £29, with a slogan 'London to Glasgow for cheaper than a pair of jeans!'. It was an immediate success with both business and individual customers, the flights being completely full. easyJet had picked the most appropriate time slots, the service was quicker door to door, and cheaper than the train. This first operation was run on two leased planes with Luton based staff, who like Stelios were generally very young. The growth and success exceeded the business plan and by the end of the second year easyJet was making a profit. This was a contradiction to the traditionally held beliefs that airline profits took years to develop, due to the long-term payback of the high investments, infrastructure, support service, etc. The autumn of 1997 saw the next bold entrepreneurial venture, with the placing of a US $500 million order with Boeing for new aircraft, to provide the capacity for planned expansion to carry 6 million passengers by the start of the year 2000.

To the initial single route of Glasgow, easyJet added routes to Edinburgh, and Aberdeen. During 1998, easyJet owned and operated a fleet of six Boeing 737–300s and this single plane type strategy was to be maintained until Boeing no longer produced the 737–300, with easyJet buying the last ones produced. The single plane type strategy was the sort of low cost strategy that underpinned the operation, and illustrates the level of detail that was necessary for the company to succeed – each plane exactly the same, therefore everyone knew it, the staff, regular fliers, etc. There was only one seating arrangement. Only one type of spares was required, maintenance being simpler and more cost effective. All this reduces costs, thus making the yield management programme universal. Companies with a range of planes have different capacities for each plane, and thus often each route, adding complexity to many of the operations, from catering to the yield management programme.

This was no hit or miss strategy. Stelios planned the company in great detail, he studied the reasons for the success of Southwest Airlines in detail and adapted them to suit his market: one type of plane, same number of seats per plane, point-to-point routing, not the much discussed and recommended hub and spoke system preferred by most operators, no agents, no tickets, no in-flight meals, a very high plane utilization and rapid aircraft turn-around at airports that would support these operational needs. The main variation from the Southwest approach was that no sales agents were used, easyJet would only accept direct bookings, paid for as the seat was booked, over the phone. This was to change to web and phone based sales bookings, as the business developed. EasyJet sold its first on-line seat in April 1998, and was quick to realize the potential and importance of this approach. By April 2002, 90 per cent of all seats sold were via the web.

The development of easyJet has been continuous, and it reached the point where at the start of 2002 easyJet operated from three English airports, Luton, Liverpool and Gatwick. Gatwick's growth started after the 11 September New York terrorist attacks which caused huge problems for the major airlines, when British Airways released slots at Gatwick in their cost-cutting programme. easyJet were quick to respond, so much so that by February 2002, when easyJet opened another five routes at Gatwick, they became the second largest scheduled carrier at Gatwick. A similar story unfolds at Liverpool, where easyJet started to operate at the John Lennon airport in 1997. The year before easyJet's arrival, the airport handled 500,000 passengers; by the end of 2001 this had grown to 2.35 million passengers, with easyJet accounting for 75 per cent of them.

The latest developments came in May 2002, when easyJet bought rival low cost airline GO and became the largest low cost airline in Europe. At the same time easyJet were negotiating with British Airways to acquire their German based company, Deutsche BA (DBA), at any time in the future up until March 2003 (BBC Business News, 8 May 2002). Perhaps the must unexpected news, for many of the easyJet customers, came in April 2002 when Stelios announced that he was to step down as Chairman of easyJet at the end of the company's next financial year. This was mainly due to pressure from the financial institutions, who were unhappy with a chairman also holding such a large percentage (in Stelios' case over 20 per cent) of the shares in the company.

By spring 2002 easyJet operated flights out of 19 European airports, Aberdeen, Amsterdam, Athens, Barcelona, Belfast, Edinburgh, Geneva, Glasgow, Inverness, Liverpool, London Gatwick, London Luton, Madrid, Malaga, Nice, Paris Charles de Gaulle, Paris Orly, Palma, and Zurich. They fly a combination of 90 routes, with Luton providing 15, and Gatwick, Liverpool and Amsterdam nine each.

LOW COST STRATEGY

An organization competing on low fares will naturally attempt to develop a low cost strategy, but it is necessary to realize that the two are not necessarily synonymous. To be successful it is necessary to look at all aspects of the business and to seek to operate them at the lowest possible cost base (Porter 1985): to look at where you add value, and where you do not, and if possible to remove those areas where you cannot add value and if not outsource them.

To this end, there were two were main differences between easyJet and most of its European competitors: first, the airports it flew from and to, and the fact it was point to point and not a hub and spoke system; and, secondly, it offered no catering services. By selecting Luton as opposed initially to Gatwick, its fixed cost per seat were reduced by approximately £10, and by having no meal or drinks service it saved the cost of the meal, the equipment, the extra staff needed to ensure speedy service and the storage and handling. This was followed by looking at the process and service delivery systems to see where other savings could be made. The two areas that easyJet changed were, first they issued no tickets, thus reducing the cost of production, and no boarding cards, since once the duty free status was removed from the EC countries there was no requirement for boarding cards other than for seat placement. So the easy answer was to allow customers to select their own seat location on boarding the plane, on a first come first served basis, all very simple changes but ones that reduced unnecessary costs. Similarly the bookings were to be direct, with no agents, thereby eliminating the need to pay agency fees, passing the saving back to the customer. Figure 2.1 outlines the difference in operating costs between easyJet and a conventional carrier.

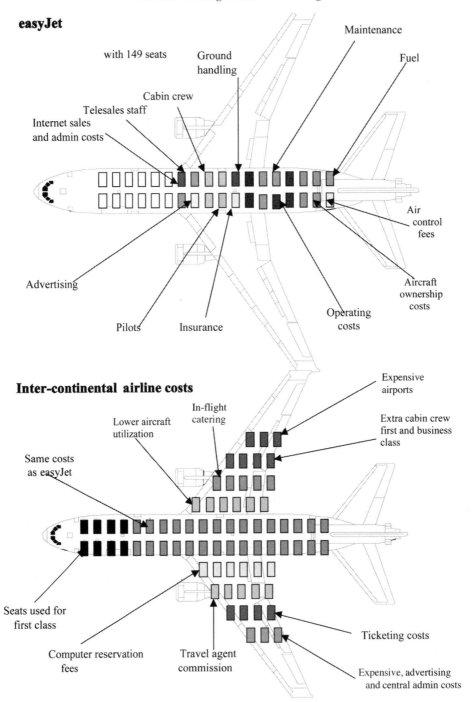

easyJet

with 149 seats

Ground handling

Maintenance

Fuel

Cabin crew

Telesales staff

Internet sales and admin costs

Air control fees

Advertising

Aircraft ownership costs

Pilots

Insurance

Operating costs

Inter-continental airline costs

In-flight catering

Expensive airports

Lower aircraft utilization

Extra cabin crew first and business class

Same costs as easyJet

Seats used for first class

Computer reservation fees

Travel agent commission

Ticketing costs

Expensive, advertising and central admin costs

Figure 2.1   The costing of running a budget airline, compared with a conventional carrier, based on easyJet Boeing 737–300 with 149 seats
Source: easyJet interview, subsequently published in easyRider, Spring 1998

One of the unnoticed strategies that easyJet developed was a psychological approach to its customers, 'yes we are low cost, yes the price is cheap, that is what we want it to be, we are happy with that, we shout about it'. But many early customers expected to find a 'cheap cut price' operator running old, crowded planes with unhappy, unhelpful staff, after bad experiences on some of the 1970's and 1980's low cost holiday flights. To get on a new plane with happy cheerful staff was not just unexpected, it exceeded many customers' expectations. The initial customers' perception, however, resulted in easyJet dropping one of its early advertising approaches featuring a dumpy easyJet cartoon plane, and replacing it with photographs of the actual planes. To ensure the message got across, Stelios flew on many flights every week in the early days of the airline; later, he took the risk of inviting a television series to be based around the company, which filmed in the airports, on the planes, and with actual staff and customers, and ITV's 'Airline' programme was born. In the early days Stelios always seemed cautious of marketing and preferred the direct approach, using simple advertising, word of mouth, lots of personal publicity and his personal touch. He not only flew on his own planes, on all the routes, but also interacted with the customers, happy ones and not so happy ones. He answered the letters personally, dealt with all customer communications, saw them not only on the planes, but in the waiting areas – he wanted to explain what he and easyJet was about.

BOOKING AND SALES POLICY

In the early days all bookings were by telephone, and payment was by credit card, with a reference number being given out and confirmed in a booking letter. This changed in April 1998 when the first ticket was sold via the web. This approach soon grew to make easyJet the world's largest seller of airline seats on the web, and become 'the web's favourite airline'. The telephone sales staff were all employed on a commission basis and were paid commission for every seat sold, so again controlling costs.

All journeys were, and still are, one way, and all are one class with the same regulations, whatever the prices. There is no reimbursement for no show passengers, there was no overbooking policy as a result, and very few customers fail to turn up. A customer can change a flight up to two hours prior to take off but must pay a £10 charge plus the price difference in the ticket, or if the price is lower, the original price is kept.

The company offers no seating reservation and uses a first come first served basis for seat allocation, which is dealt with via the boarding card, a hard reusable plastic-covered numbered card, subject to local airport regulations. The customers simply get on in blocks of arrival/boarding card numbers and select an available seat.

Sales were monitored in the early years by having a variety of phone numbers to observe the response rate to their advertising.

YIELD MANAGEMENT AT EASYJET

One of the first people employed in the early days of easyJet was an operational research specialist with experience in yield management at British Airways, and in setting up the Yield/Revenue Management programme for the Channel Tunnel. It was decided that the best approach was to write a programme for easyJet, a complex issue but made far more difficult because there was no past history of customer demand or flights on which to base the programme. A good history of past knowledge, events and demand is one of the key elements identified by both Kimes, (1989a and b) and Arthur Andersen (1997) for the success of a yield management programme. easyJet considered using an 'off the peg' programme, like 'Rembrandt', or another similar programme available at the time, but felt that in order to be truly successful they needed their own dedicated programme that could be easily modified as the company grew and learned more about its market. This decision, along with acquiring an experienced operational researcher with both BA experience and Channel Tunnel experience of creating a new yield management programme, was a wise and beneficial move.

The yield management programme at easyJet has one principal aim, to maximize revenue per flight, while ensuring an overall balance of customers per route. Each flight is treated as a separate event, unlike most airlines, and most airline yield management systems, which take into account the related flights and the interconnecting flight system.

Within their yield management system, easyJet consider they have only two kinds of destination, business-focused destinations, for example Glasgow, and non-business or leisure destinations, for example Malaga. Along with this, easyJet segment their flights into two categories of take-off timing. Early morning, and early evening week-day flights, are regarded as business sector flights. The remaining times, late morning, middle of the day, early afternoon, late evening, and weekend flights are non-business and leisure flights, or a mixture of the two. There are a number of destinations which straddle both categories, for example Edinburgh or Paris, and here the flight timing the segmentation takes place.

It is interesting that these two groups of travellers have different patterns of booking, and, despite the fact that all bookings are in general being made later, the pattern has changed little – that is, both segments are booking later, but still in the same set pattern as seen in Figures 2.2 and 2.3. Figure 2.2 shows the non-business/leisure traveller who tends to book earlier, so being more price sensitive, and who aims to take advantage of the pricing structure rather that the take-off time and date. Whereas the business traveller (Figure 2.3) is more concerned with the date and times of take-off and arrival than the price, which is not to say that price has no importance to the business traveller but that the element of time is more important. Hence the two differing booking curves, with the non-business customers' bookings building up much earlier.

The process of yield management within these two segments can be seen by the seat pricing structure on the web for two separate flights on the same day, for two different destinations, over the same period of time, up until take-off. Table 1.1 shows this for Glasgow with a flight at 7.45 and one at 20.30, and a flight to Malaga with flights at 9.40 and 20.50. Both of these destination pricing structures were for 2 July 2002 and show how the price varies not just upwards over the period prior to take-off. The non-business destination would undoubtedly look somewhat different if the take-off date had been in the winter. The Glasgow booking pattern may well have been different for a date, say, in September or October, when less people are likely to be on holiday. But this shows the differing pattern of bookings – clearly few bookings were received much in advance for the Glasgow flight.

The important difference between how easyJet and most other companies operate yield management is that easyJet do not recognize any market segmentation which directly relates to their customers. Even though they describe them as business and non-business, this relates more to destination and take-off time than the actual customer. In

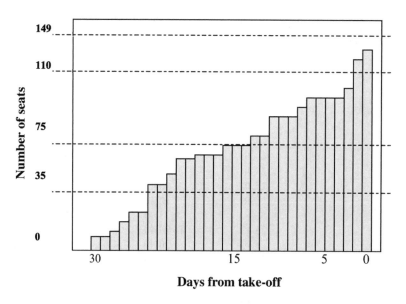

Figure 2.2   Typical non-business or leisure booking pattern

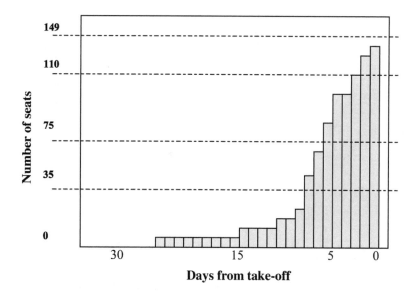

Figure 2.3   Typical business booking pattern

the case of most other airlines, segments often fall into a number of different areas; initially three main segments are generally recognised, First class, Business class, and Economy; then into types, business, non-business, commercially important people (CIP), accompanied, unaccompanied, suitable for upgrades, leisure, weekend leisure and so on. Most carriers then segment their routes: with high profit (transatlantic for

Table 2.1   Seating pricing seen via website over 45 days (http://www.easyjet.com/en/)

Days before take off	Luton to Glasgow		Luton to Malaga	
	Time: 07.45	Time: 20.30	Time: 09.40	Time: 20.50
	£	£	£	£
0	50.40	20.50	170.40	140.40
1	90.40	130.40	140.40	140.40
2	50.40	130.40	170.40	200.40
3	40.40	130.40	170.40	110.40
4	40.40	34.40	90.40	90.40
5	40.40	30.40	140.40	90.40
6	25.40	25.40	70.40	70.40
7	25.40	30.40	60.40	60.40
8	25.40	30.40	70.40	70.40
9	25.40	25.40	90.40	90.40
10	25.40	20.40	90.40	60.40
11	25.40	20.40	90.40	70.40
12	25.40	20.40	90.40	70.40
13	20.40	20.40	90.40	70.40
14	15.40	20.40	90.40	90.40
15	15.40	20.40	90.40	70.40
16	15.40	20.40	90.40	110.40
17	15.40	20.40	70.40	70.40
18	15.40	20.40	70.40	60.40
19	15.40	20.40	90.40	110.40
20	15.40	20.40	90.40	110.40
21	15.40	20.40	110.40	90.40
22	15.40	10.40	110.40	90.40
23	5.40	10.40	90.40	60.40
24	5.40	20.40	110.40	70.40
25	5.40	20.40	90.40	90.40
26	5.40	20.40	140.40	90.40
27	5.40	20.40	90.40	70.40
28	5.40	20.40	70.40	70.40
29	5.40	20.40	90.40	70.40
30	5.40	20.40	90.40	70.40
31	5.40	20.40	90.40	110.40
35	5.40	20.40	60.40	70.40
40	5.40	20.40	70.40	60.40
50	5.40	10.40	40.40	40.40

example) non- or low profit, and interconnecting (feeder routes, helping to supplement high profit flights).

OPERATIONS

As stated earlier, easyJet have tried wherever possible to simplify their operations. Such key areas are as follows.

Flights
All routes are standalone, that is there are no interconnecting flights, and all must be cost effective. The planes must be in the air for as long a period as possible, to make the capital investment pay for itself!

In-flight
All planes are the same, same cockpit details, same seating arrangement, same crew arrangements, same storage area arrangement. This means that all the Boeing 747–300 planes seat 149 passengers. If a major carrier were to use this plan they would have at least two different classes, separated by the curtain, and with higher priced areas having fewer seats, more leg room, and different services. In some cases this would be three classes, First, Business and Economy, with different seats, seat space, and seating planning, and three types of food and drink service. The result could mean easyJet having 149 seats, carrier B with two classes might have 129 seats, and carrier C only 105 seats.

Services
Again easyJet differentiated itself – Stelios' argument is 'there is no such thing as a free lunch', so don't expect one. The point made initially was that the flight is only one hour (Luton–Glasgow) so you don't really need a snack. This was then extended to the European flights, where the question was, can't you go for two and a half hours without eating a meal or snack? They found that many customers were happy to fly easyJet, but they brought their own snack, so they decided to offer snacks and drinks but as an extra, to be paid for during the flight, just as customers do in the airport (see Figures 2.4 and 2.5). These show the in-flight easyKiosk menu, indicating the range of items and the price structure over the four-year period 1998 to 2002.

Flight crew
The noticeable difference here is in the cabin crew. Initially they were all young, and there were fewer than on the traditional carrier of the same size, because there is only one class of service, and no in flight catering service.

Secondly, their uniform was more relaxed, in orange and black which consisted of a shirt, trousers or skirt, and jumper or waist-coat, and a top coat, similar to a sailing jacket. Compare this to the 'British Airways style uniform', consisting of a range of clothing, including a top coat, hat, gloves, in-flight baggage, *males*, trousers, shirt, tie, and jacket, *females*, skirt, jacket, blouse, scarf, summer weight suit of dress uniform, plus service uniforms of tabard or apron etc.

Pre-flight arrangements
Check-in: Initially, this was operated by outsourced ground handling staff, subsequently at the major bases like Luton easyJet operated their own check-in staff. Ground handling for luggage, etc., is outsourced.

Boarding pass: Wherever possible, mainly in the UK, this is a simple reusable plastic laminated numbered card. This was made possible when duty free was removed from European flights, so eliminating the need for a boarding pass to permit the purchase of duty free goods (this explains why a different boarding system is necessary on flights to Switzerland).

Tickets: easyJet operate a ticket-free service. On booking your flight you receive a unique flight number for each flight, this is received on the web site and a letter of confirmation is sent out confirming the details and the booking number/code. This

easyKiosk

Soft Drinks & Mixers	£0.50
Pepsi	£0.50
Diet Pepsi	£0.50
Tonic Water	£0.50
Lemonade	£0.50
American Ginger Ale	£0.50
Tango Orange	£0.50
Orange Juice	£0.50
Sparkling Mineral Water	£0.50

Champagne 20cl
Moet & Chandon, Brut Imperial NV £8.00

Ernest & Julio Gallo Wines

Chardonnay (White)	£2.50
Cabernet Sauvignon (Red)	£2.50

Spirits

Brandy	£2.00
Gordon's Dry Gin	£2.00
White & Mackay Whisky	£2.00
Smirnoff Vodka	£2.00
Barcardi	£2.00

Lagers

Budweiser	£1.50
Stella Artois	£1.50

Hot Drinks

Kenco Coffee	£1.00
Kenco Cappuccino	£1.00
Typhoo Tea	£1.00
Suchard Hot Chocolate	£1.00

Snacks & Confectionery

Walkers Shortbread Rounds	£0.80
Terry's Chocolate Bar	£0.40
Terry's Waifa (plain)	£0.40
Toblerone Chocolate Bar	£0.40
'24 Carat' Cake	£0.80
Raspberry Flapjack	£0.80
Kelloggs Rice Krispies 'Squares'	£0.50
Whitworths Sun Dried 'Frootz'	
Jumbo Raisins & Sultanas	£0.60
Smints	£1.00

Savouries

KP Peanuts 'Tubes' Salted, Dry Roasted	£0.50
Peperami – Original, Hot	£0.80
Cheez Dippers	£0.60
Pringles 56gm tubes Sour Cream & Onion, Original	£0.80

Gifts

EasyJet Model Aircraft	£8.00
Phonecards	£5.00/£10.00

Figure 2.4   In-flight service on easyJet, Summer 1998

system is possible because any and all bookings are made directly with easyJet, either over the phone or via the web site, no agents are used anywhere. Consider the saving made by easyJet against the traditional airlines. First the ticket: for the traditional airlines this is a multi-part ticket, expensive to print, produce and post. It is also a negotiable product as tickets can be and often are transferable. Secondly, there is the agent's commission. Finally, easyJet have no retail outlets like many of the traditional airlines, with sales offices, in high streets and at airport terminals – eastJet simply offer a booking computer sales desk.

Head Office
Known as easyLand, this is located at Luton Airport and is easily recognized by its orange external appearance. easyLand mirrors the overall easyJet approach to business, everything is simple and 'no frills'. The employees are encouraged to dress casually, it is based around open plan office environment, with Stelios himself having a desk within the main open plan office area. The business is operated on a paperless system wherever possible and the concept of low cost strategy is encouraged throughout.

easyKiosk

Hot Drinks					**Snacks**
Nescafe	Nescafe	Tetley Tea			Kit Kat
Coffee	Chocolate				Chunky
£1.50	£1.50	£1.50			£0.60

Soft Drinks					Pringles
Pepsi	Pepsi Max	Still Water	Tonic Water	Orange Juice	Original
300ml	150ml	330ml	150ml	150ml	£1.00
£1.00	£0.60	£1.00	£0.60	£0.60	

Sandwiches (*on some flights, sandwiches may be a different make and variety, subject to availability*)

Original
Mighty Oat
Flapjack
£1.50

Hovis			
Cheese and Pickle		Chicken and Bacon	
Sandwich	£2.50	Sandwich	£3.50
Tuna & Sweetcorn Bap	£3.00	Ham and Cheese Roll	£3.00

Alcoholic Drinks				
Wine: Merlot	Chardonnay	Whisky	Gin	Beer
187ml	187ml	White & Mackay	London Dry	Red Stripe
		50ml	50ml	300ml
£2.50	£2.50	£2.50	£2.50	£2.00
		Vodka	Brandy	Budwiser
		Smirnoff	Polignac	330ml
		50ml	50ml	
		£2.50	£2.50	£2.00

Figure 2.5 In-flight service on easyJet, April 2002

COMPETITION

Ryanair

Until the take over of GO airlines in May 2002 Ryanair were the largest low cost airline in Europe. Ryanair started in 1985 with flights between Waterford, Ireland and Gatwick, London, and a year later managed to break the stranglehold operated between BA and Aer Lingus on the Dublin–London route. In the early days Ryanair was offering the full traditional airline service, but changed in 1990/1 to become a low cost airline, again adopting the approach developed by Southwest Airlines. They cut the non-profit routes, reducing their routes from nineteen to five. By spring 2002 Ryanair had developed into Europe's largest low cost carrier, operating 76 routes, to thirteen countries, carrying an estimated 12 million passengers. By the summer of 2002 Ryanair will operate a fleet of 44 Boeing 737s.

buzz

buzz commenced business in a burst of publicity as the new entrant to the low cost air market in September 1999. Based at Stanstead Airport in Essex, buzz operates to 21 destinations, three in Germany, and Spain and fifteen in France. The airline is owned and operated by KLM, who already operated a low-cost operation KLM UK, which flies to Amsterdam. As a result buzz do not fly to either Holland or Belgium.

Virgin Express

Based in Belgium, Virgin Express was established in 1996 when the Virgin Group gained a controlling interest in Euro-Belgian Airlines. The airline flies fifteen routes to nine countries in Europe. Virgin Express is also based around the Boeing 737 jets running both 737–300 and 737–400 series planes. It operates similarly to easyJet in that it has no tickets, but does reserve seats and does have boarding cards. It offers no private lounges or extras like newspapers but does offer in-flight snacks like tea/coffee, bottled water and sandwiches or rolls. Unlike its major competitors Virgin Express flies into main airports such as Heathrow and Fiuicino at Rome.

HOW DOES EASYJET MATCH REQUIREMENTS FOR A SUCCESSFUL YIELD MANAGEMENT SYSTEM?

In a recent Radio 4 interview ('On the ropes', 9 July 2002), Stelios acknowledged two factors as being important in operating a low cost business. The first was the economic laws of price elasticity; the second the use of the technique of yield management. Both are very important to easyJet's success.

How well does the easyJet model follow the accepted required approach for the successful implementation and operation of a yield management programme?

Sheryle Kimes (1989a and b) and Arthur Andersen (1997) identified a number of key elements for yield management to be successful. How well do these fit into the easyJet model?

Arthur Andersen suggested the following five key functions:

1. Market segmentation
2. Price management
3. Demand forecasting
4. Availability, and/or capacity management
5. Reservation negotiation

They also put forward four preconditions for yield management to operate:

1. Perishable inventory or seasonal demand
2. High fixed costs or sunk costs
3. Fixed capacity either overall or in the short term
4. Advance purchase of service/product

Kimes (1989a) identified seven key techniques necessary for the success of a yield management system:

1. The ability to segment
2. Perishability of inventory
3. Product sold in advance
4. Fluctuation in demand
5. High fixed costs
6. Low marginal sales costs
7. High marginal production costs

Kimes (1989b) went on to identify five core requirements for the operation of a yield management system:

1. Booking patterns
2. Knowledge of the demand patterns by market segments
3. An overbooking policy
4. Knowledge of the effect of price changes
5. A good information system

The Common Features and how easyJet fits them

Perishable inventory: very clearly any airline running a scheduled service has a highly perishable service. Once the check-in gate has closed, any unsold seats are lost forever. An empty seat on a specific route at a specific take of time can never be sold later. No opportunity exists to oversell the next flight, unlike, say, a retail shop, where extra sales can always be accommodated.

Market segmentation: both Kimes and Arthur Andersen state that the ability to segment your market and the practice of doing so is a requirement for the successful operation of a yield management programme. However, easyJet do not segment their market in terms of customer segmentation, and they only operate a small segmentation in terms of their operation, in that they recognise two segments, business routes and take-off times, and non-business or leisure routes and their time slots.

Demand forecasting: this is an interesting area. In order to forecast demand accurately, the normal approach is good historic information, which Kimes effectively mentions in three different areas. But every time easyJet open up a new route, they will have no direct history or knowledge related to demand, so they have to be able to gain this through knowledge/experience of other similar routes. Initially even this was not available, but they used past experience or other forms of forecasting.

Fixed capacity: the capacity is undeniably fixed, there is no opportunity of adding just one extra seat, unlike a hotel where they might be able to add an extra bed.

Negotiable pricing structure: easyJet's price structure is open to all, visit the web site and see; it is negotiable in so far as you can pick the time of the flight when you book and so adjust the price to suit personal needs to some extent. But, if negotiation is taken as haggling and bargaining, then there is little negotiation in that sense of the word.

High fixed costs: the fixed cost is exceedingly high, the cost of a new or extra plane starts in the region of £50–100 million once the plane, package and engines have been agreed, so that is high.

Reservation system: clearly easyJet has a reservation system, either via the web or over the telephone, but not as wide and accessible as many airlines, for example retail outlets, airport reservation desks, telephone, travel and booking agents, company web sites, agents' web sites, cheap travel web sites, but it is very easy to access, understand and operate.

Low marginal cost of sales: the cost to easyJet of one extra passenger is very low – the cost of the booking, one confirmation letter, maybe commission if taken on the phone, the cost of the additional fuel for the extra weight, and that is about all.

From these specific elements, we can see that easyJet do not meet all the established criteria for a successful yield based operation, but few would disagree that easyJet is now a successful and profitable airline, despite very adverse conditions for the whole industry. easyJet have shown that by good, effective management and planning, a small business (remember that easyJet started with one route and two leased planes) can effectively use yield or revenue management as one of the tools to achieve successful a operation.

Richard Branson, one of the men Stelios Haji-Ioannou aspires to, said, 'if you want to become a millionaire from the airline industry, start off as a multi-millionaire'. Well, again, Stelios and easyJet are showing that being a millionaire, or having access to the funds of one, does help, but he is also showing that you can make a million or more out of running an airline.

DISCUSSION QUESTIONS

1. What are the potential negative effects that yield management can have on customer relations?
2. Select one of the easyJet routes (for example Luton–Nice) and track the prices for the 45 days until take-off. Having selected the route, record the price every 5 days for the first 15 days, then every 2 days until 14 days from take-off, then every day. You need to record the prices for three different time slots, say early morning, mid-afternoon, and the last flight. Comment on your observations and the possible reasons for the price variation between days until take-off.
3. What problems do you envisage easyJet may have with the addition of a company like GO? (GO, an ex-BA company, used a BA-type of yield management programme and alternative sales outlets, rather than simply the Internet and phone sales).

REFERENCES

Arthur Andersen (1997) *Yield Management in Small and Medium-sized Enterprises in the Tourist Industry*. Brussels: Directorate-General XXIII, European Commission.

Kimes, S. E. (1989a) 'The basics of yield management', *Cornell Hotel and Restaurant Administration Quarterly*, **30**(3), 14–19.

Kimes, S. E. (1989b) 'Yield management: a tool for capacity-constrained service firms', *Journal of Operations Management*, **11**(4), 348–63.

Porter. M. (1985) *Competitive Advantage*. New York: Free Press.

easyRider, easyJet in-flight magazine, also available via easyJet web site

Web sites
http://www.buzzaway.com
http://www.easyjet.com
http://www.ryanair.com
http://www.virgin-express.com

Other sources of relevant information

Belobaba, P. P. (1989) 'Application of a problematic decision model to airline seat inventory control', *Operational Research*, **37**(2), 183–97.

Berge, M. E. and Hopperstad, C. A. (1993) 'Demand driven dispatch: a method of dynamic aircraft capacity assignments, models and algorithms', *Operational Research*, **41**(1), 153–68.

Bonnisseau, J. and Cornet, B. (1990) 'Existence of marginal costing pricing equilibria: the non-smooth case', *International Economic Review*, **31**(3), 685–708.

Larsen, T. D. (1988) 'Yield management and your passengers', *ASTA Agency Magazine*, June, 46–8.

Orkin, E. B. (1988) 'Boosting your bottom line with yield management', *The Cornell Hotel Restaurant and Administrative Quarterly*, **28**(4), 52–6.

Orkin, E. B. (1990) 'Strategies for managing transient rates', *The Cornell Hotel Restaurant and Administrative Quarterly*, February, 34–9.

Rothstein, M. (1971) 'An airline overbooking model', *Transportation Science*, **5**, 182–92.

Schlifer, E. and Vardi, Y. (1975) 'An airline overbooking policy', *Transportation Science*, **9**, 101–14.

Vohra, R. (1992) 'Marginal cost pricing under bounded marginal returns', *Econometrics* **60**(4), 859–76.

Weatherford, L. R. and Bodily, S. E. (1992) 'A taxonomy of research overview of perishable asset revenue management: yield management, overbooking and pricing', *Operations Research*, **40**(5), 831–44.

Wheelwright, S. C. and Makridakis, S. (1989) *Forecasting Methods for Management*. New York: John Wiley and Sons.

Williams, L. (1987) 'Dark science brings boost to airline profits', *Sunday Times*, 27 November, 94.

3

The Wedding Bell Blues

Sheryl E. Kimes

Revenue management, or yield management, is commonly practised for hotel guest rooms, but has not yet been systematically applied to hotel function space (Hartley and Rand, 2000; Kimes and McGuire, 2001). Function space provides a substantial revenue stream for hotels and could benefit from the application of revenue management[1].

The goal of function space revenue management is to maximize contribution per available space for a given time (ConPAST) by manipulating price and event duration. ConPAST has three components: contribution, space and time. Contribution is preferable to revenue because of the varying profit margins of the different streams of function space revenue. Space refers to the number of square feet or metres in the function room, and time refers to the time-segment for which contribution is measured.

In this case study, you will analyze how function space revenue management can be applied to the weddings at a large convention hotel. We will first discuss revenue management in general, then cover duration and pricing management tools that function space managers can use, and then present the case study. The goal of the case study is to help you understand how revenue management can be applied to function space.

REVENUE MANAGEMENT

Revenue management is the application of information systems and pricing strategies to allocate the right capacity (in this case, function space) to the right customer at the right place at the right time (Smith *et al.*, 1992). The determination of 'right' entails achieving both the most contribution possible for the hotel while also delivering the greatest value or utility to the customer. In practice, revenue management has meant setting prices according to predicted demand levels so that price-sensitive customers who are willing to purchase at off-peak times can do so at favourable prices, while price-insensitive customers who want to purchase at peak times will be able to do so.

Restaurants

The application of revenue management has been most effective when it is applied to operations that have relatively fixed capacity, demand that is variable and uncertain, a perishable inventory, an appropriate cost and pricing structure, and varying customer price sensitivity (Kimes, 1989; Cross, 1997a and b). Those attributes are found in the function space industry.

Different industries are subject to different combinations of duration control and variable pricing (see Figure 3.1) (Kimes and Chase, 1998). Industries traditionally associated with revenue management (hotels, airlines, car-rental firms, and cruise lines) are able to apply variable pricing for a product that has a specified or predictable duration (Quadrant 2 of Figure 3.1). Function space, movie theaters, performing-arts centres and arenas, charge a fixed price for a product of predictable duration (Quadrant 1), while restaurants and golf courses charge a fixed price but face a relatively unpredictable duration of customer use (Quadrant 3). Many health care businesses charge variable prices (e.g., Medicare versus private pay), but do not know the duration of patient use, even though some may try to control that duration (Quadrant 4). The lines dividing the quadrants are broken because in reality no fixed demarcation point exists between quadrants. Thus, an industry (such as function space) may have attributes from more than one quadrant.

		Price	
		Fixed	Variable
Duration	Predictable	Quadrant 1 Movies Stadiums/Arenas Function space	Quadrant 2 Hotel rooms Airline seats Rental cars Cruise lines
	Unpredictable	Quadrant 3 Restaurants Golf courses	Quadrant 4 Continuing care hospitals

Figure 3.1 Typical pricing and duration positioning of selected service industries

Successful revenue management applications are generally found in Quadrant 2 industries, because they can manage both capacity and price. To obtain the benefits associated with revenue management, non-Quadrant 2 industries should attempt to move to Quadrant 2 by deploying the appropriate strategic levers. This implies that Quadrant 1 industries, such as function space, should concentrate on developing demand-based pricing approaches. This is not to say that duration management cannot be improved, but only that most of the benefits associated with revenue management will be obtained from differential pricing.

FUNCTION SPACE REVENUE MANAGEMENT

Function space is more difficult to revenue manage than transient guest rooms because of its interaction with both rooms and food and beverage demand. While function space will reap most of its revenue management benefits from pricing, this is not to downplay the role of duration control.

Duration Control

Duration can be managed in four ways (Kimes and Chase, 1998): refining the definition of duration, reducing arrival uncertainty, reducing duration uncertainty, and reducing the amount of time between functions. Each will be briefly described and the issues associated with each discussed.

Definition: Most hotels define function space duration as a day-part but the definition of day-part and the number of day-parts varies by hotel. Since events can span multiple day-parts or use only part of a day-part, hotel function space managers should consider defining duration as an hour. Most computerized systems track this information, but it may be difficult to retrieve.

Arrival uncertainty: Arrival uncertainty can be defined in two ways: the timing and quantity of requests and the no-show and cancellation rate of booked events. Determining the timing and number of requests from different market segments is a challenging task. Hotels still have a great deal of difficulty with forecasting their demand for group rooms (Kimes, 1999a), and most have not even attempted to forecast their function space demand. If a hotel can obtain information on the lead time and the amount of business of major market segments, it can make better decisions on demand they will have, when they will have it and when to release space to other market segments.

While hotels have a difficult time in forecasting function space demand, they do a good job of reducing cancellation and no-show rates by requiring non-refundable deposits and pre-payments for function space. In some high-demand cities, hotels even require pre-payment for the requested number of guest rooms. This protects them from saving guest rooms for room blocks that do not materialize at the agreed upon rate.

Duration uncertainty: Since events can span multiple days or day-parts, hotels must ensure that the guest rooms associated with the event do not unnecessarily displace higher paying transient business and must ensure that the event lasts for the agreed length of time. Hotels do a good job in ensuring that the contracted function space is used for the required length of time by requiring deposits and pre-payment. They have a much more difficult time ensuring that the guest rooms are occupied for the specified length of time. Many groups, particularly conventions, suffer from high room attrition on the last day or two of the event. If group members check out early, the hotel is usually stuck unless they use early departure fees (with their associated customer satisfaction issues) or require pre-payment for all rooms.

Time between functions: In high demand periods, the set-up and breakdown time requirements can impact demand. Hotels that try to minimize the labour cost associated with set-up and tear-down often end up turning down business that could have been accommodated if more labour was deployed. For example, a hotel that requires a two-hour set-up and two-hour break-down for all events would not be able to book a meeting that ended at 5 p.m. and a dinner that began at 6.30 p.m. in the same room. If more employees were assigned to speed the transition between events, the labour cost would be more than covered by the increased revenue associated with the incremental event.

Pricing

Function space pricing is complicated by the fact that function space cannot be priced without considering the impact on room sales and food and beverage. A price that may seem too low for the function space when considered alone may more than compensate for itself when room and food and beverage revenue are considered. Similarly, a high function space price may be unprofitable for the hotel if it displaces potentially higher paying business.

Function space managers face two types of pricing decisions: what price to charge and how to determine who pays which price. When analyzing which business to accept, the manager must assess the days and day-parts requested, the number of function rooms required, the expected number of guest rooms and the expected food and beverage and other expenditures. Since the profit margins for different revenue streams vary, the manager must determine the expected contribution associated with each event and compare that with any potential displacement of other business. If the expected contribution is higher than the potential displacement, the group should be accepted, and if not, it should be rejected or referred to another time.

Along with determining the appropriate price to charge, the hotel must also justify the prices charged to different clients. Rate fences (both physical and non-physical) can be used to determine who pays which price. Physical rate fences might include the presence of certain amenities (i.e., high-tech rooms command a premium) or location (i.e., rooms on the first floor command a premium). Non-physical rate fences might include customer characteristics (i.e., repeat customers receive a discount), transaction characteristics (i.e., customers booking events through the Internet receive a discount), or day of week or time of day (i.e., customers booking events on weekends or mornings receive a discount).

DEVELOPING A REVENUE MANAGEMENT PROGRAMME

To develop a function space revenue management programme, managers should (1) establish the baseline of performance, (2) understand the drivers of that performance, (3) develop a revenue-management strategy, (4) implement that strategy, and (5) monitor the strategy's outcome (Kimes, 1999b).

THE ROLE OF FUNCTION SPACE

Function space provides a significant revenue stream for most hotels. Function space demand consists of both groups who both rent space and guest rooms (typically conferences and meetings) and groups who rent only space (usually social events). Generally, function space is managed by the Sales and Marketing department and is broken into four or more groups, including weddings, conventions/exhibitions, meetings and social, each with its own director and team of sales managers.

PROBLEM SETTING [2]

The Director of Marketing of a large convention hotel was looking at the financial aspects and noticed that the revenue from social catering had dropped from $5,116,174 to $5,021,195. Occupancy was slightly up (1999, 59.64 per cent; 1998, 59.57 per cent), but the average rate (1999, $0.597 per square foot; 1998, $0.609 per square foot) and the revenue per available square foot (1999, $0.356; 1998, $0.363) were down. What was even more surprising was that the average guest room rate had increased by 8 per cent and RevPAR had increased by 12 per cent. How could they be making less money when there were more weddings this year? What was going on?

Currently, the sales managers are given a set of dates to book weddings (some dates are not available because other events require the use of the ballroom). The sales managers can book one large wedding in the whole ballroom or have two smaller weddings in each half. The whole ballroom can fit 500 covers while each half can fit only 220 covers. Sales managers have two sets of menus with a low budget option and a high budget option. The sales manager is expected to get $21,000 in revenue for Saturday nights for the ballroom or $12,500 for half the ballroom. The sales manager can discount on all other time periods.

Demand varies by month with most weddings occurring during May through October (Figure 3.2). Saturday nights are the most popular time to hold a wedding, followed by Saturday afternoons.

Upon careful study, the Director of Marketing found that many clients were having difficulty in meeting minimum revenue requirements and that sales managers were offering expensive (but unprofitable) upgrades such as ice carvings and sweet tables in an attempt to qualify the client and to meet their monthly revenue quota.

In addition, sales managers were booking the weddings very far out (Figure 3.3). About half of all weddings were booked more than a year before the event.

The staff has been noticing that they have been turning away many unexpected short-term weddings. In fact, turndown and lost revenue far exceeds the amount of revenue booked (Figure 3.4). A turndown is counted when there is no space to offer the guest or when the guest does not meet the hotel's criteria. Lost business refers to when the client chooses not to book the hotel. In addition, groups which wanted to use guest rooms have been turned down when the ballroom was needed but was already booked for a wedding.

The reasons for turndown and lost business vary, with some clients simply 'shopping' and others not meeting the hotel's criteria (Table 3.1).

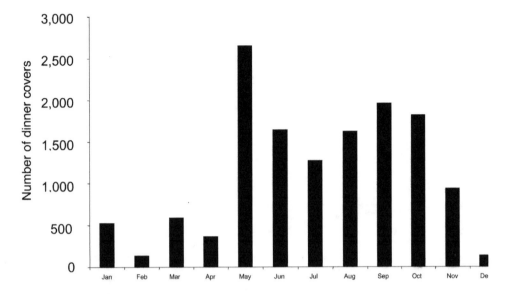

Figure 3.2   1999 dinner covers

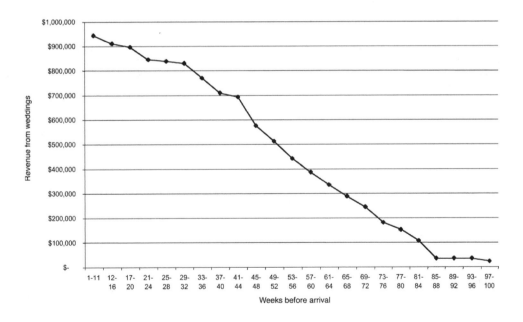

Figure 3.3   Wedding booking pace

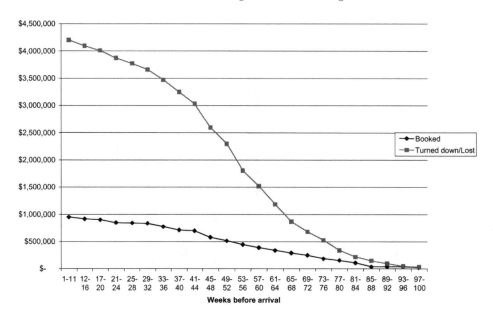

Figure 3.4 Wedding booking pace

Table 3.1 Reasons for turndowns and lost business

Type	Turndown (T) or Lost (L)	Dinner covers	Revenue ($)
Postponed	L	700	37,159
Ambiance	L	350	21,103
Food price too high	L	965	45,978
Left message/no response	L	16,478	866,412
Minimum guarantee	L	915	49,714
Far from airport	L	100	5,805
Location	L	350	12,935
Other–lost	L	49,513	2,519,306
Rate conscious	L	250	8,571
Dates changed	T	810	28,085
Sleeping rooms n/a	T	25	625
No space–sales	T	846	34,583
Other–turndown	T	620	39,503
Too far out	T	200	2,125
No space–catering	T	9,482	479,429
Total		81,604	4,151,333
Turndown		11,983	584,350
Lost		69,621	3,566,983
Actually booked		13,609	

DISCUSSION QUESTIONS

The Director of Marketing has asked you to analyse the current situation and develop a revenue management strategy for weddings. Specifically:

1. What is causing the problem?
2. What pricing and duration control management strategies do you suggest?
3. What implementation issues will she face? How should she handle them? How will she be able to measure her success with her revenue management programme?

Be specific on how she can take your recommendations and implement the suggested policies in her hotel.

NOTES

1. Much of the first section of this chapter comes from Sheryl E. Kimes and Kelly A. McGuire (2001) 'Function Space Revenue Management: A Case Study from Singapore', *Cornell Hotel and Restaurant Administration Quarterly*, **42**(6), 33–46.
2. I would like to thank Carolyn Fredey for her assistance with this section.

REFERENCES

Cross, R. G. (1997a) 'Launching the revenue rocket: how revenue management can work for your business', *Cornell Hotel and Restaurant Administration Quarterly*, **38**(2), 32–43.

Cross, R. G. (1997b) *Revenue Management*. New York: Broadway Books.

Hartley, J. and Rand, P. (2000) 'Conference sector capacity management', A. Ingold, U. McMahon-Beattie, and I. Yeoman, (eds), in *Yield Management: Strategies for the Service Industries*, 2nd edn, pp. 315–38. London: Continuum.

Kimes, S. E. (1989) Yield management: a tool for capacity-constrained service firms', *Journal of Operations Management*, **8**(4), 348–63.

Kimes, S. E. (1999a) 'Group forecasting accuracy for hotels', *Journal of the Operational Research Society*, **50**(11), 1104–10.

Kimes, S. E. (1999b) 'Implementation of restaurant revenue management: a five-step approach', *Cornell Hotel and Restaurant Administration Quarterly*, **40**(3), 15–22.

Kimes, S. E. and Chase, R. B. (1998) 'The strategic levers of yield management', *Journal of Service Research*, **1**(2), 156–66.

Kimes, S. E. and McGuire, K. A. (2001) 'Function space revenue management: a case study from Singapore', *Cornell Hotel and Restaurant Administration Quarterly*, **42**(6), 33–46.

Smith, B. C., Leimkuhler, J. F. and Darrow, R. M. (1992) 'Yield management at American Airlines', *Interfaces*, **22**(1), 8–31.

4

The Right Price Consultants

Julie Swann

INTRODUCTION

In recent years, a number of industries have turned towards innovative pricing strategies such as revenue management or dynamic pricing to manage their inventory effectively. Firms are employing such varied tools as dynamic pricing over time, target pricing to different classes of customers, or pricing to learn about customer demand. The benefits can be significant, including not only potential increases in profit, but also improvements such as reduction in demand or production variability, resulting in more efficient supply chains. Ford Motor Company used pricing initiatives to match supply and demand and target particular customer segments, and executives credit the effort with $3 billion in growth between 1995 through 1999 (Leibs, 2000).

Dynamic pricing, where price changes over time in response to variability in supply or demand, has long been applied in retail industries, e.g., in the form of markdown pricing. For many firms, the Internet has also presented new opportunities for dynamic pricing, since price changes are inexpensive, and demand data is easier to collect. For instance, Boise Cascade Office Products has stated that prices for the 12,000 products that they offer online could change as often as daily (Kay, 1998). For additional examples, see Baker *et al.* (2001) for industry applications, or Elmaghraby and Keskinocak (2002) for academic research in this area.

Even manufacturing companies have begun to explore new pricing opportunities. A significant example is Dell Computers, who segment customers by type (industry, government, academic, etc.), where the price of a product may differ according to the segment. Furthermore, even the price of a product within a segment may change over time (McWilliams, 2001).

Existing pricing and revenue management research has largely focused on industries such as the airlines, hotels, and even retail sales (see the above-mentioned authors for some reviews). However, there are a number of characteristics that distinguish general manufacturing industries from other industries, including the non-perishability of products and the ability to vary production levels. Furthermore, manufacturing differs from most retail environments in its reordering and capacity characteristics.

Thus, the *integration* of pricing with production in manufacturing is still in its early stages, and coordinating these aspects with the supply chain offers significant opportunity to improve efficiency and profits. This is especially true for manufacturers who sell through electronic channels, since this medium offers additional flexibility for price and demand management.

In this case study, we focus on dynamic pricing in manufacturing, where the pricing decision is coordinated with production (see Chan *et al.* (2002) for a review of this area). We develop a simple operations model, and present computational results obtained from a number of experiments. We focus on motivating general insights for managers, such as when it makes sense to use dynamic pricing, and what impacts it has on a supply chain or organization.

CASE STUDY

Natasha Lee, VP of Operations at JJT, Inc.[1], left the meeting deep in thought. She was a little shocked at the ideas that she had just heard, and she had to admit the ideas made her a little nervous.

The consultants at the meeting had just suggested that JJT consider a new dynamic pricing strategy, where prices of their products would fluctuate over time in response to system variability. It wasn't just the new strategy that made Natasha nervous; it also was the thought of JJT, an established manufacturer of widgets, being the first in the industry to try such a strategy. She also knew that the new strategy had the potential to impact the supply chain she managed, and she was worried that the consultants hadn't considered all of the potential impacts of the strategy.

Company JJT had manufactured widgets and similar products for 30 years. They were a corporate conglomerate, selling many kinds of products in a variety of different markets. The company had established itself early in the industry and held the largest market share in many areas, as well as having a good reputation among its clients. Yet the management at JJT knew that business models at many traditional companies were beginning to change, driven in part by the expansion of e-commerce, and they wanted to make sure that JJT continued to be successful. JJT had hired outside consultants to help position the company for the future, and the consultants were given a broad mandate to consider many aspects of business at Company JJT.

'Their ideas certainly are bold', Natasha thought to herself, as she walked the corridor to her office. She knew that some industries used dynamic pricing, but the idea had not yet established itself in traditional manufacturing firms. The consultants' idea was simple though: allow prices to change over time while trying to maximize the profit of the system. The consultants had coordinated the pricing and sales decisions with production as well, taking into account inventory holding costs, production costs, and production capacity during each period of time.

Natasha suddenly remembered where she had heard about dynamic pricing. Her daughter had told her at dinner not long ago that Amazon.com had tried dynamic pricing, with customers paying different amounts for the same DVD based on demographics or even the browser they used. Customers had responded negatively to the strategy, and Amazon.com had stopped the pricing tests. 'But that's not the same as the pricing strategy the consultants are suggesting', Natasha realized. Amazon.com tried

pricing based on differences among customers, really a form of differential pricing
rather than dynamic pricing. However in the consultants' pricing strategy, all customers
paid the same price at a particular time, and the prices could vary over time.

In her office, Natasha began to look at the material prepared by the consultants. The
consultants first explained the nature of the relationship between price and demand.
Generally, as the price of a product increases, the demand for the product decreases.
JJT, like many companies, assumes that the structure of this relationship is linear,
yielding linear demand curves for each product. An example of a linear demand curve
for a particular product as a function of price is shown in Figure 4.1. In this case the
linear demand curve is such that $D = -10 \times P + 30,000$ (where $D =$ demand and $P
=$ price)[2]. JJT has limited the price to be between \$1200 and \$2200, so the corre-
sponding limits on demand are 18,000 and 8000 units; these bounds may be determined
because of concerns about market share or about the accuracy of the demand model
outside of a reasonable range.

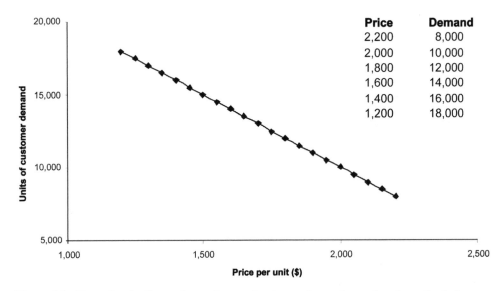

Price	Demand
2,200	8,000
2,000	10,000
1,800	12,000
1,600	14,000
1,400	16,000
1,200	18,000

Figure 4.1 Example of a linear demand curve (customer demand as a function of price)

The demand curve also takes into account customers' sensitivities towards the price,
often measured in the form of 'demand elasticity', which is the percentage change in
quantity/percentage change in price. Natasha knew that customers were quite sensitive
to the price of some of their products (luxury gifts, with elasticity around 3.5), especially
if substitutes for the products were available, but in other cases price changes didn't
affect demand as much (brand-name beer for which many customers had loyalty, with
elasticity around .25).

The material prepared by the consultants continued. The revenue generated by sales
of the product is $R(D) = D \times P$, or $-10\,P^2 + 30,000 \times P$. Figure 4.2 shows revenue as
a function of product price, within the bounds indicated before. If the production
capacity was not limited, then the revenue curve indicates that setting the price to be
\$1500 (thus selling 15,000 units of demand) provides the maximum amount of revenue
(\$22,500,000). However, this is not the demand level that provides the most profit, since
costs also need to be considered. With unlimited production capacity, the demand that

provides the most profit can be calculated using derivatives, and for this example the optimal price is $1750 (corresponding to demand of 12,500). The consultants also called this the *optimal uncapacitated demand*. However, JJT only has the capacity to produce 12,000 units of this product in a particular month, so the optimal price for this production period alone is $1800.

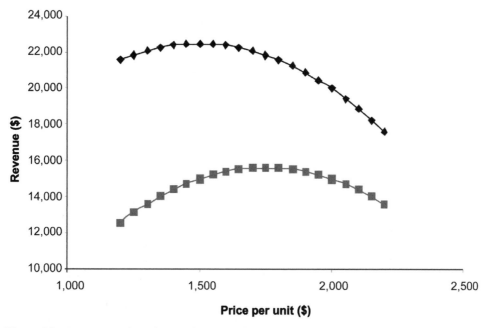

Figure 4.2 Revenue and profit as a function of price

Of course, Natasha realized this representation was just for a particular month out of the year. For many of their products, JJT experienced significant variability in sales over the course of the year. The consultants classified the products at JJT into five categories and focused on general characteristics of products within these classes to demonstrate this effect. The consultants first estimated linear demand curves in each month where the parameters were multiplied by seasonality factors, then calculated the optimal uncapacitated demand in each period. The result, shown in Figure 4.3, demonstrates the nature of the variability of the classes of products over a year.

The first class of products, Seas1, includes items like tennis racquets – generally demand is low in the winter, higher in late spring and summer, and lower again in the fall. The second class of products (Seas2) exhibits the opposite effect, where demand is generally higher in the winter and lower in the summer, e.g., sports equipment. Both classes include quarterly seasonality factors, as well as additional variability from month to month. Some of the products at JJT experience a learning or word-of-mouth effect, where sales increase over the year, music CDs for instance might fall into the IncMean class. High technology products like computers generally see decreasing demand over their lifetime, where sales decline as new products cannibalize sales of older products (DecMean class). For comparison, the consultants also created a class called Sawtooth with some randomness, which is not motivated by particular products but was chosen as a contrast to the other demand scenarios.

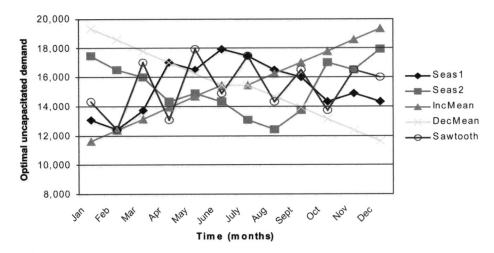

Figure 4.3   Demand variability by product class

Natasha mulled over the report as she headed to the cafeteria for lunch. The consultants claimed that dynamic pricing could significantly increase profit, particularly under certain kinds of demand variability. Natasha saw that the strategy allowed for a better matching between system capacity and customer demand. The consultants had even tried to quantify the increase in profit from dynamic pricing. Natasha suspected that the numbers were high, but she was sure that there were gains in profit to be achieved through dynamic pricing. However, they also claimed that pricing might be able to help with the variability that JJT experienced, an idea that hadn't occurred to Natasha. That could mean an opportunity to reduce the supply chain costs at JJT, and perhaps pass the savings on to customers as well.

She continued to pore through the materials over lunch. The consultants had developed a simple mathematical model to try to quantify the impact of dynamic pricing. The objective was to maximize profit over time, represented by the following:

$$\text{Maximize profit: } \sum_{t=1}^{T} R_t(D_t) - h_t I_t - k_t X_t$$

where I was for inventory, X indicated production, and h and k were the costs associated with each of the activities. The system was also subject to constraints in each period $_t$, described as below:

$$I_0 = 0 \qquad \text{(1) Beginning Inventory}$$
$$I_t = I_{t-1} + X_t - D_t \qquad \text{(2) Inventory Balance}$$
$$X_t \le q_t \qquad \text{(3) Production Capacity}$$
$$I_t, X_t, D_t \ge 0 \qquad \text{(4) Positive and Integers}$$

Natasha remembered seeing similar models when she studied Operations Management in an MBA programme. Although price didn't appear explicitly in this one, the consultants explained the price was calculated from the demand curve since demand was the decision variable.

Using this model, the consultants solved for the best price that would match supply and demand, and they estimated the profit for each of the product classes. They also developed the following performance metric, which they called the profit potential:

$$\text{Profit potential:} \frac{\text{Profit under dynamic pricing}}{\text{Profit under fixed pricing}} - 1$$

The result was an estimate of the percentage increase in profit if JJT went to a dynamic pricing strategy, and the results for the five classes are shown in Figure 4.4 for three different levels of variability. (All remaining results are based on the case of medium variability.)

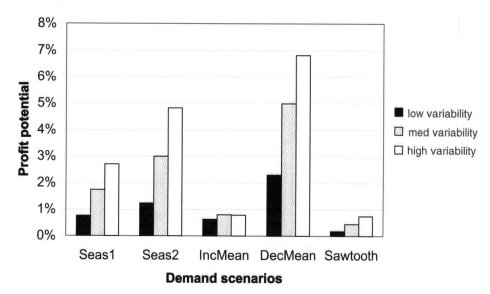

Figure 4.4 Profit potential by product class and variability level (dynamic pricing over fixed pricing)

The results indicated that dynamic pricing could mean increases in profit from 1–5 per cent, no small change for products with low profit margins at JJT. Of course, these numbers were a bit optimistic; for one thing the consultants assumed that the demand could be entirely predicted, and the reality was that one never knew just how many orders would come in at any time. Furthermore, they hadn't made any mention of competitors' reactions if JJT started changing prices, or whether customers would start behaving strategically. Still, even a percentage or two improvement could mean significant gains for JJT.

Natasha also noticed that dynamic pricing had quite different impacts depending on the type of product being considered. For realistic variability, the impact ranged from 1 per cent improvement (IncMean) to a maximum of 5 per cent profit potential (Dec-Mean). Clearly, the nature of the demand characteristics was a significant parameter in the performance of dynamic pricing relative to fixed pricing.

Her brow furrowed as she finished off a slice of key lime pie. Where did the increase in profit come from anyway, was it just from increased sales or were there other factors?

'Maybe they're thinking too much about profit', Natasha almost said aloud. 'What would this dynamic pricing idea do to the production schedule?' She knew if dynamic pricing increased the variability it could mean real trouble for her supply chain team.

The consultant team focused on many of these questions next in the report. They carefully considered the source of the increase in profit, since changes in market share were of significant interest to JJT, as well as changes in costs. First they defined two performance metrics to calculate the change in revenue due to dynamic pricing:

$$Revenue\ change\ due\ to\ sales = (Dynamic\ sales - Fixed\ sales) \times Dynamic\ price$$
$$Revenue\ change\ due\ to\ price = Fixed\ sales \times (Dynamic\ price - Fixed\ price)$$

where the dynamic price is calculated as the weighted average price over the horizon. They also calculated the change in production cost and inventory holding cost under a dynamic pricing strategy compared to fixed pricing. The results are shown in Figure 4.5; note that the total contribution to profit potential is normalized to 100%. Contributions above the x-axis indicate an increase in profit potential due to dynamic pricing; contributions below the x-axis show a decrease in profit potential. For instance, if the contribution of inventory cost appears above 0, it implies that inventory costs for dynamic pricing were lower than for fixed pricing.

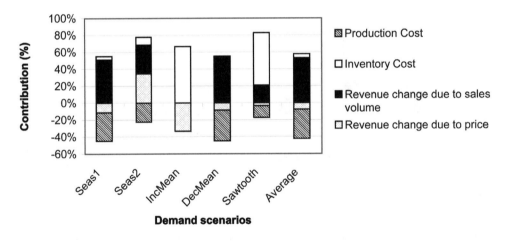

Figure 4.5 Sources of profit potential by product class (as percentage of total contribution)

As the consultants pointed out, and as Natasha saw in the Figure, profit potential from dynamic pricing could come from a variety of sources. For example, in Seas1, the potential is largely due to increased revenue from increased sales volume, but in the IncMean product class, the potential is attributed to a decrease in inventory costs.

While the sources of profit potential are not the same for every product type, in most cases revenue due to sales volume shows a positive profit contribution. This implies that sales volume (and thus market share) is generally higher for dynamic pricing than for fixed pricing. Of course, an increase in sales volume is accompanied by an increase in production cost and a decrease in price. Natasha guessed that the increase in sales volume was due to the better match of supply and demand that the consultants were claiming.

Natasha was pleased to see that the team had addressed variability as an important factor. Typically, JJT had set a single fixed price over the lifetime of each product, based on demand curves, production and holding costs, and available production capacity. All of the management at JJT knew that their customer demand fluctuated over time; it was a constant source of worry for the production team. Some months their overtime charges shot through the roof! Worse, at some times the production team was under-utilized, so it was difficult to justify the expensive labour costs during other times.

The consultants graphed the predicted sales over a year for each of the five classes of products under the best fixed price policy (see Figure 4.6). Natasha could see that the sales were all over the board, and the production schedule reflected similar kinds of variability. She was familiar with the bullwhip effect as well, which implied that the variability increased going up the supply chain, so she knew that there were hidden costs to this effect.

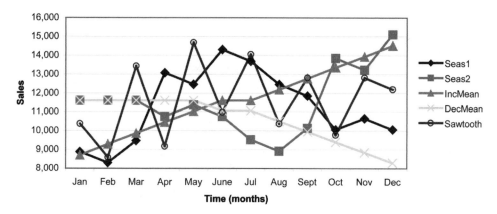

Figure 4.6 Variability of sales under fixed pricing policy

Using the same demand, the consultants looked at the resulting sales under the best dynamic pricing policy (displayed in Figure 4.7). Natasha could see that the sales variability under dynamic pricing was less, which also meant the production schedule should have less variability. The consultants argued that pricing allowed the company to utilize their capacity more efficiently, rather than putting in overtime in periods of high demand, or rather than building up expensive inventory. Natasha thought to herself, 'I certainly believe this works when capacity is fairly constant over time, but I'm not sure we'd see the same effect if capacity fluctuates, and who knows what happens if both demand and capacity are variable.'

Natasha left the cafeteria and headed back to her office. 'And what about our customers?' Natasha asked herself as she turned the corner to her office. She guessed they would be willing to accept some price changes, but not if they were too large or too often, especially if JJT could reduce costs through the new strategy and pass on some of the savings to the customers. She had heard rumours that Doug Ivester, the former Chairman of Coca-Cola Company had considered a dynamic pricing strategy (Cortese and Stepanek, 1998), and that Ivester had left Coca-Cola in part due to customer dissatisfaction over the pricing strategy. She certainly didn't want that to happen to herself! Yet, she knew that JJT needed to consider new strategies to remain successful in the changing market.

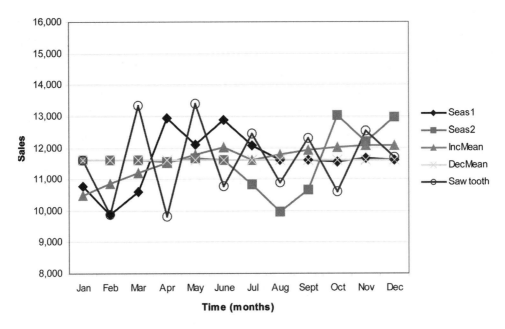

Figure 4.7   Variability of sales under dynamic pricing policy

She flipped through the report until she found more sections that interested her. Natasha chuckled as she saw the consultants had predicted many of her questions about price changes. The next portion of the report addressed the variability of the optimal prices under dynamic pricing (see Figure 4.8). For the sample products, the optimal price varied in a range as big as 11 per cent total around the optimal fixed price. For example, Widget 5.0 had a list price of $500, and the dynamic prices varied from about $475 to $525, which was pretty close to the size of rebates that JJT sometimes used for promotions.

But more than just the actual percentages, which Natasha knew were affected by the sample products chosen, the graph provided additional useful information. The Figure also indicated the direction of the price changes: increasing in the IncMean class for instance, but decreasing for the DecMean class. This meant dynamic pricing would probably be easier to implement for DecMean, since customers are more likely to accept price markdowns than steady price increases (e.g., laptops or fashion clothing). Of course, the price tended to follow the direction of the demand as well, so if demand really increased for the IncMean products, perhaps implementation would be okay. The consultants pointed out that this kind of price structure held for certain kinds of products, airline tickets for instance. The other classes experienced a similar effect where price tended to track the direction of demand (e.g., low, high, low for Seas1). This suggested that some rules of thumb might be appropriate for the directions of price changes.

The consultants also asked the question of what would happen if price changes weren't made in every production period, since customers might object to prices changing frequently. To look at this, they examined various pricing strategies for each of the product classes, where price changes were allowed 0, 1, 2, 3, 5, or 11 times during the 12 periods (0 corresponds to a fixed price, and 11 changes is full dynamic pricing). Since customers might be sensitive to the frequency of these changes, they required that

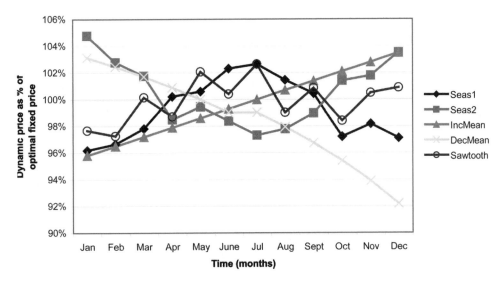

Figure 4.8 Variability of optimal prices under dynamic pricing policy

the changes be evenly spaced over the entire time horizon: that is, if 1 price change is allowed in a year, the change occurs after 6 months, so the profit increase is a lower bound on the profit if the price change can occur at any time in the year.

For each of the product classes, the consultants determined the percentage of profit potential under limited price changes relative to the profit potential under full dynamic pricing (see Figure 4.9 for the results). The results indicate that in many cases, significant profit can be achieved with fewer price changes. In most of the cases, a price change every three production periods achieved 75 per cent or more of the total profit potential.

Natasha immediately noted that this did not hold for the Sawtooth class of products. Not only was full dynamic pricing needed for that class, in some cases fewer price changes were better! The consultants addressed the last issue by noting that they only considered price changes that were evenly spaced, so the price periods would not necessarily match the pattern of demand variability well. To address the first issue, they also provided another graph (see Figure 4.10), which shows the profit potential over fixed pricing (but not relative to the total dynamic pricing profit potential). The Sawtooth class, with demand alternating between high and low in successive periods, had the lowest profit potential of any of the classes (one explanation for why full dynamic pricing is needed). Since the demand changes were frequent, it is also likely that price changes are also needed frequently to match the variability. Figure 4.10 also demonstrates that a few number of price changes can result in significant profit potential.

Natasha was quite interested in the results so far ... dynamic pricing might have some potential for JJT. However, the analysis so far considered the products completely separately. In reality, similar products often shared assembly capacity, so she didn't think this should be completely ignored. She was curious what would happen with dynamic pricing of multiple products, and she was pleased to see that the team had at least begun to address this question.

The consultants considered a portfolio of products sharing production capacity, where pricing, inventory, and production decisions were made on each product. They

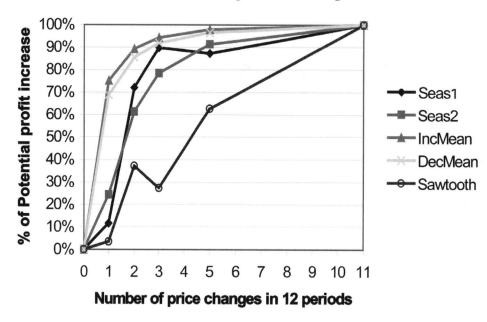

Figure 4.9 Percentage of potential profit increase due to number of price changes

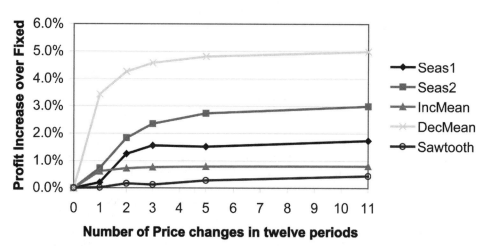

Figure 4.10 Profit potential due to number of price changes (increase in profit due to dynamic pricing policies)

assumed that products sharing capacity experienced similar types of demand variability, so they were competing for limited resources at the same time. However, they also assumed that there were no demand diversions among products, i.e., that the demand for each product was independent of the prices of the other products. For some products, Natasha felt this was reasonable – customers who wanted to buy Widget L would not substitute with Widget S, because they served different purposes. But for products such as Widget 5.0 and Widget 5.5, she was sure there were customers who wanted 5.0 but would switch to 5.5 if the price was right. The consultants focused on two of the product classes as an example (Seas1 and DecMean), and looked at the performance of dynamic pricing relative to fixed pricing as the number of products in the portfolio increased (see Figure 4.11).

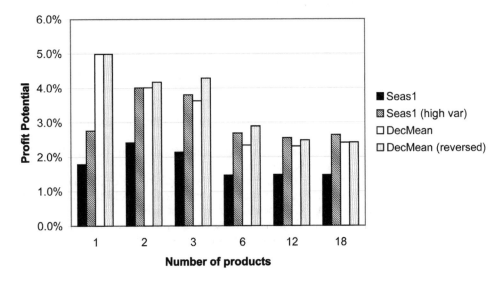

Figure 4.11   Profit potential for multiple products sharing capacity

The first thing the team pointed out was that the profit increase of dynamic pricing over fixed pricing tended to decrease with the number of products. They explained this further: both fixed and dynamic pricing strategies needed to determine the mix of products in a portfolio by determining the base price of a product (and thus the level of demand). Since some products are more profitable than others based on production costs, determining the product mix is an important component of profit, particularly when the products share limited capacity. The graph suggests that determining the mix of products in the portfolio may be as important or more so than tweaking the price of each product over time, which is the additional flexibility allowed in dynamic pricing.

Of course, this doesn't hold all of the time. In particular, dynamic pricing over two or three products often has greater profit potential than only one product. One possible explanation is that a little flexibility may have a significant effect, as Natasha had seen for the frequency of price changes. However, much of this could also be due to the relative profitability of the products that are added to the portfolio, so the consultants considered the DecMean class with the order of products reversed as their final example.

The team also examined the Seas1 class with higher demand variability, and saw that the results were similar, except that the higher variability implied a higher profit potential as well. Finally, the consultants also pointed out that whereas the profit potential decreased with the number of products, the potential by product class may stabilize. This is likely to be due to the idea that a little flexibility helps a lot, but the marginal contribution of flexibility probably decreases.

Natasha closed the binder to the report and leaned back in her chair thoughtfully. She certainly was intrigued with some of these innovative pricing strategies, and she thought some of them had potential applicability to JJT. She didn't want to accept the consultants' recommendations immediately however; they had a vested interest in convincing her to try the new strategy, since JJT would probably pay the same company to implement it if they moved forward! Also, she still had plenty of questions she wanted them to address. She turned to her computer and began composing an email of some of her many questions to the consultants.

DISCUSSION QUESTIONS

Below are some of Natasha's questions outlined to you, a member of the consultant team.

1. Why do different product classes exhibit different results (particularly for profit potential, sources of profit potential, etc.)?
2. What would happen if some of the assumptions were relaxed? For instance, what if customers planned their buying strategically, what impact would this have on the pricing strategies and results? Competition from other firms?
3. What are some guidelines on when it might make sense to use dynamic pricing and when it wouldn't make sense? What would JJT need to think about if they wanted to implement dynamic pricing?

NOTES

The graphs and some other portions of this case study are based on research that appears in Biller *et al.* (2003). An industrial partner provided the initial data set that we use for the experiments, and the data was further manipulated for the study. Related research by the author and others also appears in Chan *et al.* (2002).

1. The case is loosely based on discussions with several companies.
2. The linear demand curve in the function $D = a \times P + B$ can be derived from the definition of demand elasticity. This curve is formed with a demand elasticity of -2.0, a base price of \$2000, and a base demand of 10,000.

REFERENCES

Baker, W., Marn, M. and Zawada, C. (2001) 'Price smarter on the net', *Harvard Business Review*, **79**(2), 122–6.

Biller, S., Chan, L. M. A., Simchi-Levi, D. and Swann, J. (2003) 'Dynamic pricing and the direct-to-customer model in the automotive industry', to appear in *E-Commerce Journal*, Special Issue on Dynamic Pricing.

Chan, L. M. A., Shen, Z. J., Simchi-Levi, D. and Swann, J. (forthcoming) 'Coordination of pricing and inventory decision: a survey and classification', in Z. J. Shen, D. Simchi-Levi and D. Wu (eds), *Handbook on Applications of OR in E-commerce*. Kluwer Academic Publishers.

Chan, L. M. A., Simchi-Levi, D. and Swann, J. L. (2002) 'Dynamic pricing models for manufacturing with stochastic demand and discretionary sales'. Working paper, Georgia Institute of Technology.

Cortese, A. E. and Stepanek, M. (1998) 'Goodbye to fixed pricing?', *Business Week*, **3576**, 70–84.

Elmaghraby, W. and Keskinocak, P. (2002) 'Dynamic pricing: research overview, current practices and future directions'. Working paper, Georgia Institute of Technology.

Kay, E. (1998) 'Flexed pricing', *Datamation*.

Leibs, S. (2000) 'Ford heeds the profits', *CFO The Magazine*, **16**(9), 33–5.

McWilliams, G. (2001) 'Lean machine: how Dell fine-tunes its PC pricing', *Wall Street Journal*.

5

Revenue Management in Restaurants: A Case Example from Bornholm, Denmark

---

Nick Johns and Charlotte Rassing

INTRODUCTION

Interest in revenue management in the restaurant sector has intensified in recent years, as evidenced by work from Donaghy *et al.* (1998) and Kimes *et al.* (1998, 1999). Desinano *et al.* (2000) consider the approach one of the most promising process innovations in the hospitality industry in recent years. However, despite considerable theoretical input from these groups and the great need for restaurant revenue control worldwide, there is relatively little in the way of documented practical application.

Revenue management is often said to be a matter of allocating the right capacity to the right customer at the right time (e.g., McEvoy, 1997; Smith *et al.*, 1992) with the aim of maximizing the 'yield' of possible revenue. It is essential for the competitiveness of capacity-constrained businesses (Hoseason and Johns, 1998) especially those such as airlines and cruises where time-constrained 'seats' are sold. In principle the restaurant industry also comes into this category, since service depends upon seating customers within a constrained time frame and physical capacity. However, from the operator's point of view there are significant differences between places on a flight or cruise (or for that matter a hotel) and restaurant seats. The former are charged primarily by the space customers occupy, but the revenue-generating potential of restaurants depends upon food sales, and is only indirectly related to seating capacity. Thus in the restaurant industry, revenue management includes issues of menu planning and pricing.

Another way to regard revenue management is providing the right service to the right customer at the right time for the right price (Kimes, 1989). The relevance of this to restaurant operations can be made still clearer using Kimes' typology of service industries (see Figure 5.1).

Kimes' model reduces revenue management to two components: the duration of the service and the price that is charged for that service. Restaurants are characterized by having relatively fixed prices and unpredictable service duration. The aim of revenue

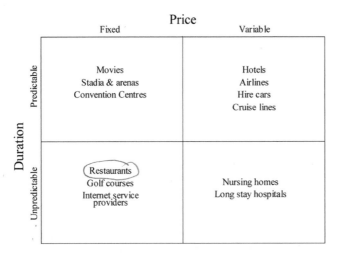

Figure 5.1 Typology of revenue management, after Kimes (2001)

management is to obtain higher revenue for a given capacity, and in restaurants this can be achieved by maximizing the yield per seat-hour. This involves managing the time for which seats are occupied and at the same time optimizing menu options and prices.

The 'occupation' of restaurant seats may be virtual or real. For instance, no-shows, late arrivals and periods of low demand all have the effect of tying up capacity even though they do not physically occupy the space. Part of the process of managing 'service duration' is to reduce this virtual occupation, which may be achieved by improving booking procedures, through more accurate forecasting and (perhaps) through overbooking. The management of actual seat occupation is also very important. The time customers take to choose can be reduced by redesigning menus, and service times can be cut with better schedules and communication. Time can also be saved by timely billing and by redesigning premises, for instance to provide a drinks bar to buffer arrivals and a coffee/desserts bar to free up tables. Fast food restaurants often use subtle cues such as bright décor and slightly hard seats to discourage guests from lingering (Johns, 1999).

Optimizing revenue through restaurant prices is related partly to rate fences and partly to menu design. Rate fences are often tied to specific dates or times of day, for instance lunch is often priced differently to dinner and meals on Valentine's or Mother's Day are usually at a premium compared to those on other days. It is also possible to charge different rates depending upon the party size, the type of booking, the location of the table, or the provision of particular amenities. These approaches aim to maximize revenue by raising prices across the board (see also Nagle and Holden, 1994). Menu design on the other hand aims to optimize prices in relation to the demand and profitability of each item, so that the price/opportunity relationship inherent in revenue management is devolved to the level of individual customers and what they wish to eat. Some approaches to menu design are discussed in the next section.

Revenue management is a particularly attractive tool in situations of rising costs, falling income or high competition. Therefore it is particularly relevant to the Danish restaurant industry. In recent years restaurants in Denmark have experienced an increase in the number of businesses against a background of declining earnings, and in addition taxes and labour laws keep operating costs very high. Thus each year sees the arrival of hundreds of new or re-opening restaurants, while slightly fewer disappear from the market-place. However, despite struggling with declining earnings and the competitive environment, most Danish restaurants react conservatively towards their problems. Typically they attempt to cut costs rather than raising revenue. They often ignore opportunities for up-selling to their customers, and attach only secondary importance to in-house merchandizing devices such as the menu. Thus revenue management in restaurants can be viewed as menu engineering, a matter of combining the right menu items with the right prices in a way that makes customers choose the items the restaurant wishes to sell. Ultimately this is what maximizes the revenue that can be derived from a restaurant's limited seat capacity.

This much is true of the restaurant industry throughout Denmark. The study presented in this chapter took place on the Danish island of Bornholm, which is located in the Baltic Sea, about 100 miles east of Copenhagen and close to the South East coast of Sweden. Bornholm is unspoiled and enjoys good summer weather, as a result of which it has become a mature resort area for fairly constant annual numbers of Germans and Scandinavians. The restaurant industry on Bornholm reflects the relatively isolated, static nature of the destination, being highly seasonal, quite highly priced and rather traditional and conservative in outlook. Thus, even more than other Danish restaurants, the industry on Bornholm typically pays little attention to the composition of the menu and to the prices charged for different items and there is often little or no attempt to investigate market trends or to seriously forecast sales. Restaurants typically base the composition and design of the new menu on last year's menu without any critical examination of the different dishes' sales performance. Therefore they presented a suitable opportunity for the revenue management trials discussed in this chapter. The objective of this work was to identify and pilot a suitable, practicable revenue management approach in Bornholm restaurants and thereby to help the industry become more effective and profitable.

THEORETICAL BACKGROUND

Various researchers have sought to optimize restaurant revenue through menu design, and at least three mature analytical approaches are available for research use, which are considered in this chapter. They all aim to compare the profitability of different menu items so that menus can be developed in a way that maximizes revenue. All three techniques compare some aspect of profitability with item turnover in a four-cell matrix. This comparison makes it possible to group menu items according to their relative score on each criterion and to decide what to do with them. The three menu analysis systems considered here are derived from the work of Miller (1980), Kasavana and Smith (1982) and Pavesic (1985).

Miller's (1980) matrix uses food cost percentage as the profitability criterion, and compares this with sales volume. The mathematics underlying this process are shown in Table 5.1, and on the basis of the comparison, Miller classifies menu items into 'winners', 'marginals' and 'losers'. A 'winner' is distinguished by having relatively low food costs and high sales volume, while 'losers' are characterized by higher cost and lower sales volume. 'Marginals' may be of two possible kinds, since they may have a combination either of lower cost/lower sales volume, or alternatively of higher cost/higher sales volume. This may be seen in Figure 5.2, which compares the three revenue management approaches.

Table 5.1 The mathematics behind Miller's approach

Menu items	P Selling price	Q Numbers sold	R Revenue	F Food cost per item	FM Food cost margin per item
1	p_1	q_1	$r_1 = p_1 \cdot q_1$	f_1	$fm_1 = \dfrac{f_1}{p_1} \cdot 100$
2	p_2	q_2	$r_2 = p_2 \cdot q_2$	f_2	$fm_2 = \dfrac{f_2}{p_2} \cdot 100$
3	p_3	q_3	$r_3 = p_3 \cdot q_3$	f_3	$fm_3 = \dfrac{f_3}{p_3} \cdot 100$
Cut-off points		$\dfrac{Q}{N}$			$\dfrac{FM}{N}$

The average sales volume of all items is employed as the criterion for considering a food item to have a 'high' or 'low' sales volume. Average sales are calculated as $\dfrac{Q}{N} = \dfrac{\Sigma_q}{N}$ where N is the number of items in the specific menu group (starters, entrées, desserts, etc.). Thus items in the upper and lower half of the matrix (Figure 5.2) are those with above and below average volume respectively. In the same way a food item is considered to have a 'high' food cost if its food cost margin is above average, calculated as $\dfrac{FM}{N} = \dfrac{\Sigma_{fm}}{N}$. Together these two tests place the item within the matrix and label it a 'winner', 'marginal' or 'loser'.

Kasavana and Smith (1982) offer a somewhat refined version of Miller's matrix. They present a more critical analysis of the process, noting the need to compare the sales mix (i.e., an analysis of customer preference and demand) critically with some suitable function of the gross profit margin (i.e., some kind of item pricing analysis). However, instead of using the simple cost/price ratio, they calculate item contribution margins as shown in Table 5.2.

Table 5.2 The mathematics behind the Kasavana-Smith approach

Menu items	Q Numbers sold	$Q\%$ Numbers sold (%)	P Selling price	F Food cost (item)	CM Contribution margin	CM_i Item CM
1	q_1	$\dfrac{q_1}{\Sigma q} \cdot 100$	p_1	f_1	$cm_1 = p_1 - f_1$	$cm_{i1} = q_1 \cdot cm_1$
2	q_2	$\dfrac{q_2}{\Sigma q} \cdot 100$	p_2	f_2	$cm_2 = p_2 - f_2$	$cm_{i2} = q_2 \cdot cm_2$
3	q_3	$\dfrac{q_3}{\Sigma q} \cdot 100$	p_3	f_3	$cm_3 = p_3 - f_3$	$cm_{i3} = q_3 \cdot cm_3$
Cut-off point		$\dfrac{1}{N} \cdot 0,7 \cdot 100$				$\dfrac{CM}{Q}$

Kasavana and Smith (1982) use a weighted criterion system, rather than the straight averages employed by Miller. An item is considered to have a 'higher' sales volume if its selection rate ($q\%$) exceeds 70 per cent of the average popularity for the group (100%

divided by the number of menu items in the group). A menu item is considered 'less popular' if its selection rate is less than 70 per cent of the average popularity.

In order to classify menu items according to their profitability the average contribution margin is calculated as $CM/Q = \frac{\Sigma cm_i}{\Sigma q_i}$. An item with a contribution margin above, or below, the average for all items is classified as having a 'higher' or 'lower' food contribution margin respectively.

These two criteria are used to classify the menu items using a four-cell matrix, as shown in Figure 5.2. The cell categories are 'stars' (i.e., high volume, high contribution margin), 'plowhorses' (high volume, low contribution margin), 'puzzles' (low volume, high contribution margin) or 'dogs' (low volume, low contribution margin).

Although the Miller and Kasavana-Smith classification systems are derived from very similar basic data material, there are some important differences between them. For instance Miller's food cost margins are calculated only by dividing cost by price, so they are independent of volume. The Kavana-Smith item contribution margins are calculated by multiplying the price–cost difference by the volume, so that both the volume and the margin with which it is compared are functions of volume. This has the effect of pushing all item scores diagonally up towards the top right-hand cell, for which Kasavana and Smith compensate by weighting the volume criterion to 0.7 rather than taking the average. However, this is a rather ad hoc approach. The classification system (into 'stars', 'dogs', etc.) is more detailed and leads to a greater range of possible management actions: one seeks to promote 'stars', to exploit 'plowhorses', to solve 'puzzles' and to eliminate 'dogs'. Miller's system permits the manager to back 'winners' and eliminate 'losers', but there is not much to be done for 'marginals'.

Pavesic (1985) has further developed the Miller and Kasavana-Smith approaches by weighting item contribution margins according to sales volume, providing a more objective criterion for classifying the items. The mathematics underlying Pavesic's approach are shown in Table 5.3.

Table 5.3   The mathematics behind Pavesic's approach

Menu items	F Item food cost	P Selling price	Q Numbers sold	WF Weighted food cost	WQ Weighted sales	CM Weighted contribution margin	$F\%$ Food cost $\%$
1	f_1	p_1	q_1	$wf_1 = f_1 \cdot q_1$	$wq_1 = p_1 \cdot q_1$	$cm_1 = wq_1 - wf_1$	$f_1 = \frac{wf_1}{wq_1} \cdot 100$
2	f_2	p_2	q_2	$wf_2 = f_2 \cdot q_2$	$wq_2 = p_2 \cdot q_2$	$cm_2 = wq_2 - wf_2$	$f_2 = \frac{wf_2}{wq_2} \cdot 100$
3	f_3	p_3	q_3	$wf_3 = f_3 \cdot q_3$	$wq_3 = p_3 \cdot q_3$	$cm_3 = wq_3 - wf_3$	$f_3 = \frac{wf_3}{wq_3} \cdot 100$
Cut-off point						$\dfrac{CM}{N} = \dfrac{\Sigma cmi}{N}$	$\dfrac{Wf}{Wq} = \dfrac{\Sigma wfi}{\Sigma wqi} \cdot 100$

Pavesic's classification is based upon somewhat different criteria from the other two. The food cost criterion is taken as the weighted average food cost percentage, calculated by dividing total weighted food cost (W_f) by total weighted sales (W_q). An item with a food cost percentage below the weighted average is classified as having a 'low' food cost. A second criterion is calculated by dividing the total weighted contribution margin (CM) by the total number of menu items (N), thus measuring an item's performance in relation to its contribution margin. Menu items that exceed this criterion are classified as having a high contribution margin. Pavesic's system employs a four-cell matrix in which menu items are classified as 'primes', 'standards', 'problems' or 'sleepers'. Although the determinants of Pavesic's matrix do not exactly overlap those of the other authors discussed, his categories may be compared with theirs, as summarized in Figure 5.2. It is legitimate to do this on the presumption that profit margin is likely to be broadly inversely proportional to food cost, while weighting gross profit contribution renders them a function of sales volume.

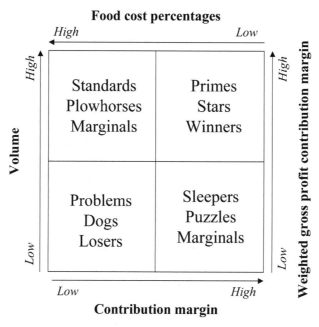

Figure 5.2 Comparison of Miller (1980), Kasavana and Smith (1982) and Pavesic (1985) matrices

Management actions suggested by Pavesic's classification are broadly equivalent to those for the Kasavana-Smith system. Items classified as 'prime' should be emphasized, and 'standard' items exploited. 'Problem' items may be modified, or dropped from the menu, while 'sleeper' items represent development opportunities.

However, these are very simplistic notions, based upon an operational view of restaurant management. Atkinson and Jones (1994) suggest a more detailed series of actions, based upon the 'four Ps' of marketing theory. These are outlined in Figure 5.3.

Because they have the greatest sales and margins, cell 1 items ('winners', 'stars' or 'primes') carry a disproportionate share of the overall gross profit contribution. A corresponding proportion of management effort should be devoted to the promotion, quality, quantity and presentation of these items. They should be highlighted on the menu and their consistency closely monitored. These are usually the restaurant's signature items, i.e., the house specialities, and because of this they are less price-sensitive than the rest of the menu. Therefore the price should be varied in order to test elasticity of demand, since any increase in volume or price will provide a healthy contribution to net income targets. In contrast the aim for menu items in cell 2 ('marginals', 'plowhorses' or 'standards') is to raise the average gross profit margin by capitalizing upon

Performance A
(food cost percentages, contribution margin)

Poor   *Good*

	2 Price: Up Product: Modify Promotion: Do nothing Place: Do nothing	**1** Price: Up/down Product Do nothing Promotion: Sell Place: Do nothing
	4 Price: Review Product: Replace Promotion: Do nothing Place: Do nothing	**3** Price: Down Product Rename Promotion: Sell Place: Reposition

Good ... *Poor*

Performance B
(volume, weighted gross profit contribution margin)

Figure 5.3 Suggested management action for menu item matrix groupings (adapted from Atkinson and Jones (1994))

their popularity, which can be done for example by relocating them on the printed menu, adjusting portion sizes or modifying standard recipes. Cell 2 menu items attract price-sensitive customers and are therefore often referred to as demand generators. Therefore their prices must be competitive with those of other nearby restaurants.

Menu items in cell 3 ('marginals', 'puzzles' or 'sleepers') are often the most difficult and frustrating group but at the same time provide the best opportunities for menu development. These items frequently include new items that are being test-marketed to see how customers respond to them (Pavesic, 1985). Management action should focus upon improving their sales volume, which can be done by promoting, repricing or repositioning them. For example they can be renamed or made the subject of special promotions, actions which have the potential to move them up into cell 1. Items in cell 4 ('losers', 'dogs' or 'problems') could in principle be removed from the menu, or the restaurant might continue to carry them without a listing on the menu. Many of them are worth little if anything to the operation, but there are generally a few that still have some market potential, and these may be moved to cell 2 by increasing the price. However, some of these are likely to be items that have to be kept on the menu, even though their contribution is low. For instance they may aimed at special groups of visitors, i.e., children or vegetarians, or they could be so-called decoy anchors – products without which other items are less acceptable such as coffee, an adjunct for cake. If these items must be retained on the menu, the manager should seek to reduce food cost or increase popularity and gross profit margin, thus effectively moving them towards other cells of the matrix.

Every item on the menu must fall into one or other of the four cells in Figure 5.3, but the items within a single cell cannot be considered equivalent, and it is possible to identify more specific actions by considering the relative rankings items within a given cell (Kasavana and Smith, 1982). Within the cells themselves, it is permissible to have a low gross profit margin on items in cell 1. Items in cells 2 and 3 should have a medium-to-high gross profit margin, while those in cell 4 should have a high gross profit margin, if they are to stay on the menu.

In practical terms, menus often do not function simply at the level of individual items. According to Bayou and Bennett (1992) the performance of item groupings should be considered in any analysis of restaurant profitability, as well as that of the individual menu items themselves. Groupings that should be considered include categories based upon the type of dish (e.g., appetizers, entrées) and those relating to meal periods or business categories (breakfasts, lunches, banquets and so on). Menu matrix analysis can be refined to consider the positioning of individual items within menu groupings of this kind. Hayes and Huffman (1985) also suggest an alternative approach, in which mini profit and loss accounts can be drawn up for each separate menu item. In principle this is appropriate for analysing groupings within the menu, but it does not provide such convenient categories for management decision-making as the four-cell techniques discussed here.

On the other hand the four-cell techniques have a number of shortcomings that should be mentioned. They are based on average sales volumes, average food cost percentages and average gross profit margins. This may result in the unhelpful clustering and generalizing of menu item profitability. In addition they are normative in concept, and some items must always fall into the less-desirable categories. Hayes and Huffman (1995) note that if the less desirable items in the matrix are eliminated, the overall average will change, rendering some of the remaining ones less desirable, and every time the consequence of the analysis is that some items are removed without being replaced, the menu will end up with just one starter, one entrée and one dessert. Thus matrix analysis results in an endless battle if the recommended management actions are carried out without considering the whole picture, and decisions about eliminating, repositioning, or price changes should not be made solely on the basis of quantitative data. Subjective and psychological aspects of the customer's purchase decision also have to be taken into account.

Miller's method identifies the low food cost items as the ones to sell, an approach that is often criticized because it is based on food cost percentages rather than food cost: 'you can't bank percentages – only dollars' (Pavesic, 1985: 71). Both the Kasavana-Smith and the Pavesic approach use a market share cut-off point of 70 per cent of average sales, implying a skewed demand distribution. Skewing demand towards lower priced items avoids elimination of the more highly priced menu items that make a major contribution to revenue. However, the 70 per cent cut-off point does not take into account the specific circumstances of each restaurant. The Miller, Kasavana-Smith and Pavesic categorization systems are all ultimately based upon averages and therefore always identify some less desirable (i.e., below average) menu items. Hayes and Huffman (1985) attempt to remove this focus on averages with an alternative system, in which individual profit-and-loss statements are drawn up for each menu item. Unlike the other systems discussed above, this analysis takes into account fixed costs, which are shared equally among all the menu items. It is often difficult for a restaurant manager to apportion variable costs such as labour, electricity and water to individual menu items. However, Hayes and Huffman (1985) suggest that labour and other non-food costs are likely to vary with production volume, and hence with quantity of sales so that these variable costs can be realistically estimated as 35 per cent of gross sales. The result of Hayes and Huffman's profit-and-loss method is independent of cost classification (i.e., as variable or fixed) since the result is based on gross profit (i.e., selling price minus food cost). Hayes and Huffman's (1985) analysis identifies the 'best' items as those which contribute the greatest profit. This allows the restaurant operator to examine each menu item independent of the rest of the menu and avoids dependence on averages. However, this is a rather more complicated process than that required for the classification techniques described above. For the purposes of the present study, the three classification techniques were applied to a restaurant on the island of Bornholm, with the aim of identifying an acceptable, user-friendly approach suitable for the managers of small businesses in this environment.

THE BORNHOLM CASE

Several Bornholm restaurants were contacted in early 2000 in order to assess interest for a revenue management project. The restaurant in which the trials discussed here took place was one of those that replied positively. It is located in the northern part of the island and at the time of the project had space for 125 covers. The style of food was (and is) traditional Danish, with a static menu that does not change the selections except for seasonal changes. Thus the menu scenario was similar to that described by Miller and Pavesic (1996). At the time of the study the restaurant offered six starters, fourteen entrées and five dessert items, and the manager considered that the prices reflected what the market could bear. From time to time prices were reviewed in an informal way to ensure that they were broadly workable in relation to food costs.

During 2000 the restaurant provided regular data concerning the sales volume, food cost and selling price of each menu item, which were analysed using the three matrix approaches discussed above. The full menu analysis involved all items, including starters, entrées and desserts, but this generated a large amount of information. In the interests of simplicity and to provide a clear demonstration of the techniques, only the results from the starters are presented here.

Results

Results from classifying the six starters separately according to the Miller, Kasavana-Smith and Pavesic systems are presented in Table 5.4 and 5.5; in Table 5.5 they are adjusted to conform with one (i.e., the Kasavana-Smith) terminology.

The two tables show a broad agreement (goodness of fit 0.958) in the way the three methods classify the six menu items (a) – (f). In principle, the salmon platter is the house speciality and 'star' dish, while the deep-fried prawns and lobster soup are 'old faithfuls'. The smoked venison and chicken represent up-and-coming new products and the shellfish platter is apparently declining. It is important to note the discrepancies with regard to items (b) and (c), which tend to 'normalize' items.

Table 5.4 Classification of starters (original terminologies)

Menu item	Miller	Kasavana-Smith	Pavesic
(a) Smoked venison	Marginal	Puzzle	Sleeper
(b) Shellfish platter	Loser	Puzzle	Problem
(c) Salmon platter	Marginal	Star	Prime
(d) Chicken breast	Marginal	Puzzle	Sleeper
(e) Deep-fried prawns	Marginal	Plowhorse	Standard
(f) Lobster soup	Marginal	Plowhorse	Standard

Table 5.5 Classification of starters (adjusted to Kasavana-Smith terminology)

Menu item	Miller	Kasavana-Smith	Pavesic
(a) Smoked venison	Puzzle	Puzzle	Puzzle
(b) Shellfish platter	Dog	Puzzle	Dog
(c) Salmon platter	Plowhorse	Star	Star
(d) Chicken breast	Puzzle	Puzzle	Puzzle
(e) Deep-fried prawns	Plowhorse	Plowhorse	Plowhorse
(f) Lobster soup	Plowhorse	Plowhorse	Plowhorse

DISCUSSION

The fact that the three techniques classified the dishes in a very similar way suggests that the classification is accurate. On the other hand the differences in classification of items (b) and (c) (the shellfish and salmon platters) suggests that the designation of these dishes may be only marginal. This is significant, since these are the two 'outlying' items: the 'star' and 'dog' in the upper right and lower left-hand cells. The normative nature of matrix classification, discussed already, is evident here, but in addition there is a clustering tendency, in which a 'dog' is almost a 'puzzle' and a 'star' almost a 'plowhorse'. Closer inspection of the items reveals that they are in fact quite narrowly spread in relation to one another, so that the four-way classification is a matter of fine distinction, rather than one for major management action.

According to the simplest theoretical considerations, the manager of this restaurant should capitalize upon the 'star' dish (the salmon platter). The deep-fried prawns and lobster soup should be exploited and the shellfish platter dropped from the menu. The smoked venison and chicken breast should be promoted. Atkinson and Jones (1994) would augment these with some further actions. The highly successful salmon platter should be promoted vigorously; perhaps service staff can recommend it when they take guests' orders. It should be tested for demand elasticity by raising the price; if the latter can be raised significantly in relation to the other items this dish will offer service staff an opportunity for upselling. Little if anything should be done with the deep-fried prawns or lobster soup at the present time, but the two meat dishes (the smoked venison and chicken) should be heavily promoted, by putting them in a conspicuous place on the menu, or by providing special merchandizing on the table. It may also be possible to make them more attractive by changing their name, or description. For instance the menu might emphasize their provenance as a 'fresh local speciality'. Finally they could be placed on special offer, bearing in mind that any price cut will also affect their perfomance in profit margin terms. The greatest challenge is the shellfish platter. Depending upon demand elasticity its price should be raised to make it more profitable, but in addition it must be much more effectively promoted, and many of the already mentioned techniques (i.e., name/description change, menu prominence, merchandizing) could be used for this purpose. Only if all these fail should the item be dropped and replaced with an alternative, since to do this brings a considerable risk of non-acceptance.

The relatively bunched nature of the classification suggests that in fact the menu may already be working quite effectively within its parameters, and means that management action needs to be even more circumspect. Of course, in theory it is possible that the whole menu is inappropriate, but this is very unlikely in the restaurant discussed here, which has survived successfully for more than five years. This exposes a weakness of matrix menu analysis systems. They are incapable of identifying an inappropriate menu, and can only compare existing items. In the present case it is probable that menu development could benefit as much from a qualitative market analysis. For instance, customers probably expect to find seafood on the menu because the restaurant is on an island. Customers may on the whole prefer fish to shellfish, because for cultural reasons it is regarded as 'safer', hence the preference for salmon over shellfish. It would be unwise to remove the shellfish option, because it is expected, and in any case its 'dog' status is marginal. It, like the two meat items, should be marketed more aggressively, in a way that emphasizes their 'authenticity' as typical produce of Bornholm.

CONCLUSIONS

The study discussed here represents an initial attempt to provide a working management tool for the Danish restaurant industry. Menu analysis is by no means the whole story in revenue management in the restaurant industry, but the scope for some of the techniques mentioned in the introduction is limited. Bornholm is a mature market where demand is relatively limited, even during high season, and this makes it impracticable to gain much revenue advantage by managing bookings or service duration times. The scope for raising prices on specific dates is limited by the shortness of the season, and at the time of writing the prevailing dining culture makes it impossible to use the other criteria discussed above for rate fences. This leaves menu analysis. It is clear that matrix analysis of this type, and indeed revenue management in the broader sense, may not be the perfect means of improving menu effectiveness. However, this study has demonstrated that such techniques have something useful to say, that they are relevant and understandable to local revenue managers, and that they at least serve to focus management attention upon the menu and its revenue-maximizing potential. Even if this only highlights the need for more effective marketing, it will have provided a substantial benefit to the industry and to the local economy.

DISCUSSION QUESTIONS

Discuss the following:

1. How does the restaurant industry compare/contrast with airlines and hotels in terms of capacity and price management?
2. In what ways does menu engineering equate to revenue management in the restaurant industry? In which ways does it not do so?
3. Is menu engineering an appropriate way to approach revenue management in restaurants of the kind found on Bornholm?

REFERENCES

Atkinson, H. and Jones, P. (1994) 'Menu engineering: managing the foodservice micro-marketing mix', *Journal of Restaurant and Foodservice Marketing*, **1**(1), 37–55.

Bayou, M. E. and Bennett, L. B. (1992) 'Profitability analysis for table-service restaurants', *Cornell Hotel and Restaurant Administration Quarterly*, **32**(2), 49–55.

Desinano, P., Minuti, M. S. and Schiaffella, E. (2000) 'Controlling the yield management process in the hospitality business'. Paper presented at the Fifth International Yield and Revenue Management Conference, Assisi, Italy, September.

Donaghy, K., McMahon-Beattie, U., Yeoman, I. and Ingold, A. (1998) 'The realism of yield management', *Progress in Tourism and Hospitality Research*, **4**(3), 187–95.

Hayes, D. K. and Huffman, L. (1985) 'Menu analysis: a better way', *Cornell Hotel and Restaurant Administration Quarterly*, **26**(3), 64–70.

Hayes, D. K. and Huffman, L. M. (1995) 'Value pricing: how low can you go?', *Cornell Hotel and Restaurant Administration Quarterly*, **36**(1), 51–6.

Hoseason, J. and Johns, N. (1998) 'The numbers game: the role of yield management in the tour operations industry', *Progress in Tourism and Hospitality Research*, **4**(3), 197–206.

Johns, N. (1999) 'The meal experience: a matter of signs', *The Hospitality Review*, **1**(4), 50–4.

Kasavana, M. L. and Smith, D. I. (1982) *Menu engineering*. Hospitality Publishers.

Kimes, S. E. (1989) 'Yield management: a tool for capacity-constrained service firms', *Journal of Operations Management*, **8**(4), 348–63.

Kimes, S. (2001) CHR Reports: Yield Management. http://www.hotelschool.cornell.edu/chr/research/yieldmanagement.pdf, last accessed 15/05/02.

Kimes, S. E., Barrash, D. I. and Alexander, J. E. (1999) 'Developing a restaurant revenue-management strategy', *Cornell Hotel and Restaurant Administration Quarterly*, October, 18–29.

Kimes, S. E., Chase, R. B., Choi, S., Lee, P. Y. and Ngonzi, E. N. (1998) 'Restaurant revenue management: applying yield management to the restaurant industry', *Cornell Hotel and Restaurant Administration Quarterly*, **39**(3), 32–9.

McEvoy, B. J. (1997) 'Integrating operational and financial perspectives using yield management techniques: an add-on matrix model', *International Journal of Contemporary Hospitality Management*, **9**(2), 60–5.

Miller, J. E. (1980) *Menu Pricing and Strategy*. New York: Van Nostrand Reinhold.

Miller, J. E. and Pavesic, D. V. (1996) *Menu Pricing and Strategy*, 4th edn. Canada: John Wiley and Sons.

Nagle, T. and Holden, R. (1994) *The Strategy and Tactics of Pricing: A Guide to Profitable Decision-Making*, London: Prentice-Hall.

Pavesic, D. V. (1985). 'Prime numbers: finding your menu's strengths', *Cornell Hotel and Restaurant Administration Quarterly*, **26**(3), 70–7.

Smith, B. C., Leimkuhler, J. F. and Darrow, R. M. (1992) 'Yield management at American Airlines', *Interfaces*, **22**(1), 8–31.

6

Dynamic Pricing of Distillate Products at Petroleum Terminals

Douglas Harvey, Nicola Secomandi and Theodore V. Valkov

INTRODUCTION

This case study describes a systems-based process for optimally managing the pricing and allocation of inventory across the network of terminals through which petroleum refiners and marketers sell petroleum products to distributors and large customers. The process consists in optimally managing the posted prices for product at the terminal with the objective of maximizing profits, while at the same time managing demand so that the upstream supply schedules are met in the most economically efficient way possible. The methodology is based on several stages of demand analytics followed by network optimization. A live test of the process was conducted across ten terminals in the US throughout the early summer of 2001 with a major petroleum company. The results of the live test did show an 11.5 per cent increase in profit, a 3.1 per cent increase in liftings, an 8.1 per cent increase in margin, and a 19 per cent decrease in daily demand volatility relative to a control group that employed the current business practices. These results can be directly attributed to the systematic optimization processes with confidence levels ranging from 61 per cent to 78 per cent. Throughout the live test, upstream supply schedules were respected, and the systems-based process was also able to meet the usability, throughput, compatibility and reaction time requirements of the actual downstream business environment of an oil major. Current work is underway on a complete systems solution for the refined products Marketing and Supply sector, as well as on further live tests with other major petroleum companies.

BACKGROUND TO THE CASE

Pricing and Revenue Optimization for Refined Products

If the world oil executives were polled to describe the petroleum products business in one brief sentence, the words 'big' and 'hard to make money' would probably make the top of the list. There is no debate that the business is big – in 2000 for instance, the US met 38.5 per cent of its total energy needs by consuming 37.96 quadrillion BTUs of petroleum products (DOE/EIA 2001).

To meet this need, the oil industry has made major capital investments in creating a global supply chain of which the major segments are crude oil exploration and production (the 'upstream'), and transportation, refining and distribution (the 'downstream'). While the dollar amount invested per barrel is roughly the same in the upstream and the downstream portions of the chain, it has been a long-standing fact that the 'downstream' is characterized by low profitability due to a complex combination of overcapacity, volatile demand and structural factors. In the recent few years however, oil companies have begun to seek solutions to increase the economic efficiency of their downstream operations and improve results. The work described in this case study is part of a joint effort by leading industry players and **PROS** Revenue Management, Inc., to implement systematic pricing and revenue optimization techniques towards this end. Downstream petroleum is rife with optimization opportunities, and it is beyond the scope of this case study to describe them all. We refer the reader to Klingman *et al.* (1987), Bodington and Baker (1990), and Ronen (1995) for discussions and examples of optimization in the petroleum industry. The authors have chosen to describe a relatively small component of the overall optimization work, focusing solely on the optimization of refined product pricing at the downstream terminal level.

Pricing and the Refined Products Value Chain

The standing of this particular optimization problem within the industry can be described in terms of following the downstream value chain from the refinery onward. The major refined products (gasoline, diesel, jet fuel) account for roughly 75 per cent of the product stream obtained from crude fractionation. As shown in Figure 6.1, the bulk of these products enter a primary distribution network of long-haul pipelines, barges and other shippers, which deliver them to distribution terminals located throughout the country. At these terminals, the products are sold to a broad array of large end-users (e.g., transportation companies, power plants, and industrial plants), distributors and re-marketers. The products reach their end use through local secondary distribution networks that reticulate from each of the above terminals (tanker trucks are a familiar component of these secondary networks).

A typical large oil refiner and marketer in the US may thus sell through a network of several hundred primary terminals using a complex commercial structure of spot sales, term contracts and swaps (exchanges) applied across several channels of trade. There is an entire hierarchy of optimization opportunities to be found when one examines the variety of commercial arrangements under which product is sold.

Within this hierarchy, the optimization of spot pricing has proven to be a very effective lever to improve performance, and create a foundation for bringing systematic revenue optimization techniques into the downstream petroleum sector. The importance

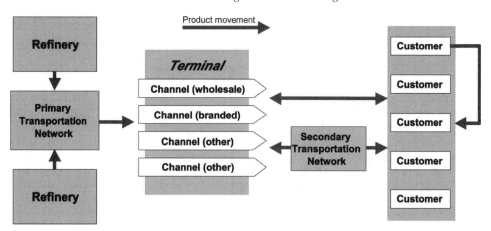

Figure 6.1 Schematic representation of the downstream refined products chain, showcasing the role of the terminals at which product pricing is being optimized.

of optimizing spot prices can be explained by three reasons. First, refiners and marketers price the product dynamically[1] with regard to competition, local supply–demand balance, commodity indexes for refined products[2] and several other market factors. Second, spot sales are on average the dominant sales arrangement. Finally, the publicly posted price for spot purchases (a.k.a. rack price) is used by both customers and industry as a key price indicator. Daily posted prices for each product by all major suppliers at each terminal can be publicly obtained from several data providers.

Commercial Problems Addressable by Pricing Optimization

It is clear that managing posted prices is a challenging task even for large companies, owing to the frequency of pricing decisions, number of products and points of sale. The need for good price management extends far beyond this challenge however, because of some fundamental problems particular to downstream petroleum. The real benefit of the optimization solutions described herein is the management of these fundamental problems through the lever of pricing. The fundamental problems in question are as follows:

● The downstream business operates largely in a 'supply push' mode, determined on a large scale by refinery operating plans and long-haul pipeline capacity bookings. In simplified terms, the 'product has to move'. On a small scale, this modus operandi translates into individual operating plans for each terminal. Deviations from the plan generally have undesirable results[3]. Unfortunately, such deviations are frequent for two reasons. First, demand at the terminal level is intrinsically highly volatile and influenced by a host of factors. Second, local operating plans are based on simplistic legacy demand forecasting methods (such as those embedded in supply chain software) combined with heuristic views on demand that aim to palliate forecasting inadequacies. As a result, pricing is often used as a relief valve for staying within the plan, rather than as a lever for managing demand in a proactive and optimally profitable manner.

● The operating plans are generally based on historic sales information and static forecasts. Thus they do not take into account the dynamic nature of the market, where product may be highly valuable on one day, and undesired on the next. As a result, companies operate under plans that fail to send the most product to the highest value areas. The companies also fail to systematically take advantage of the synthetic flexibility of re-routing supply on a short-term basis, which is made possible by the storage capacity in each terminal and the physical transportation network.

- Because of staffing and information technology limitations, refiners and marketers generally cannot respond as fast to overall market changes as their customers can. The result again is lost profit and inefficient allocation of product. For instance, a sharp upward intraday move in a given product commodity index will generally make the customers rush to lift as much product as possible before the next day, when the seller will typically reflect this move in its posted price. As a result, a refiner that is slow to react may end up selling a significant amount of product below its real replacement cost. Conversely, a sharp downward index move may virtually halt liftings (the amount or volume of petroleum products released to customers) at a given location.

- There is little price differentiation between customers, and as a result refiners and marketers generally fail to capture the additional willingness-to-pay of customers who attach importance to the non-commodity attributes of the product (e.g., brand, delivery time, volume reliability, price guarantee). This fact further contributes to low margins (differences between cost and selling price) in the downstream products marketing business.

The optimization of product pricing offers a highly leveraged opportunity to address these problems on a global scale. First, optimal control of pricing based on a detailed modelling of demand behaviour can help refiners and marketers *to execute the operating plan in a more profitable and stable manner*. Second, the detailed modelling of demand can be used to *arrive at better operating plans that adapt to where the market values the product most, and use pricing proactively to capture this value*. Third, the understanding of demand at the customer level of resolution can help identify opportunities for pricing segmentation and thereby help *maintain margin*. Finally, a system implementation of this process enables refiners and marketers to *respond to market changes in real time in a locally focused manner without an increase in staffing levels*.

The present case describes the methodology and results from a live exercise in posted price optimization[4] conducted in cooperation between PROS and one of the world's oil majors in the early summer of 2001.

AIMS AND OBJECTIVES OF THE CASE

The successful adoption of optimization technology in a new industry is contingent on a carefully orchestrated incremental process. Pilot tests of how the technology performs in the intended business setting are an important step in this process. The case describes the pilot test of posted price optimization technology in the actual business setting of a large refiner and marketer of petroleum product. There were several objectives and goals of the pilot process. The first was to design an appropriate optimization process that would support the business goals of the refiner/marketer. Another objective was to calibrate the optimization process using actual data and create an environment where the system could be presented with live market data to obtain a pricing recommendation that would be usable by the business. The final objective of the pilot was to assess the performance of the technology in a live setting, where the optimized prices would be used to actually drive sales, and compare this performance to a control reflecting the results from the existing price process.

PRICING OPTIMIZATION LIVE TEST METHODOLOGY

Optimization Process

The first objective was achieved by means of business process analysis executed through interviews with focus groups across the downstream business responsible for supply, marketing, distribution and trading. From a technical standpoint, the optimization process designed to manage spot prices was arranged in five steps:

- *Demand modelling:* Using available transaction and demand determinant[5] data, a quantitative model describing the relationship between seller price and own demand within a given market context is constructed. The market context refers to a particular group of customers (e.g., regular wholesale customers at the Savannah, GA terminal) and set of market conditions.
- *Demand reaction forecast:* A forward-looking estimation of how liftings for every terminal and customer segment would react to changes in the seller price structure (including rack price) is performed using the foregoing causal models.
- *Pricing and inventory allocation optimization:* Subject to operational constraints and the volume targets of the plan, the foregoing demand model is used to determine the optimal prices that maximize dollar profit. In the case where the business objective is to meet the supply plan for the terminal in the most profitable manner, the objective function is to maximize expected daily dollar profit adjusted for a dollar penalty for deviating from the plan daily liftings target[6]. In the case where the business objective is to establish *and* execute the optimal short-term supply plan (as opposed to just execute an externally-determined plan), the objective function is to maximize the expected daily dollar profit subject only to the physical infrastructure constraints. Other objective functions can be specified if deemed conformal to the objectives of the business[7].
- *Execution:* Wherein the prices derived from the foregoing analytical process for every terminal in the scope of the pilot are published by the seller at the same time and in the same manner as prices at terminals outside of the pilot scope.
- *Real-time calibration:* Within a certain period following execution, data is collected that enables comparison of how the market actually reacted to the optimized prices relative to the reaction forecast by the models and confidence bounds thereof. This information is used to recalibrate the demand model of step 1 above (demand modelling) and enable the optimization process to adapt itself to the unavoidable changes in the market-place dynamics.

To accomplish the remaining two objectives of the pilot, project teams from PROS and from each refining and marketing company involved established a regular data extraction and exchange process which simulated the flow of information that would be experienced by an enterprise version of a pricing optimization system built around the foregoing process:

- Current liftings data at every terminal considered
- Current and historical transaction data
- Market intelligence on competitor posted prices at the terminals considered
- Market information on commodity index movements (e.g., Platt's)
- Terminal inventory data and supply plan
- Configuration tables for channels of trade, customer segments and other structural business rules impacting pricing points.

This information is manually translated and input into the core demand analysis and optimization modules of the application by PROS personnel, and the results are communicated back to the client. This arrangement enables the calibration process and a test of the live performance of the system without an on-site installation, GUI configuration and enterprise data interface design. The arrangement is suitable for a small number of terminals (e.g., three to ten) such as that used in the live test.

A stream of historical data covering a period of approximately one year is used before the live test to calibrate the demand analysis modules. This historical data is also analysed to gain prior insight into customer segmentation and market patterns. Examples of such analysis include identification of customer groups with differentiated price/rack position sensitivity, and identification of locations where target rack position has been difficult to achieve. The data examined also allowed for the identification of factors explaining competitor behaviour, such as the correlation between Platt's directional moves and competitor pricing moves. Several other components of the analysis include insight into demand volatility and market share with large customers, and the development of performance indicators.

During the live test, current information is exchanged through the same channels used to extract and transfer historical data, and the results of the optimization are communicated electronically to the refiner/marketer. If the data exchange processes are thoroughly tested beforehand, the refiner/marketer can receive optimized prices within five to ten minutes after the input data is sent out. This time delay is well within the needs of the live test, and is also suitable for production pricing over a small number of terminals (e.g., three to ten).

Performance Assessment Methodology

Petroleum product markets are highly volatile due to the underlying commodity price movements, the intricate competitive dynamics of rack ranking, and a broad array of exogenous demand drivers such as weather, economic growth, etc., For this reason, one cannot rely on a simple method – e.g., comparing the profit from a given period of time with optimized prices to the profit from the same period a year ago, or to the profits from a nearby 'non-optimized' terminal – for assessing the performance impact of optimization. A more sophisticated approach is required, which allows clear isolation of the impact of optimization from the other influences, and compares observations on an equal basis.

A live testing period of approximately two to three months is necessary for collecting enough samples for making a good statistical comparison and experiencing a varied range of market conditions. The live testing should be conducted over as many terminals as reasonably possible given the manual nature of data exchange. In practice, we have found that a judiciously chosen four to ten terminals can capture a representative cross-section of the business.

During the foregoing period, a testing pattern whereby optimization is cyclically applied over a shorter sub-period (over one or two supply cycles, i.e. one or two weeks) followed by a similar period without optimization, can be applied at randomly selected locations. This enables removing the effect of short-term market trends from the comparison.

Over the testing period, a set of test samples will thus be obtained. Each sample is a financial performance indicator (e.g., profit) over a short time interval when optimized prices were used (e.g., a day). Let the set of these samples be denoted as $[P]_o$ and the set of time intervals (e.g., days) for their collection be denoted by $[D]_o$.

Using historical data and data taken during those intervals of the live test period when no optimization was used, a control set of time intervals $[D]_C$ is constructed, which is structurally equivalent to $[D]_o$ from a market environment standpoint. Structural equivalence is achieved by selecting from the full set of historical data a subset of time intervals such that the set of market condition vectors[8] $(x_1, x_2, x_3 \ldots)$ for this subset is closest in the Cartesian sense to the set of market condition vectors associated with the set $[D]_o$. Furthermore, because of the strong day-of-the-week effect on volume in the business, the control and test data sets should have an equal number of holidays, Mondays and normal business days. Let $[P]_C$ denote the set of performance indicators for each of the time periods of the set $[D]_C$. One thus has a set of time intervals over which prevailing market conditions were the most similar to those during the optimization time period from a structural and quantitative standpoint, and can proceed to compare the two sets of results $[P]_o$ (with optimization) and $[P]_C$ (without optimization) to assess the impact of pricing optimization on economic performance[9].

A two-tailed heteroscedastic t-test is used for comparing the means and the standard deviations between the test and control performance sets $[P]_o$ and $[P]_C$, and for determining the degree to which differences in means and standard deviations can be attributed to chance. In this manner, one can obtain not only a measure of the impact of optimization, but also a measure of the reliability of the comparison made[10].

ANALYTICAL METHODOLOGY

There are two main components to the quantitative analysis. The first component is the demand modelling, which involves estimating demand functions by maximum likelihood procedures. The second component is the optimization process, which employs a deterministic non-linear optimization model.

Demand Modelling

Following Luenberger (1995: 126–7) we employ a demand model that consists of two components: number of arrivals and willingness-to-pay. This approach has also been employed by Bitran, Caldentey, and Mondschein (1998). The two components are modelled as independent random variables.

We employ one of the models presented in Secomandi, Abbott, and Harvey (2002). We assume that the number of arrivals N during a period of length t is Poisson distributed with a mean equal to λt and that the probability density function of the willingness-to-pay W is:

$$f_w(p) = 0 \qquad\qquad\qquad \text{if } 0 \leq p < p_0$$
$$f_w(p) = \frac{\epsilon_0}{p_0} \exp[-\epsilon_0(p/p_0 - 1)] \qquad \text{if } p_0 \leq p \leq \infty$$

The model is based on the behavioural assumption that a purchase occurs whenever $W > p$. Hence the number of purchases in a period of length t at price p is:

$$N(p) = N\text{Pr}\{W > p\}$$

Including the size component S, modelled as a random variable independent of N and W, the demand at price p in a period of length t is:

$$D(p) = SN(p)$$

Therefore, it is easy to see that the mean demand $\bar{D}(p)$ is:

$$\bar{D}(p) = \lambda t \bar{S} \qquad\qquad\qquad \text{if } 0 \leq p < p_0$$
$$\bar{D}(p) = \lambda t \bar{S} \exp[-\epsilon_0(p/p_0 - 1)] \qquad \text{if } p_0 \leq p \leq \infty$$

Here p_0 is a reference price and ϵ_0 is its associated elasticity. This demand function is known as the log–linear demand and has been used in Example 1 in Gallego and van Ryzin (1997). It also has the property of having a linear price elasticity given by the following expression:

$$\epsilon(p) = \frac{\partial D(p)/\partial p}{D(p)} p$$

The elasticity thus has the following property:

$$\epsilon(p) = 0 \qquad\qquad\qquad \text{if } 0 \leq p < p_0$$
$$\epsilon(p) = -\frac{\epsilon_0}{p_0} p \qquad\qquad \text{if } p_0 \leq p \leq \infty$$

The demand model can be estimated using maximum-likelihood techniques as shown in Secomandi, Kambour and Harvey (2000), and Secomandi, Abbott and Harvey (2002). More specifically, the parameters of S and $N(p)$ are estimated separately. Estimation of $N(p)$ yields estimates for the quantities λ, ϵ_0, and p_0. While this entails solving a nonlinear optimization problem, knowledge of these parameters provides management with valuable market intelligence.

The Optimization Model

Following Gallego and van Ryzin (1997), inverting $\bar{D}(p)$ and letting d denote the mean demand yields:

$$p(d) = \left[1 + \epsilon_0^{-1}\ln\left(\frac{\lambda t \bar{S}}{d}\right)\right] p_0$$

This allows formulating an optimization model in terms of mean demand d_k accepted in period T_k. Let c be the initial capacity and r_k be the planned replenishment occurring at the beginning of period k. The following non-linear deterministic pricing optimization problem is a simple adaptation of the model proposed by Gallego and van Ryzin (1997):

$$\text{NLP}: \text{maximize} \sum_{k \epsilon K} p_k(d_k)d_k$$

Subject to:

$$\sum_{k \epsilon K : k \leq k'} d_k \leq c + \sum_{k \epsilon K : k \leq k'} r_{k'} \quad \forall k' \epsilon K$$

$$0 \leq d_k \leq \lambda t_k \bar{S} \quad \forall k \epsilon K$$

This is a non-linear program with a concave objective function subject to linear constraints. Hence it can be readily solved by standard non-linear programming methods. The model objective function can easily be extended to accommodate variable costs for each time period and penalties for violating inventory targets in each period.

RESULTS

Table 6.1 summarizes the results from the comparison of test periods (with optimization) to control periods (without optimization), using the above approach at all terminals where the statistical confidence in the t-test results exceeded 50 per cent. To protect confidential data, individual terminals are identified by test codes alone, and the results are provided in dimensionless form in terms of percentage change of test relative to control.

The results show that using systematic daily optimization of the rack price increased the average dollar profit at the terminal by 11.5 per cent. The confidence levels of these findings ranged from 61 to 78 per cent. Thus, the primary objective of the live test – to determine whether systematic optimization can increase profits in the downstream – was achieved successfully. In business terms, the live tests showed that systematic optimization can generate very substantial benefits with a high degree of certainty.

The results also indicate the increase in profit could be achieved on average without a sacrifice in volume or margin. Average liftings increased by 3.1 per cent and average daily margin increased by 8.1 per cent when prices were determined with the aid of the systematic optimization tools. It is to be noted that volume targets were considered in all live tests.

The increase in profit seen in the live test can be attributed to the use of a systematic, quantitative process for estimating the willingness-to-pay of customers, assessing the market conjecture and competitive positions, and relying on a scientific, balanced framework for determining the desired price levels. This systematic process can be highly complementary to the current business process of pricers in the downstream refining/marketing sector, who have a strong experience base and good 'feel' for the market, but cannot integrate large volumes of quantitative information in the time required for making decisions.

Table 6.1 Results from the comparison of daily profit averages, daily lifting averages and daily margin averages in the test sample (days with pricing optimization) and control sample (days with comparable market environment when pricing decisions are made using current business processes) across terminals. Comparison confidence levels are determined by means of a two-tailed heteroscedastic t-test using the variances of the samples, and can be thought of as a probability that the change in performance can be attributed to optimization as opposed to random chance. Only tests where the confidence level exceeded 50 per cent are considered.

Terminal test ID	Average daily profit change over control (%)	Average daily liftings change (%)	Average daily margin change (%)	Profit comparison confidence level (%)
A	+21.8	−6.5	+30	78
B	+17.0	+3.5	+12	71
C	+9.0	+37	−17	63
D	−9.0	−53	+92	61
E	+12.4	−7.5	+4.7	78
F	+7.4	+11	−3.6	71
G	+11.5	−23	+45	71
H	−0.6	+18	−16	74
Volume-weighted average	+11.5	+3.1	+8.1	61 to 78

Table 6.2 Performance of the systematic optimization process in terms of reduction of demand volatility and compliance with predetermined volume targets. To measure the former, the standard deviation of daily liftings in the test sample (days with pricing optimization) is compared to the standard deviation of daily liftings in the control sample (days with comparable market environment when pricing decisions are made using current business processes). To measure target compliance, terminals where total liftings over the test period were within 30 per cent of the target were considered to be compliant.

Terminal test ID	Change in standard deviation of daily liftings (%)	Compliance with volume targets
A	−17	Yes
B	+5.6	No
C	+43	No
D	−14	Yes
E	+26	Yes
F	−42	Yes
G	−73	Yes
H	−38	Yes
Volume-Weighted Average	−19.3	Yes on 6 out of 8

The conditions of the live test did not allow for changing prices intra-day or optimizing in the context of the entire network of terminals. It is expected that these capabilities of the process should yield additional profitability enhancements relative to the results above. These capabilities will be available upon full-scale enterprise deployment.

An important collateral measure of performance in the downstream refined products marketing sector is the ability to meet volume targets at each terminal predetermined by the supply operations. Another important measure is day-to-day variability in liftings. If this variability can be reduced, supply planners can reduce the reserve stock of product held in the terminal tanks, thus reducing the carrying and capital costs to the business.

Table 6.2 summarizes the results from the live pilot in terms of these two measures. To protect confidential data, individual terminals are identified by test codes alone, compliance with volume targets is indicated by simple 'yes/no' codes, and the change in standard deviation of daily liftings is expressed in percentage change between test sample and control sample.

These results show that the increase in financial performance was achieved concomitantly with a modest decrease in demand volatility. Furthermore, liftings at the terminals priced using the systematic optimization process complied with the target volumes set by the business.

CONCLUSIONS

A wide range of market conditions, including severe shortage, oversupply and deep price competition were encountered across the different locations where the systems-based price optimization process was tested live. The process performed satisfactorily across the range of these conditions.

From an economic performance standpoint, the live test did show that the systematic rack price optimization process led to:

- 11.5 per cent increase in average daily profit
- 3.1 per cent increase in average daily liftings
- 8.1 per cent increase in average daily margin
- 19.3 per cent decrease in demand volatility (daily liftings standard deviation)

relative to a control group that employed the current business practices. Translated over the volume of the refined petroleum products business, this finding makes a very strong economic case for the adoption of systematic optimal management of prices and demand at the downstream terminals.

Furthermore, throughout the live test, upstream supply schedules were respected, and the optimization process was able to meet the usability, throughput, data, compatibility and reaction time requirements of the actual downstream business environment of an oil major.

These results raise the possibility that the petroleum industry is a candidate for joining the list of other industries, such as airlines, natural gas, electricity, retail goods, travel and entertainment, health care and so forth, who have considerably benefited from the systematic practice of scientific optimization embedded in software products tailored for the needs of the specific users.

Current work is under way on the development of a complete systems solution for the refined products Marketing and Supply sector, as well as on further live tests with two other major petroleum companies.

DISCUSSION QUESTIONS

There are some common questions that downstream petroleum marketing practitioners ask when introduced to the new technological approach for pricing presented in this case.

1. Can margins be increased without sacrificing volume?
2. Where does the additional profit come from? Is it from selling more or selling at a higher price?
3. Are the benefits of pricing optimization sustainable in the long term?

NOTES

1. Generally, prices for refined products are determined on a daily basis, and several companies have the ability to change prices intra-day. There is a general drive in the industry to develop fast intra-day pricing capabilities to better match demand swings driven by movements in commodity prices.
2. Commodity indexes for refined products are based on wholesale trading prices at major regional supply hubs such as New York Harbor. These indexes are publicly available for each region in the US (e.g., Midwest, Gulf Coast, etc.) and are important proxies of the cost of the product from a marketer standpoint under standard cost of replacement accounting practices. Thus, the optimization of prices is carried out in a stochastic cost environment.
3. For instance, a terminal where sales are below target will experience inventory buildups in the short term. Because of the upstream 'product push', limited flexibility in re-routing product, and terminal capacity limitations, excess inventory is often passed on to the trading arm of the organization, which effectively liquidates it at a sub-premium price (conversely, when the trading arm is asked to procure product to remedy a shortage, premium prices will be paid by the organization). To avoid shortages and meet highly volatile demand, terminal operators may have to carry significant amounts of reserve in the tanks. The carrying cost of this inventory is substantial and further reduces economic performance.
4. The complete exercise involved the optimization of the entire pricing structure at the terminal, of which the posted price is one particularly important component. Not all spot sales at the terminal take place at the posted price owing to a complex interplay of channel tiers, discounts and adjustments particular to each seller. It is beyond the scope of this case study to discuss the optimization of the entire spot pricing structure, owing to space and confidentiality considerations.
5. Demand determinants are external parameters that influence demand, e.g., competitor price levels, index directional moves, etc.
6. Virtually all the pricing decisions made in the live pilot were based on maximizing this objective function. In parallel, an optimization without penalty for plan overruns and underruns was also carried out. A comparison between the recommendations of the two optimizations indicates that there is significant revenue enhancement opportunity from using the analysis to establish an optimal short-term plan rather than as a tool to simply execute an externally determined plan.
7. For instance, one may seek to maximize the revenue generated per barrel of equity

petroleum as it moves through the value chain. In this case, the objective function would be total expected revenue adjusted for equity stake.

8. A market condition vector is a series of data points that characterize the market at a given time instant (or a brief period). For instance, it was found that rack rank, average rack posted margin, own posted margin, Platt's level, Platt's directional move, season and inventory level relative to average level were suitable data items to use to satisfactorily describe the business context of any given day.

9. It may seem at first that this method for creating test and control samples is excessively convoluted, until one takes into account the nature of the business. For instance, Thursday, 12 May, when Platt's moved up 5 cents and rack rank was 2 is a fundamentally different market from the preceding Wednesday, 11 May, when Platt's moved down 1 cent and rack rank was 11. There is no business basis for comparing performance between these days. On the other hand, Tuesday, 15 June, with similar Platt's directional move and rank is more comparable to 12 May than 11 May. Because the market is 'memory-less' and reactive to short-term conditions, the approach outlined herein is robust. This is easily demonstrated by comparing the performances between randomly extracted control samples – in most cases, the differences in performance between such randomly pulled controls are within the tolerances of statistical significance for the test. It may be also thought unusual that control samples are determined after the test is complete. This is necessary because there is no way of knowing what the market conditions will be exactly during the test.

10. This is another advantage of the comparison approach adopted relative to simpler comparison methods.

REFERENCES

Bitran, G. R., Caldentey, R. and Mondschein, S. V. (1998) 'Coordinating clearance markdown sales of seasonal products in retail chains', *Operations Research*, **46**, 609–24.

Bodington, C. E. and Baker, T. E. (1990) 'A history of mathematical programming in the petroleum industry', *Interfaces*, **20**(4), 117–27.

Department of Energy–Energy Information Administration (DOE/EIA), *Annual Energy Review 2000*, DOE/EIA-0384(2000), Washington, DC 2001.

Gallego, G. and van Ryzin, G. J. (1997) 'A multi-product, multi-resource pricing problem and its applications to network yield management', *Operations Research*, **45**, 24–41.

Klingman, D., Phillips, N., Steiger, D., Wirth, R., Padman, R. and Krishnan, R. (1987) 'An optimization based integrated short-term refined petroleum product planning system', *Management Science*, **33**(7), 813–30.

Luenberger, D. G. (1995) *Microeconomic Theory*. New York: McGraw-Hill, Inc.

Ronen, D. (1995) 'Dispatching petroleum products', *Operations Research*, **43**(3), 379–87.

Secomandi, N., Abbott, K. and Harvey, D. (2002) 'Business-to-business energy revenue management: models, Java design, and examples', Working Paper, PROS Revenue Management, Inc., Houston, TX, USA.

Secomandi, N., Kambour, E. and Harvey, D. (2000) 'Dynamic pricing algorithms in revenue management', Technical Report, PROS Revenue Management, Inc., Houston, TX, USA.

7

Free Nelson Mandela? The Politics and Pricing of Culture Within Society

Elizabeth Carnegie

The winter sun is shining on a Sunday morning in Cape Town as the boat leaves for the half hour trip to Robben Island, and the prison that held Nelson Mandela for many years which is now a museum.

The audience is mixed. Many are South African from other states paying homage, some are African Americans bringing children, a smaller number are white European visitors. But all were going with a reason, a sense of purpose. Yet for all, the experience was not the same. Essentially, how we perceive, receive and understand the cultural messages and monuments that reflect the past and make sense of the present are determined by our relationship to that past. This case study aims to outline not just what and how culture is developed, determined and understood within society at local, national and international level, but also attempts to offer a rationale for why our cultural heritage and access to it cannot be measured simply in cash terms, hence the inclusion of this chapter in a book on pricing strategies. It argues that our cultural heritage and access to it in its many forms is fundamental to human development and community success and sets out to examine the role of culture within society, emphasizing and exploring the need to subsidize cultural activities, events and institutions in order to ensure that they are available to all regardless of their ability to pay. Through an examination of diverse institutions such as Robben Island and Edinburgh's Museum of Childhood, this case study aims to consider ways in which heritage institutions attempt to offer a shape to the past, to give meaning to a challenging present and uncertain future. It will argue that culture is something that cannot be easily financially evaluated and will consider the role of free and subsidized access to cultural institutions and the expectations of an increasingly sophisticated public when faced with cultural representations. Lastly, it will look at what true access means within the modern world.

Not all cultural activities or the monuments that symbolize them represent the best of human achievement, in many cases places such as Robben Island remain to remind us of the darker side of human activity from which we need to learn from the past to develop as individuals, groups or nations. Therefore places like Robben Island can convey a message of hope as well as human suffering.

Whilst Robben Island is a monument to the success of the anti-apartheid movement, its mission, to reflect on the past but also to move forward, does not offer a comfortable experience. Some 20 per cent of the guides are ex-prisoners telling and retelling their stories in an attempt, as our guide put it, to 'get the anger out'. For some visitors that anger was still too strong to bear as one girl cried, 'there is no reconciliation' as her friend said, 'hush, now you are on Robben Island you are not supposed to feel that here'. Whilst Robben Island has become an established part of the tourist trail in Cape Town since it opened as a museum in 1987, becoming a World Heritage Site in 1999, and having recently celebrated their one millionth visitor, the site is first and foremost a monument, a place to remember as is voiced by Amdimda Toivo ya Toivo, former political prisoner and now the Namibian Minster of Labour.

> *Robben Island is a symbol, not only for South Africa and Namibia but also for Africa and the World. It was here that we learned that adversity could be overcome by commitment and vision. It was here than pains of individuals could be soothed by the unity of groups. It was here that we were reminded that freedom had a price. We must never forget what the Island represents.* (Amdimda Toivo ya Toivo, Ilifalababtu, 2002)

Those who undertake them – regardless of their race, background or country of origin – view visits to the Island as pilgrimages. The need to have a place to remember so that we never forget is indeed the key reason why Robben Island is a museum and why prison camps such as Westerbock in Holland, Auschwitz-Birkenau in Poland, have also been preserved as museums. As heritage becomes increasingly commodified we are in greater need of access to the real.

Thousands of miles away an elderly woman looks at a doll fashioned from an old shoe, a vestige of a working-class nineteenth-century childhood which has survived to be viewed within an Edinburgh museum and she smiles at her own memory of a clothes-peg doll. Then she recalls her mother and domestic toil. Then she feels sadness at the memory of loss, before moving forward as a small hand pulls her to the next case.

Thus memories are forged and felt through our relationship to places and things in the past, present and over time. Some memories, such as those deeply felt in pilgrimage to Robben Island, need to be healed. Others are more personal, a natural part of a life lived around people and things in a rapidly changing society.

Memories, then, some personal, others dealing with the magnitudinal events which shaped our lives, our countries and the world, are contained within the cultural institutions, the museums, the heritage centres, the simple objects and the prison walls. How are we to access that past to understand the present, face an uncertain future? Is culture, as Marx would argue, simply a commodity, part of the mechanics of a capitalist society or is access to culture vital, rendering the cultural institutions custodians of the material evidence of such human activity?

In the UK, as elsewhere in the world, most state-run cultural institutions, while they might wish to be free, charge for access in a number of ways: through taxes, entrance fees, school visits and merchandizing. A shrinking public purse coupled with the need to be competitive within a growing, if not overcrowded, market has long been an argument for the need to charge.

However, given Blair's Labour Administration's emphasis on education and the potential educational role of museums, extra funding was secured for at least the short term to ensure free access to all national museums in Britain.

National museums and galleries in Britain being funded directly from Whitehall can be viewed as having a distinct advantage over large municipal collections such as Glasgow Museums, which although still free to the public, are reliant on local authority funding. Where access is wholly free to the public, running costs are being met or subsidized by other organizations or individuals through grant awards and sponsorship. Equally important has been the role of volunteers within cultural attractions which heavily subsidized the running costs and indeed this is still the case with for example National Trust properties. However, changes in the pattern of volunteering, essentially a postwar movement, suggests that there will soon be a shortage of volunteers within the current and successive generations, which may well create running problems for some types of visitor attraction.

Free access however, has had a dramatic and immediate effect on visitor numbers as Anna Southall, Director, National Museums and Galleries of Wales commented in the *Museums Journal*, December 2001.

> *The return ... to free admission had been a stunningly successful policy ... With 90% increase on visitor numbers since its introduction, the success of the policy has far outstripped what we predicted and hoped for.*

The figures for the National Museums for Scotland also show a significant increase, even allowing for the loss of visitors after the foot and mouth epidemic in Britain and the September 11th terrorist attacks in the United States which severely affected UK tourism during 2001. However, increased numbers of visitors who are tourists, whilst important to the economy, do not provide sufficient argument for the existence of cultural institutions.

A large percentage of museum audiences to the local authority-run museums are visitors to the city. Derek Janes, Director of Edinburgh City Museums, acknowledged that the museums' proximity to the tourist high spots inevitably influence not just the content but the way they are received and understood by audiences

> *Inevitably the city museums of Edinburgh, because of their physical location, are traditionally aimed at the tourist market – there has been a change over the last fifteen to twenty years where there has been a more conscious decision to target local audiences – also museums have become clearer in their individual purposes. It started as a political agenda when the political control of the council changed in 1984 and there was then a political decision to create the People's Story museum – or Museum of Labour History as it was originally intended and the impetus towards creating that museum led to a social history ethos within a lot of the work of the museums service and that has had some influence on other parts of the service as well.* (Janes, 2002)

A good museum or heritage attraction need not sacrifice authenticity in order to be a successful tourist attraction. To do so is to underestimate the needs and abilities of visitors, many of whom may in fact be expatriates seeking to find some sense of belonging.

People are also perfectly capable of and willing to visit institutions such as those associated with dark tourism in order to understand and learn from the devastating effects of war and social injustice. Almost two thirds of the visitors to Robben Island for example are not South African yet they make the journey for the reasons highlighted above. Of the 750 daily visitors to Robben Island just under a third are South African: 15 per cent are from the United Kingdom, 23 per cent from the rest of Europe,

8 per cent from the United States, almost 12 per cent from Asia and about 3.5 per cent are from Australia, New Zealand and the rest of Africa.

It is possible that some visitors visit more for curiosity than from any deeply felt sense of place or occasion but few fail to be moved by their visit. The trip to Robben Island including the ferry is not free but at 100 rand (c. £6.50 at the time of writing) is cheap to tourists but could represent a significant outlay for locals who also have to pay. As the South African Government wishes that all school children should visit Robben Island at least once this is no small commitment from a country that has devastating poverty and inequalities.

Deidre Prins, Chief Education Officer at Robben Island, believes that if people are asked to make a small contribution in the form of entrance fees they will value the product more. This is not a new argument. Glasgow Museums found that free work-shops for children were often less well attended that those for which a nominal charge was made. In Scotland, which has a tradition of free entry to museums in the larger cities, many believe that whilst locals having already paid through taxes should be given unrestricted access it would be fair to put a levy on visitors.

However, local government's commitment to free access to the larger municipal collections, whilst not directly mandated, in the main is part of an ongoing commitment to culture. As cultural activities are the key tourist product of both Edinburgh and Glasgow such a move would almost certainly limit visitors and there would be a sub-sequent loss of goodwill. Also it can be argued that money not spent on entrance fees is freed up for other tourist spends in shops and cafes or at least the locality.

Given the nature of audiences, the people less likely to pay admission are those for whom museum and heritage attraction visiting is not part of their culture and gov-ernment access initiatives are aimed at widening access within the community.

Audiences to traditional museums in the UK and indeed the western world, have been largely middle class, often women of a certain age (60 per cent of visitors to the now National Trust-run Pollock House in Glasgow were women of a pensionable age (Carnegie, 1996), so unsurprisingly there are large numbers of the public who are consciously non-users of museums. The question it seems is not whether people should have to pay for culture, but whether they want to access it at all. It seems that it is not enough for an institution to offer free or heavily subsided access in order to attract visitors.

How then do organizations break down barriers to inclusion so that people can value a cultural experience that is readily available to them for free or for little financial outlay?

As the National Museums of Scotland audience grew, Edinburgh City Museums lost visitors as a consequence of the growth of alternative visitor attractions in the locality such as the science centre Our Dynamic Earth and the overpriced Edinburgh Dungeon which is of dubious historical integrity with fairground effects and yet it often has queues for admission when the City Art Centre across the road is half empty. This raises interesting arguments about what people want from culture which is inevitably tied in with ideas about class, leisure and consumption but also highlights the fact that a large percentage of people who attend Edinburgh attractions are visitors to the city. Is it that the majority of museums and visitor attractions have been planned with tourists in mind rather than prioritizing local people and that there are in fact only a certain number of potential visitors to go round? Derek Janes argued that Edinburgh City Museums have been targeting locals for a number of years but as Edinburgh is a tourist city tourists will make up a substantial part of the visitor figures particularly during the summer months.

We did do some work a number of years ago and in fact what that illustrated was the profile of visitors to the People's Story was no different from the profile of visitors for the Museum of Childhood. Makes the point that People's Story is a bit of a creature of its location. I think people do have concepts, because people who run museums are largely middle class, there is perhaps a romanticization of what people want. I suspect what they want is an interesting story about where they lived that they can quite enjoy and will give them happy memories – you know, cinemas, pubs, football. Things they do. Things that mean something to them and not horrible living conditions and dying and stuff. (Janes, 2002)

One of key challenges facing heritage professionals is how to break down the class and cultural barriers associated with museums and other 'high art' forms. For many people, crossing the threshold of institutions that reflect the state authority or, in the case of some museums, represent colonial rule, can take a lot of confidence and courage. World wide, city museums are often situated in prime city centre spaces and have imposing facades that can be threatening or off-putting.

Not only are there audiences we are not attracting but that there are audiences who even if they came would not really be quite confident enough to know what to do. There is still a problem with threshold. It is still there, we still haven't learned. It is very much class units. (Janes, 2002)

Nor are museums and heritage institutions unique in having clear non-cash based barriers to access. Lynne Halfpenny, Arts Outreach Development Officer for Edinburgh City Council who looks after the Council's £2.6 million budget that is dispersed across the cultural arts sector, acknowledges that theatres also have the reputation of being elitist.

People are perfectly comfortable to part with money and go to the cinema with friends or whatever. There is something to be learned about why this is a perfectly acceptable pastime and they are potentially absorbing culture and receiving feedback and an expanded view. There is something about how they are programmed and who you can go with and the fact that you are not expected to come out the end of it a critic. There appears to be very different rules about being a critic of certain art forms and a critic of others and the fear of the Emperor's New Clothes syndrome is still there very much with the arts. (Halfpenny, 2002)

Audience participation and consulting with advocacy groups is deemed a key way to encourage and widen participation amongst groups who have been traditionally non-museum-goers. To learn from their audiences Derek Janes and other senior museum staff from Edinburgh City Council Museums went on placements with various groups who do not make use of the department's facilities.

We had a very interesting exercise of senior staff going on placements with mainly advocacy groups and I went on an advocacy group for people with mental distress and that was interesting and they were a very disenfranchized group as far as museum visiting was concerned as a lot of them don't like crowds so that makes it very difficult for them to come to our big exhibitions. What became very clear and which is very interesting and what we all need to learn from is – they said it about museums and they said it about libraries – is that what do you do when you go to a museum, what do you do when you go into a library – how do you see them? What do you do? How do you use them? (Janes, 2002)

If Halfpenny and Janes are right and people feel that they are not equipped with the necessary skills, education and knowledge to be comfortable users then surely the fault lies with institutions that play to their peers and by limiting access, limit knowledge. Huntly House in Edinburgh provided an interesting example of increasing access by simply changing the name of the museum.

> *We have recently changed the name of Huntley House museum which doesn't mean anything – it is not even a real name, it is a mistake – to the M of Edinburgh, that is a good clear name for a museum. Some of the consultation we did on that – people up in arms – no you can't change HH museum because it, it is HH. The very act of changing the name of the Museum has actually increased the visitor figures by 50 per cent since it happened, which is quite startling. Since the beginning of April 2001 visitor figures went up 50 per cent month by month just by changing the name. A bit of work inside but people don't know that when they come in. Now it has a clear name people go there.*
> (Janes, 2002)

The message is clear. People are able to deal with threshold issues if they know what to expect from the museum or heritage attraction. It can be argued though that access should also mean more than simply being able to view those collections on display.

Many more institutions are aiming to be 'museums without walls'. Some recent examples of this are the Open Museum at Glasgow who work closely with local groups creating exhibitions and events held off site in community or shopping centres. Glasgow Museums and the National Museums of Scotland are planning to allow public access to their brownfield stores. Robben Island also ensures that the message of the site is carried into the schoolroom and overseas and is keen to forge links with other groups and currently they are in partnership with the Anne Frank House in Amsterdam and an educational establishment in Devon, England.

Elsewhere access is only allowed to that which it is deemed suitable for the public to see. All museums hold collections that are considered not readily accessible to the public for a variety of reasons; for example, sexual or political material or human remains that also raise ethical issues about the right to hold such material in a museum in the first place.

Museums that are in the main state funded institutions reflect the cultural values of the people they represent. Victorian museums obsessed with discovery and the culture of the 'other' will inevitably be faced with the problems of how to reconcile their past policies, politics and collections with a present which has revaluated their involvement in such countries. It is for this reason that recent years have seen debates centred round the ownership and ultimately repatriation of the material, cultural and human remains of other cultures.

As the public become more knowledgeable, attitudes by professional bodies have to change in step with this, thus forcing a more open approach. This is particularly true of the medical profession and the appropriation and subsequent storage of human remains. Hence, the repatriation in 2002 of Tasmanian Aboriginal remains by the Royal College of Surgeons of England. In 1998 Glasgow City Council approved the return of what was believed to be a Sioux warrior shirt from the 1890 Wounded Knee battle. The shirt had been in Glasgow Museums collections since 1891 when it arrived as part of a collection donated from Buffalo Bill Cody's Wild West Show, and was the subject of repatriation campaign that began in 1991.

Glaswegians were canvassed on what they thought should happen to the shirt and the majority were in favour of repatriation. Museums rarely encourage the kind of open debate witnessed in case of the Ghost Shirt and the larger, more auspicious British Museum is very circumspect when considering any repatriation claims. A case in point being the Benin bronzes taken by the British after the punitive strike of 1897, many of which are the British Museum and other institutions in the UK and Europe.

A willingness to enter into public debate shows a commitment to access to collections in line with the Museums Association strategy for future development within the sector. As is an acknowledgement that cultural institutions need to reflect all visitors at a local level and in particular to create a focus for an expression and celebration of multiculturalism. The Edinburgh City Council Policy Document, 2002, sets out priorities identified by the council and recognizes the need to:

> *Promote locally, nationally and internationally the expression of Edinburgh's diverse cultural identity, and to recognise the reciprocal benefits of widening cultural experience through international contacts.*

> *Support and develop those cultural activities which enrich and extend personal and community development.*

This is both an expression of multiculturalism at home and an acknowledgement that Edinburgh as the Festival City has strong international links. Edinburgh City Museums in common with other cultural agencies within the city have been working towards creating a forum for multi-ethnic and indeed socially excluded groups within the city.

Museums, heritage attractions, even visitor centres, can and indeed should be accessible to all groups within society and no one should be or feel excluded on the grounds of race, class or poverty. Price is clearly an issue and the benefits of access must surely be balanced against the economic issues. The Museums Association Ethics Committee maintains that:

> *All members of society have a right to visit and use them (museums) ... What does it mean to be accessible? There are two elements: the physical and the philosophical. Museums are coming to terms with the first. ... As important are the philosophical assumptions. Why and how are objects acquired? What criteria are used in documentation and display? What values drive publicity campaigns? How do we select the language of our labels and publications? The health and vitality of museums can best be judged by the quality of their relationships with people. The stronger a museum's commitment to improved access, the better those relationships will become.*
> (www.museumsassociation.com)

In conclusion then, this chapter has argued that everybody should have the right of access to culture and that the public should have the right to decide not just what and how cultures are represented but also the right to participate in the debates which will decide the future of collections and representations in the United Kingdom and all over the world.

Emotional, cultural access is only possible if there is an easy path to physical access that is about more than simply being able or prepared to pay for entrance. If museums and other heritage and cultural institutions are to attract wider audiences which truly reflect society both locally and internationally then their ethos, messages and rationale must be more about the need to share and learn from the past through collections, buildings, memories and each other rather than simply exist to attract tourist gold.

Through representations of political and global concerns we learn to understand the powers and processes of the world and through the personal we can have an understanding of ourselves and feel empathy for others.

The 'apple boxes', which held the meagre possessions that each prisoner of Robben Island left with, highlight the power and yet humility of possessions, yet are nothing without the human stories behind them. These boxes illustrate the point that objects are the result of human activity, sites and monuments the glorious achievements of humankind, the prisons and camps the physical representations of the dark side of human behaviour.

How can we put a price on culture, a price on learning from the past? Cultural activities should be priced not according to market forces but as a crucial, important aspect of our lives.

DISCUSSION QUESTIONS

1. Should access to culture in its many forms be related to ability to pay and if not should such activities be subsidized by the public purse? Consider the implications for the withdrawal of public money.
2. Without a sense of the past and an understanding of where we came from people would have no sense of community. Discuss with reference to how your community emphasizes and interprets its unique cultural traits.
3. The material evidence of human activity is contained within cultural institutions. Sometimes our cultural identity is mixed up with the misfortunes of others and objects contained within state-run museums may be the cultural property of other countries and cultures. Consider the arguments for repatriation of such objects. Is it possible to honestly determine the issues of ownership?

BIBLIOGRAPHY

Ilifalabantu, *Heritage of the People*, Vol. 6, No. 1, South Africa, June 2002.
Carnegie, E. (1996) 'Trying to be an honest woman', in Kavanagh, G. (ed.), *Making Histories in Museums*. London: Routledge.
Voices of Young People on Robben Island, Robben Island Publication, South Africa, 16 June 2002.

Journals
Museums Journal, December 2001.
Museums Journal, July 2002.

Interviews
Derek Janes, Director of Edinburgh City Museums.
Lynne Halfpenny, Arts Outreach Development Officer for Edinburgh City Council.
Deidre Prins, Chief Education Officer, Robben Island Museum.

Websites
http//www.infosite.co.uk/masite/ethics.htm

8

Sex and Saunas

Ian Yeoman, Catherine Drudy, Ruth Robertson and Una McMahon-Beattie

Take one massage parlour boasting a five star-service behind the expensive drape of its £11,000 curtains. Add a forthcoming sex multiplex, complete with 'friction dancing', to the handful of existing lap dancing clubs and strip pubs. Throw in the 20-odd licensed saunas, a couple of hundred street prostitutes and mix with the most relaxed drinking laws in the country ... (Edinburgh Evening News, 15 April 2002)

What you have here, is an image of Edinburgh that is a mini-Amsterdam, a haven of saunas, lap-dancing, stag parties, hen parties and naughty weekends. It is a perception of a city where the sex industry thrives against a backdrop of culture, history, festivals and art that drives the city's tourism image. Edinburgh is a city of the 'Edinburgh International Festival', 'The Fringe', 'Edinburgh Castle', 'The Former Royal Yacht Britannia' and 'Holyrood Palace', where tourism is core to the city's economy. However, it is also a city where sex tourism grew up through the 1980s, when Edinburgh had the tag of the 'AIDS Capital of Europe' (*Edinburgh Evening News*, 15 April 2002), resulting in Edinburgh City Council adopting a pragmatic approach to disease prevention in order to combat a growing drugs and AIDS problem. This approach led to a policy that is managed through the licensing of saunas and massage parlours in the city that offer a range of *extras*. Hence, the emergence of an underworld perception of Edinburgh, as the UK's sex tourism capital. It is a policy that is founded on a tolerance of sex tourism, resulting in the implementation of a licensed sauna and massage parlour regime throughout the city. These saunas and massage parlours are a means by which the council can control crime, health and social issues related to prostitution across the city. With their characteristics of fixed capacity, time-varied demand and a perishable experience, these establishments have all the characteristics of industries that use revenue management. So, what are the issues of revenue management that pertain to Edinburgh's sauna and massage parlours?

SEX TOURISM

A strong link exists between sex and the tourism industry, particularly in respect of sex as a motivating factor for travel (Hall 1996). The issue of sex tourism, although a relatively modern area of research and study, is well documented in respect of structural, social and power influences it exerts on various countries, cities or areas. However, when sex tourism is under discussion, Edinburgh is perhaps not considered as a destination for this type of activity. The industry was encouraged in the 1990s to move from its original area of Leith Docks, closer to the City Centre via registered massage and sauna establishments. This move was predominately for health reasons, i.e., the spread of sexually transmitted diseases.

Sex tourism is one of the most emotive and sensational issues in tourism. It is an extremely problematic area to define (Hall 1996). Opperman (1999) sets to define sex tourism within the context of purpose of travel, length of time, relationships, sexual encounters and travel. Opperman argues that combining these variables constitutes a debate on sex tourism. Herold and Van Kerkwijk (1992) distinguishes sex tourism as sexual gratification as the main motivator for travel, whether consciously or unconsciously. It is a debate. Ryan and Hall (2001) states that the term sex tourism incurs images of the red light districts, prostitution and exploitation. Ryan argues that sex tourism is a search for identity as well as exploitation. He examined sex tourism within the realm of non-commercial versus commercial; voluntary versus non-voluntary; confirmation of identity versus assault on identity. Thus Ryan acknowledges the vast spectrum covered by the concept. Ryan and Hall (2001), Opperman (1999) and Hall (1996) highlight the problem of constructing a definition of sex tourism[1]. Ultimately, Ryan's view on the definition of sex tourism is that it should allow for discussion of different paradigms and can be described using the all-inclusive term of 'sexual intercourse away from the home'.

EDINBURGH'S SEX TOURISM

What has been the effect of Edinburgh City Council's pragmatic solutions-based policy towards sex tourism? One notable effect, is a comparison of sex tourism between Edinburgh and Glasgow. This shows a distinct difference as to why women enter this type of work between Edinburgh and Glasgow, with 62.7 per cent of Glasgow's prostitutes reporting illegal drug use. According to Councillor Phil Attridge, convenor of the regulatory committee on licensing:

> *If by minimizing prostitution on the streets we have made Edinburgh safer than Glasgow, where's the problem in that? Glasgow now has a horrendous problem, whereas Edinburgh is an absolute success story with no tags around its neck. We are taking a pragmatic approach. You can stick your head in a moral cloud, but that doesn't solve problems. Do you want the police, who are already on limited resources, rounding up girls in saunas, or do you want them solving crimes?*
>
> (Rimmer, 2000)

Plant (1997) agrees that there are distinct differences between drug taking by sex workers in Glasgow and Edinburgh. He noted that that there were high levels of intravenous drug users in Glasgow, where in Edinburgh drug usage was mostly cannabis and alcohol. He also found that there was a higher level of pimping in Glasgow than in Edinburgh. However, Ruth Morgan-Thomas of ScotPEP, argues that Edinburgh is unique in the UK for its low levels of violence, stating: 'We only see a serious level attack once a month at the most and normally once every couple of months' (Rafferty, 2001).

Violence against street prostitutes in Glasgow is stark; out of 240 prostitutes contacted by Dr Barnard of Glasgow University, 54 per cent had been slapped, punched or kicked, 25 per cent reported being raped and 23 per cent said they had been strangled (Scott, 2001; Rimmer, 2001). Barnard concludes that there are

many different triggers for violence towards prostitutes. Often these are about the type and cost of the sex the woman wants to sell and that men think they should be provided with. In her mind she is clear that this is about sex for money, not anything else, but reminding the client of this can create tension, increasing the risk that he will become irritated and possibly violent.

Men who buy sex often see it as a service. One man described sex with a prostitute as being similar to getting your car washed. As consumers they often think they have certain rights over the women. This view is completely at odds with the prostitute's view that she is in control of the encounter, not the man.

She believes that there are around 1000 prostitutes, compared to approximately 300 in Edinburgh, working in Glasgow, with approximately 90 per cent of them on drugs – mostly heroin. The lower levels of violence in Edinburgh compared to Glasgow may be due to the city policy. Scott's (2001) investigation found that in Edinburgh a policy of 'liaison and discretionary prosecution' is said to offer prostitutes better protection. Due to this tolerant policy and management, Edinburgh City Council now has 23 licensed sauna and massage parlours.

EDINBURGH'S SAUNA BUSINESS

Stephen Rafferty (1999) estimates that there are approximately 500 to 700 prostitutes working in any given year in Edinburgh, with more than 80 per cent working 'indoors' or 'saunas'. These saunas operate under the Civic Government (Scotland) Act 1982. Its aim is to:

Make provisions as regards Scotland for the licensing and regulation of certain activities; for the preservation of public order and safety, and the prevention of crime.
(Civic Government (Sco) Act 1982)

This means that in order for saunas and massage parlours in Edinburgh to conduct their business, they must apply to The City of Edinburgh Council for a licence and meet a level of criteria. This includes factors such as health and safety, working conditions and fire regulations. Rafferty (1999) believes that the licensing of saunas came about due to the first heroin explosion in Edinburgh when the police were faced with the difficult task of controlling a booming street sex trade in which many of the women were working to feed drink and drug habits. He also believes that it was inextricably linked to the murder of two prostitutes in 1981 and the upsurge of violent attacks, robberies and blackmail attempts on clients. Those events, allied with the increased health risks from HIV, focused attention on prostitution and brought realization that action was needed to bring the situation back to a manageable level. Therefore, the police and authorities turn a blind eye to the prostitution in the city, tolerating a problem in order to manage it. Margo Macdonald (2002) argues that,

> *There is no doubt about it, the policy of tolerance in Edinburgh has resulted in much lower figures as regards sexually transmitted diseases, there's much less violence, there's no pimps, there's no lassies under 16 recorded working last year and so on.*

Plans for new 'upmarket' massage parlours in Edinburgh have brought recent speculation to the issue of sex tourism. A recent article in the *Edinburgh Evening News* (Cumming, 2002) highlighted that a local firm, Club 7, plans to open a massage parlour in the New Town area by the end of April, while Spearmint Rhino, a US-based lap dancing chain, plan for a 'sex multiplex' in the capital by the end of the year.

However, many feel that Edinburgh's 'tolerant' approach is going too far. Catherine Harper, of Scottish Women Against Pornography (Cumming, 2002) feels that the city council is renowned as a soft touch by sex club owners and that the council are giving licences to too many premises, in turn turning Edinburgh into a sex tourism capital. However, a spokesman from Club 7 Leisure argued that the sex industry is no longer seedy back streets, with a lot of the 'cloak and dagger' stuff disappearing. He continued to highlight that Club 7 are 'providing services for people who are upfront about their needs – the new millennium man who isn't afraid to admit he needs a massage.'

Although many campaigners feel that the local authorities are transforming Edinburgh into a 'sex tourism' destination, backers for the new developments feel they were only attempting to bring the capital in line with other major European cities.

Edinburgh City Council's sauna policy takes a pragmatic solution approach to sex tourism and realizes that in order to control and reduce the negative impacts of the industry they must firstly recognize that the industry exists and then take measures to tackle the problems. By licensing saunas and massage parlours, the council is focusing around health issues and violence. The Council regards their approach to sex tourism as one that is strategic and that can control a problem.

THE SEXUAL ENCOUNTER

The sexual encounter or experience is highlighted through a number of reviews that are available on the web, i.e. www.worldsexguide.com, www.punternet.com. For example, Dee (2002), the name of a punter, recalls his experience of the Edinburgh sex scene.

> *It has to have the sexiest girls and most relaxing policing in the UK. ... All saunas' charging are basically the same. The set-up is also the same for most saunas. On entry you pay a set fee to the sauna manager for the time spent in the room, then you are given a key to a locker, a bag for your valuables and a towel. You change, shower and join the girls in the lounge area, where a non-alcoholic drink will be offered. You can generally spend as long as you want (sometimes you will have no choice if the place is*

busy and the number of girls is limited). You choose a girl and then go through to the room. She will tell you her prices, you choose what you want and then away you go. A reasonable example of pricing: entry fee (30 minutes, £15; 45 minutes, £20; 60 minutes, £25); services (hand relief, £30; oral, £35; sex plus oral cum twice, £50; two girl, £90– £100). Note that prices for Premier League Saunas may increase by £5–£10; for poorer saunas and older staff, they maybe cheaper. Also, if you book an hour, some of the charges for the services maybe increased by £10. Hours vary, but generally . . . between 10 a.m. – 10 p.m., with a change of shift at 4 p.m.

SEX TOURISM AND REVENUE GENERATION

Generally speaking, there has been no known literature regarding revenue generation from sex tourism. It should be noted that as it is such a delicate subject and many factors are concerned with illegality, it is virtually impossible to calculate the wealth generation made by tourists. However, Julia O'Connell Davidson (1998), a reader in Sociology at the University of Leicester, has discovered how the economics of sex tourism works for tourists, prostitutes and the travel industry. She believes that

as a whole, sex tourism flourishes in countries where a large percentage of the population live in poverty, where there is high unemployment and no welfare system to support those who are excluded from the formal economy. Those involved in tourist-related prostitution are very often migrants from rural areas or urban conurbations, and may be attempting to support several dependants as well as themselves through prostitution.

It is felt that this statement relates to Third World sex tourism destinations and does not consider those developed countries that have a high activity of sex tourism, usually behind closed doors. Unfortunately, no international figures have been published regarding the money made by sex tourism, however, O'Connell Davidson found from her research that the prime beneficiaries of sex tourism are mostly the airlines that transport sex tourists, the hotels in which they stay, and the travel agents that arrange their flights and accommodation. Other beneficiaries may include local restaurants and attractions.

Michelle Nichols (2001) recently investigated the impacts of the annual Edinburgh Festival on prostitution. From her research, she found that prostitutes from across Europe are flocking to work in Edinburgh because of increased demand on the sex industry during the festival. The same article reported Ruth Morgan-Thomas arguing that you will find with any city that has a major festival that women will travel for the event. She believes that this increase of women is not at all taking away business from the local industry as the prostitutes in Edinburgh are fairly well-used by the tourists as well. This shows that although tourists are most likely using the services of the women in Edinburgh, it is difficult to determine an exact figure for such a problem.

SAUNAS, MASSAGE PARLOURS AND REVENUE MANAGEMENT

Kimes' (1997, 2001) ingredients and preconditions of revenue management for the hotel and airline industry have been adopted as a framework in which to compare

Edinburgh's saunas and massage parlours. The framework allows for assessment of revenue management in order to discuss its practice within the sex tourism industry. Table 8.1, explains the degree of application of the principles of revenue management for Edinburgh's sauna and massage parlour business.

Conclusions are drawn that the cost structures of saunas and massage parlours typically contain a significant element of fixed costs in relation to variable costs. The capital costs of new sauna are similar to those of small hotels, plus the cost of meeting the Civic Government (Sco) Act 1982. Capacity is measured by the number of rooms in the sauna. The total capacity in Edinburgh is linked to numbers of establishments and rooms. The cost of selling an extra room for a sexual encounter has little relevance, as a fixed pricing and duration policy is operated in order to control capacity. Saunas are capacity constrained firms that have eliminated the problem of unpredictable duration of customer use, which inhibits how organizations manage revenue. By using a predictable duration policy, saunas control the length of time the punters use the service. This definition of duration, is measured in terms of 30 minutes, 45 minutes, etc. This approach to duration management reduces uncertainty of duration and also allows sauna managers to manage time. Time availability of the rooms and sex workers are the constraints upon capacity. Saunas use booking diaries and convention charts to control and log duration. Punters either reserve in advance or walk into a sauna. There is evidence to suggest advanced reservations are usually based upon preferred prostitutes/masseurs, as many prostitutes will have regular punters.

Barth (2002) examines revenue management statistics as a means of measurement. A revenue management statistic is essential in order to measure the results and effectiveness of operations. Revenue statistics are constructed with some type of rate efficiency ratio (for example, the average spend per customer) multiplied by some kind of capacity utilization ratio (for example the percentage of seating capacity utilized). Total revenue can change due to the average price alone, capacity utilisation alone, or through some combination of these. Kimes (2002) states that the unit of inventory in revenue management situations is 'time'. Therefore, as saunas operate a fixed pricing and duration policy, revenue could be measured per hour of the day per prostitute as a means of business performance. Drudy (2001), in her study of prostitution in Edinburgh, found that many saunas and massage parlours did not operate at 100 per cent occupancy. For example, establishments with seven rooms may only have four prostitutes working. So the capacity constraint is very much focused on the prostitute rather than the room availability.

Revenue management (Kimes, 2001) is based upon companies developing logical differential pricing policies. Industries actively practising revenue management use differential prices and charge customers using the same service at the same time different prices depending upon customer and demand characteristics. Within the sauna business the practice of fixed pricing is evident. Fixed pricing is both for the duration of the service, i.e., room booking and range of sexual services (Dee, 2002). This approach to pricing, reflects an informal cartel characteristic. Therefore, Edinburgh's saunas and massage parlours charge punters using the same service at the same time at the same price. There is evidence to suggest, that this approach is fair (Dee, 2002). Punters can see what they are getting and therefore 'trust' (McMahon-Beattie *et al.*, 2002) the prostitute. This element of 'trust' is highlighted by Dee, as certain saunas run scams based upon the 'look' of the punter (Dee 2002). This focus on trust and fairness works within the realms of perceptions of fairness (Kahneman *et al.*, 1986), as punters will have societal norms that govern what is fair and not fair.

According to Barth (2002), one of the goals of revenue management to is obtain the

Table 1 Application of revenue management principles to the sex industry

Characteristic	Characteristics of revenue management	
	Application in the hotel and airline industries	Application to Edinburgh's sauna and massage parlour industry
Relatively fixed capacity	Hotels and airlines tend to be capacity constrained with no opportunity to inventory their products or goods. Many hotel services and products are perishable. Capacity can be changed by, for example, adding a number of new bedrooms as this involves a large financial investment in terms of equipment and plant.	Saunas have a physical fixed capacity, similar to hotel bedrooms. Many establishments in Edinburgh operate between four and twelve rooms. Capacity constraint is associated with availability of the prostitute rather than the room.
High fixed costs	The industries are characterized by high fixed costs and, as explained above, the cost of adding incremental capacity can be very high and is not quickly adjusted. Adding new bedrooms to a hotel not only entails a large capital outlay but may involve a long planning and construction period.	As many saunas have similar characteristics as hotels, the cost of adding additional rooms is extremely high. Many saunas and massage parlours face strict planning criteria on their size of operation.
Low variable costs	The costs incurred by, for example, selling a bedroom or airline seat to a customer in otherwise unused capacity is relatively inexpensive and incurs only minor servicing costs.	The cost of selling an extra room for a sexual encounter are the same as a hotel. But most of the saunas and massage parlours operate a fixed pricing policy for different services.
Time-varied demand	Since capacity is fixed, organizations cannot easily adjust their capacity to meet peaks and troughs in demand. Therefore, demand varies: hotels can benefit from controlling capacity when demand is high and relaxing that control when demand is low. As with airlines, utilization of reservation systems can assist in managing demand since they log requests for rooms in advance.	As capacity is fixed and cannot be adjusted, many saunas and massage parlours operate very simple convention charts and booking diaries in order to manage demand and log reservations. Therefore, demand may be predictable when plotted against different certain times of the day or days of the week.
Similarity of inventory units	As a general rule, revenue management systems operate in a situation where inventory units are similar. However, it should be noted that service firms like hotels and airlines can differentiate their units by, for example,	Saunas and massage parlours sell rooms depending on the degree of luxury and facilities in the room, i.e., standard, jacuzzi, luxury, etc.

Characteristics of revenue management

Characteristic	Application in the hotel and airline industries	Application to Edinburgh's sauna and massage parlour industry
	offering add-on luxury features or the possibility of upgrades.	
Market segmentation	Hotels and airlines normally have ability to divide their customer base into distinct market segments such as leisure or business. These customers have different behaviour patterns, e.g., corporate clients are usually time sensitive, pay higher tariffs; whilst leisure travellers travelling at non-peak periods who tend to book longer in advance, are more price sensitive. Airlines have sophisticated consumer behaviour models drawn from good information management systems.	Saunas and massage parlour do not segment their market. They offer fixed capacity, based upon room type and duration room booking, i.e., 30 minutes or 45 minutes. This characteristic follows Kimes' (2001) pricing and duration of service industries. This price is based upon the room booking. Additionally, sex workers offer a range of prices depending upon the service required. In many establishments, these prices are fixed and non-negotiable.
Historical demand and booking patterns	Detailed knowledge of hotel and airlines sales and booking data per market segment should help managers predict peaks and troughs in demand and assist in effectively aligning demand and supply.	Demand is based upon experience. This is about marrying demand supply. Basically, rostering enough sex workers to service demand in saunas and massage parlours. The proprietor's expert knowledge of demand patterns is used as a rostering tool.
Pricing management	Revenue management is a form of price discrimination. In practice, hotels operate revenue management systems which depend on opening and closing rate bands. In order to stimulate demand in periods of low demand, hotels can offer discounted prices whilst during periods of high demand low rates can be closed off. Additionally, by offering a number of rates in the hotel the manager will, ideally, profitably align price, product and buyer and increase net yield.	According to Dee (2002) Edinburgh's saunas follow Kimes' fixed pricing and fixed duration pricing policy. Saunas do use price to segment or control demand. Punters pay a fixed fee to the sauna manager upon arrival based upon duration. Punters choose a girl for a massage in a private room. Once in the room, pricing is based upon the sexual services menu, i.e., 'hand relief', 'oral' or 'full sex'. According to Dee (2002), certain saunas 'rip off punters. Typical scam is asking for blatantly more than the going Edinburgh rate – £100 for sex, etc. I once chose a girl who looked fantastic – she was Brazilian or Venezuelan, but claimed to be Spanish. I liked the look of her so upgraded to a VIP room. She

Characteristics of revenue management

Characteristic	Application in the hotel and airline industries	Application to Edinburgh's sauna and massage parlour industry
		took that as her cue to rip me off. … Next time I went … I got the same hassle with a different girl.'
Overbooking	Overbooking is an essential revenue management technique. Overbooking levels are not set by chance but are determined by a detailed analysis of what has happened in the past and a prediction of what is likely to happen in the future. Predicted no-shows, cancellations, denials, all form part of a complex calculation carried out in advance. In this way the risk of disappointing a customer who has booked in advance is minimized.	There is no evidence to suggest overbooking occurs in Edinburgh's sauna business, as most business seems to be on 'demand' rather than 'advanced reservations'. Convention charts and booking diaries are used to schedule sex workers and punters.
Information systems	Effective management information is essential for successful revenue management. Information technology can assist greatly in the sorting and manipulation of required data. The use of artificial intelligence (AI) has enormous potential for handling the complexities of revenue management because of its abilities in complex problem solving, reasoning, perception, planning and analysis of extensive data. Expert systems (ES) are 'knowledge based' software packages that reflect the expertise in the area of the application and these types of systems have extensive capacity in dealing with non-numeric, qualitative data. These systems need to be integrated with property management, reservation and group systems. If this is not the case, incomplete or inaccurate information may be entered into the revenue management system.	No computerised and information systems operate in saunas and massage parlours. Knowledge based systems are very much based upon experience and intuition of the sauna manager.

highest average price for the product or service that is being sold. Evidence (Dee, 2002; McCoy, 2001) from Edinburgh's sauna and massage business, suggests that average spend per punter is based upon the sexual service offered – an encouragement to have full sex rather than oral sex only.

Yeoman and Ingold (2001) discuss the risk-taking behaviour of revenue managers in the airline and hotel businesses being concerned with overbooking. Risk-taking behaviour in saunas and massage parlours is not concerned with overbooking, but the risk the prostitute and the punter take in the terms of crime, health and social issues. Church and colleagues (Church *et al.*, 2001) suggests the risk of violence on prostitutes is greatly reduced in saunas compared to that of street prostitutes, prostitutes working outdoors in Glasgow being six times more likely to have experienced violence by clients than those working indoors in Edinburgh. Additionally, prostitutes and punters expose themselves to sexually transmitted diseases such as HIV and hepatitis C, a characteristic of risk-taking behaviour. Although prostitutes are educated and supported by ScotPEP and the health authority on safe sex practices, i.e., using condoms, there is risk arising from pressure from punters seeking sex without condoms.

ISSUES AND CONCLUSIONS

Edinburgh City Council's pragmatic solutions approach towards prostitution and the subsequent accidental label as the UK's sex tourism destination brings us into the realms of revenue management as practised within saunas and massage parlours. Edinburgh's saunas have the characteristics of small hotels, but the practice of revenue management is based upon a fixed pricing and duration policy, resulting in rooms and sexual services been offered at a fixed price. This seems to be justified in terms of perceived fairness, in which services and duration are clear to punters in order that 'scams' and negotiation are taken out of the equation. But the real issues are not the practices of revenue management, but the ethics and morality of sex tourism and prostitution within the city. These are the issues that the reader of this case study may wish to reflect upon.

DISCUSSION QUESTIONS

1. What are the characteristics of sex tourism in your destination?
2. Discuss the morality, ethics and characteristics of revenue management for the sex tourism industry.
3. Discuss Edinburgh's sauna and massage parlour business against Robert Cross's[2] core concepts of revenue management.

NOTES

1. For the purpose of this case study, one omission is made from the discussion on sex tourism, notably paedophilia. Paedophilia is a clinical term that refers to an adult personality disorder that involves specific and focused sexual interest in pre-

pubertual children (Clift and Carter, 2000). The subject of paedophilia and child prostitution is a highly emotive subject and is outwith the realms of this research.
2. Cross, R. (1997) *Revenue Management: Hard-Core Tactics for Market Domination.* Broadway Books, New York

REFERENCES

Barth, J. E. (2002) 'Yield management: opportunities for private club managers', *International Journal of Contemporary Hospitality Management*, **14**(3), 136–41.

Civic Government (Sco) Act 1982.

Church, S., Henderson, M., Barnard, M. and Hart, G. (2001) 'Violence by clients towards female prostitutes in different work settings: questionnaire survey', *British Medical Journal*, **322**, 524–5.

Cumming, J. (2002) 'Super sauna spends £11,000 on curtains', *Edinburgh Evening* News, 28 March. Accessed at *http://news.scotsman.com/archive.cfm?id=337762002&rware=JAYXKSYENZJW& CQ_CUR_DOCUMENT=10*

Clift, S. and Carter, S. (2000) *Tourism and Sex: Culture, Commerce and Coercion*, London: Continuum.

Dee (2002) Edinburgh Massage Parlour Review. *http://www.worldsexguide.com/guide/United _Kingdom/Edinburgh*

Donaghy, K. and McMahon, U. (1995) 'Yield management – a marketing perspective', *International Journal of Vacation Marketing*, **2**(1), 55–62.

Drudy, C. (2001) 'The Effects of Sex Tourism on the Health and Wealth of Edinburgh'. School of Marketing & Tourism Dissertation, Napier University, Edinburgh.

Edinburgh Evening News (2002) 'No sex tourists please', 15 April 2002, accessed at *http://news.scotsman.com/index.cfm?id=402782002&rware=ICXCPRZIVXLV&CQ CUR_ DOCUMENT=6*

Hall, C. M. (1996) 'Sex tourism in South-East Asia', in D. Harrison (ed.) *Tourism and the Less Developed Countries*. London: Belhaven Press.

Herold, E. S. and Van Kerwijk, C. (1992) 'AIDS and sex tourism', *AIDS and Society International Research and Policy Bulletin*, **4**, 8–9.

Kahneman, D. Knetsch, J. and Thaler, R. (1986) 'Fairness as a constraint on profit seeking: entitlements in the market', *American Economic Review*, **76**(4), 728–41.

Kimes, S. (1997) 'Yield management: an overview', in I. Yeoman and A. Ingold (eds) *Yield Management: Strategies for the Service Industries*. London: Cassell.

Kimes, S. (2001) 'A strategic approach to yield management', in A. Ingold, U. McMahon-Beattie and I. Yeoman (eds) *Yield Management: Strategies for the Service Industries*. London: Continuum.

Kimes, S. (2002) 'Revenue Management: An Insight into Hotels, Restaurants and Golf'. Scottish Tourism Revenue Management Conference, 20 March, Dunblane, Scotland.

MacDonald, M. (2002) 'Talks over prostitution zone', 15 November. Accessed at *http://news. bbc.co.uk/hi/english/uk/scotland/newsid_1656000/1656885.stm*

McCoy, G. (2001) *McCoy's British Massage Parlour Guide*. London: McCoy's Guides.

McMahon-Beattie, U., Yeoman, I., Parmer, A. and Mudie, P. (2002) 'Price and the maintenance of trust', *Journal of Revenue & Pricing Management*, **1**(1), 25–34.

Nicholls, M. (2001) 'Foreign prostitutes flocking to Edinburgh Festival', *The Scotsman*, 20 August. Accessed at *http://www.festival.scotsman.com/home/headlines_specific.cfm?articleid =447&rware=PWTYKTGENYLV&CQ_CUR_DOCUMENT=9*

O'Connell Davidson, J. (1998) *Prostitution, Power and Freedom*. London: Polity Press.

Oppermann, M. (1999) 'Sex tourism', *Annals of Tourism Research*, **26**, 251–66.

Plant, M. (1997) 'Alochol and drugs and social milieu', in G. Scrambler and A. Scrambler (eds) *Rethinking Prostitution: Purchasing Sex in the 1990s*. London: Routledge.

Rafferty, J. (2001) 'Danger zone', *Big Issue Scotland*. Accessed at *http://www.bigissuescotland.com/features/352/intolerance/index.cfm*

Rafferty, S. (1999) 'The pleasure industry', *The Scotsman*, 25 September.

Rimmer, L. (2001) 'The game of her life', *Scotland on Sunday*, 17 March. Accessed at *http://news.scotsman.com/index.cfm?id = 294032002&rware = KYYBILBENYLV&CQ _CUR_ DOCUMENT = 1*

Ryan, C. and Hall, M. (2001) *Sex Tourism*. London: Routledge.

Scott, K. (2001) 'Prostitutes left at risk of attack', *The Guardian*, 2 March. Accessed at *http://www.guardian.co.uk/Archive/Article/0,4273,4144767,00.html*

Yeoman, I. and Ingold, A. (2001) 'Decision making', in A. Ingold, U. McMahon-Beattie and I. Yeoman (eds) *Yield Management: Strategies for the Service Industries*. London: Continuum.

9

Hotel Demand/Cancellation Analysis and Estimation of Unconstrained Demand Using Statistical Methods

Patrick H. Liu

INTRODUCTION

This case study is based on reservation data from 23 hotels in the US of various types (downtown, resort, airport, roadside, convention, etc.), ranging in size from 62 to 4800 rooms, and spanning several seasons over a three-year period (1998–2000). In this investigation we study only the 'transient demand' defined as the request for rooms for given nights by prospective guests that are not affiliated with a group event. A transient may or may not have certain 'rights' to preferential rates or room availability based on agreements with organizations or published promotions.

Of these 23 hotels, on average, the demand data were censored (or constrained) on 61 per cent of the days by either room rates or hotel capacity or both at various booking lead-times. Table 9.1 shows, for each of the 23 hotels, the hotel size measured by the total number of rooms in the hotel, hotel type, the major seasons used by the hotel, the total number of days that we have investigated, the total number of days that demand data were censored, and the censorship percentage. The real names of the hotels are replaced by H1–H23 to protect the confidentiality of the hotels.

We attempt to accomplish the following three objectives in this case study:

1. How to estimate the unconstrained hotel daily demand based on censored booking data.
2. Analysis of unconstrained hotel demand distributions by season by day of the week, which includes mean, standard deviation, and distributional form of the demand. Regression analysis to link demand variability to hotel size.
3. Analysis of the cancellations/no-shows by season by day of the week for each of the 23 hotels.

Table 9.1 Summary information of the 23 hotels in case study

Hotel name	Hotel size	Hotel type	Major seasons used by hotel	Study period	Total number of days*	Number of days censored	Censoring (%)
H1	500	Downtown	Peak, Low, Shoulder	7/1/99–8/21/00	418	337	80.62
H2	630	Downtown	High, Low, Medium, Convention	8/30/99–8/17/00	354	275	77.90
H3	550	Downtown	Peak, Slow, Shoulder	4/5/99–8/21/00	505	443	87.72
H4	430	Downtown	High, Low, Medium, Holiday	4/20/99–8/17/00	486	355	73.05
H5	278	Airport	Regular, Summer, Convention	7/3/99–8/17/00	412	80	19.42
H6	4800	Resort	Off-Peak, High, Convention, etc.	10/24/99–8/23/00	305	240	80.00
H7	200	Resort	Off-Peak, High, Convention, etc.	10/29/99–8/23/00	300	194	64.67
H8	337	Downtown	High, Slow, Shoulder, etc.	5/24/99–8/21/00	456	306	67.11
H9	305	Downtown	High, Low, Medium	3/9/99–8/16/00	527	405	77.00
H10	895	Convention centre	Summer, Open, Shoulder, Slow	10/1/99–8/21/00	234	123	52.56
H11	131	Country Inns	Fall, Winter, Spring, Summer	7/1/99–8/21/00	418	336	80.38
H12	138	Downtown/Resort	Fall, Winter, Spring, Summer, Pre-Summer	10/17/99–8/17/00	303	168	55.63
H13	162	Resort Inn	Fall, Spring, Pre-Winter, Winter, Summer	9/16/99–8/21/00	331	87	26.28
H14	70	Downtown/Resort	Fall, Winter, Spring, Summer	8/18/99–10/4/00	414	339	81.29
H15	150	Roadside Inn	Fall, Winter, Spring, Summer	11/22/99–10/4/00	317	84	23.33
H16	370	Downtown	High, Low, Mid-High, Sellout, Shoulder	3/1/98–4/16/00	709	173	24.40
H17	100	Roadside Inn	Holiday, Low, Regular	1/1/99–10/4/00	643	56	10.24
H18	680	Downtown/Resort/Convention	Low, High, Convention	8/17/99–1/31/00	168	149	88.69
H19	191	Resort	Leisure, Peak, Summer, Value	2/23/00–10/4/00	225	186	82.67
H20	62	Resort	Leisure, Peak, Summer	2/23/00–10/4/00	218	200	88.89
H21	264	Resort	Leisure, Peak, Summer	2/20/00–10/4/00	228	206	90.35
H22	300	Resort	Leisure, Peak, Summer	3/3/00–10/4/00	216	186	86.11
H23	200	Resort	Leisure, Peak, Summer	4/5/00–10/4/00	183	136	74.32

* These are days having valid data.

Due to the large volume, only detailed analysis for hotels H3, H5, H10, H17 and H21 are given in this case study (in Tables 9.3–9.7 to represent different types of hotels; these Tables are at the end of the chapter). Analysis for the remaining 18 hotels can be obtained by contacting the author directly.

ESTIMATION OF UNCONSTRAINED HOTEL DAILY DEMAND BASED ON CENSORED BOOKING DATA

The primary basis for forecasting future unconstrained transient demand is a hotel's historical demand data. Hotels will realize unconstrained transient demand only if there are no restrictions (or constraints) placed on bookings during the entire booking process (e.g., room rate at rate threshold, no capacity limitations, no stay controls, and other explanatory variables, such as competitors' room rates, at their nominal levels).

Usually unconstrained transient demand can be observed during low seasons. During peak seasons, only the portion of the unconstrained demand that has been booked is observable – the remaining portion becomes 'lost opportunities', sometimes called denials. For many hotels during peak seasons, almost every day is constrained. Booking data are easily tracked in hotel reservation systems. Denials represent a much thornier problem, as a hotel's data on reservation requests that were turned away are invariably incomplete and often misleading. Even when reservation systems are designed to record data on lost opportunities, the data recorded are insufficient for inferring unconstrained demand (Orkin, 1998).

A great deal of effort has been made in the hotel industry to come up with the right number for the unconstrained demand for the constrained days. Some use denial data, which have been dismissed by many industry experts as grossly unreliable (Orkin, 1998). Some estimate using uncensored data only and discard the censored data. Some estimate using the data as they exist, by ignoring the fact of censorship. Others use methods such as the so-called two-stage maximum likelihood method and the 'detruncation' methods (e.g., Hopperstad, 1995, McGill, 1995, Pölt, 2000, Swan, 1990, Weatherford, 2000, Wickham, 1995, and Zeni, 2001). In this case study we use the statistical methods developed by Liu *et al.* (2002) to statistically infer the unconstrained demand based on censored reservation data. This method is more general and likely to produce more accurate and unbiased estimation than those in previous research (e.g., Brummer *et al.*, 1988, Hopperstad, 1995, Lee, 1990, McGill, 1995, Skwarek, 1996, Wickham, 1995). (See Liu *et al.*, 2002 for a literature review of these papers, a detailed step-by-step development of the deconstraining algorithms, and several numerical examples.)

In this section, we only discuss how to estimate the unconstrained total daily arrival transient demand at the gross level with all market segments and length of stays combined. The following steps are used in estimating the unconstrained demand.

Step 1: For each hotel, group the reservation data by arrival days' season (as defined by the hotel), day of the week, and room type. For example, such a group may include reservations for Monday arrivals (length of stays can be 1, 2, 3, etc.) in peak season for standard rooms. The purpose is to make the unconstrained demand data within each group 'homogeneous'.

Step 2: For a group, obtain the booking-pace curve for each arrival day. For a given arrival day, bookings requests will occur at different lead-times and can be represented by a booking-pace curve which is the graph of total bookings versus the lead-time (in days or hours) before the arrival day. The time period between the expected first reservation request and the arrival day will be referred to as the 'planning horizon'. Divide the longest planning horizon of the arrivals days in the group into lead-time intervals. It is not necessary for these lead-time intervals to be constant over different lead-times. Intervals further away from arrival day can be longer. Intervals near or on arrival day can be shorter (even in hours on arrival day). We have the following three general criteria for the lengths of the lead-time intervals: (1) the sample size in each intervals should be sufficiently large, (2) for an arrival day, room rate remains constant over the time interval, and (3) demand rate is roughly constant over the interval.

Step 3: Obtain the total number of actual bookings and their associated rate and capacity limitations in each of the lead-time intervals for each of the arrival days in the group. Capacity limitations are represented by the percentage of time during which the booking is open.

Step 4: Assume that the total number of bookings in each of the lead-time intervals for the arrival days in the group is distributed in Weibull, Poisson, or normal distributions. Pick an appropriate distribution (see Liu *et al.*, 2002 for a discussion on selecting lead-time demand distributions).

Step 5: Compute the unconstrained demand in the lead-time intervals for each of the arrival days in the group using the algorithms developed in Liu *et al.* (2002).

Step 6: For each arrival day in the group, sum up the unconstrained demands in the lead-time intervals over its entire booking lead-time to arrive at the total unconstrained daily demand.

Hotels of different type usually have very different length of 'planning horizons'. For example, quite often customers start booking rooms at resort or convention hotels more than a year in advance, while airport or roadside hotels may have only a few days' 'planning horizon'. In this case study, we have computed the total unconstrained daily demand for over 5000 arrival days. The average 'planning horizon' for the 23 hotels is about 100 days. That is, on average, for each arrival day we need to compute unconstrained demand from roughly 100 lead-time intervals (in days for long lead-time and in hours on arrival day) and then add them up to obtain the unconstrained total daily demand. The following example demonstrates the deconstraining algorithms in Step 5 above.

Example 1: Table 9.2 shows the number of actual daily gross bookings that were made at a resort hotel with a lead-time of 20 days out, for 9 arrival days (that were all Sundays in a low season) and their associated rate hurdles. Gross bookings are bookings before cancellations/no-shows. The room rates did not change during the day. The rate threshold was set at \$70. All the sample lead-days were open without capacity limitations and stay controls. Values z_i in column 4 are obtained by dividing rate hurdles by 100.

Table 9.2 Demand data and associated rate hurdles in Example 1

Sample number i	Actual gross bookings	Rate hurdle $	z_i
1	1	70	0.70
2	0	70	0.70
3	1	70	0.70
4	0	70	0.70
5	0	70	0.70
6	1	70	0.70
7	1	85	0.85
8	0	95	0.95
9	0	100	1.00

For illustrative purpose, we assume the exponential distribution (a special case of the Weibull parametric regression model) for the unconstrained gross demand. The parametric regression model for the demand density function is

$$f(x|z;\beta) = \exp(z\beta - xe^{z\beta})$$

where β is the distribution parameter and z is the actual rate hurdle divided by 100 as shown in column 4 of Table 9.2.

Since there is no capacity limitation and the rate hurdle limitations have been explicitly included in the model by z, all demand data in column 2 of Table 9.2 are complete data (i.e., not censored data). (See Liu *et al.*, 2002 for detailed discussions on complete and censored data.) We can obtain the estimate $\hat{\beta} = 1.1584$ by solving $\frac{d\log L(\beta)}{d\beta} = \sum_{i=1}^{n} z^{(i)} - \sum_{i=1}^{n} x_i z^{(i)} e^{\beta z^{(i)}} = 0$ (see equation 18 in Liu *et al.*, 2002). Therefore the exponential distribution becomes $f(x|z; \hat{\beta}) = \exp(1.1584z - xe^{1.1584z})$. By solving $f(x|z_0 = 0.70; \hat{\beta} = 1.1584) = 2.2499e^{-2.2499x}$, we obtain the unconstrained demand distribution at $z_0 = 0.70$. The expected unconstrained bookings for the constrained sample x_i, iϵ(7,8,9), are $u_{x_i} = x_i + 1/2.2499$; thus $u_{x_7} = 1.4445$, and $u_{x_8} = u_{x_9} = 0.4445$. Therefore the gross demand for the 9 samples in Table 9.2 unconstrained at rate hurdle $70 are 1, 0, 1, 0, 0, 1, 1.4445, 0.4445, and 0.4445.

For those same nine arrival days, if we continue computing the unconstrained demand in each of the remaining lead-time intervals over the entire planning horizon, we can obtain the total unconstrained daily demand for each arrival day by summing up its unconstrained 'lead-time interval' demand.

Once the total unconstrained daily demand is obtained, the mean μ and standard deviation σ of the unconstrained demand grouped by the arrival day's season (as defined by the hotel) and day of the week for each hotel can be easily computed:

$$\mu = \sum_{i=1}^{n} d_i/n \text{ and } \sigma = \sqrt{\sum_{i=1}^{n} (\mu - d_i)^2 / (n-1)}, \text{ where } d_i \text{ is the total unconstrained daily}$$

demand for arrival day i in the group. The results for hotels H3, H5, H10, H17 and H21 are shown in columns 6 to 7 of Tables 9.3 to 9.7.

The average unconstrained bookings μ in Table 9.3 indicate that H3 is a business-oriented downtown hotel because weekdays have more business than during the weekends over all seasons. Airport hotels such as H5, on the other hand, usually show little demand trend in days of the week over the seasons (though H5 shows a slight demand increase in mid-week). H10, as a convention center, shows demand changes between seasons are much greater than those among days of the week within a season. It has as much as ten times demand in the summer season as in the open season. Roadside hotels, such as H17, are somewhat similar to airport hotels in terms of demand variations among days of the week in all seasons. Resort hotel H21 shows strong weekend demand (Friday and Saturday) in all seasons, which is generally consistent with conclusions drawn from other resort-type hotels (some hotels may have weekends defined as Thursday to Sunday).

For each of the 23 hotels in the case study, we have also computed the weighted average mean $\bar{\mu}$ and the weighted average standard deviation $\bar{\sigma}$ of the unconstrained daily demand over all seasons and days of the week. The weighted average $\bar{\mu}$ and $\bar{\sigma}$ are calculated as $\bar{\mu} = \sum_{i=1}^{m} n_i\mu_i / \sum_{i=1}^{m} n_i$, and $\bar{\sigma} = \sqrt{\sum_{i=1}^{m} n_i\sigma_i^2 / \sum_{i=1}^{m} n_i}$, where i represents a given combination of season and day of the week, μ and σ_i are the mean and standard deviation of the total unconstrained daily demand for i. The values of $\bar{\mu}$ and $\bar{\sigma}$ for each of the 23 hotels are shown in Table 9.8. The weighted average values $\bar{\mu}$ help pinpoint the relative position of the unconstrained daily demand for any season/day of the week combination for a hotel.

ANALYSIS OF UNCONSTRAINED HOTEL DEMAND DISTRIBUTIONS

The distributions of unconstrained hotel transient demand by season by day of the week are very important to hotel revenue management programmes and have been assumed to be Poisson distributions in almost all hotel revenue management research in the literature (e.g., Badinelli, 2000; Bitran and Mondschein, 1995; Bitran and Gilbert, 1996; Rothstein, 1974). This assumption, if correct, can greatly simplify the computation of the hotel demand probability transition matrix because of the memoriless property of the Poisson distribution. However, this assumption has not been verified by real demand data.

Basing on the unconstrained demand data obtained from the preceding section, we have performed extensive distribution analysis of the unconstrained demand by season by day of the week by each of the 23 hotels. We have used the software package BestFit® 4.0 by Palisade Corporation to fit the distributions to the data.

Example 2: The unconstrained total daily demand from 40 Saturdays in the regular season at hotel H5 are: 156, 164, 136, 176, 125.3616, 191, 154.4457, 152.3000, 128, 79.8127, 189, 160.2763, 138, 138.1143, 132.0105, 160, 89.0547, 104.0799, 100, 133, 127, 142, 157, 133, 172.0193, 173, 157, 123, 179, 167, 172.4229, 169, 176.2579, 111, 135, 102.2031, 132.9567, 153, 158.3806, 208. The non-integer demand is due to our deconstraining algorithms discussed in the preceding section. Figure 9.1 shows the best-fitted theoretical normal distribution curve versus the actual distribution of the demand data.

The three goodness-of-fit test values generated by BestFit® 4.0 are Chi-Square = 8.8000, Anderson-Darling A–D = 0.3285, and K–S = 0.1065, with corresponding p-values at 0.2673, >0.25, and >0.15.

Based on the distribution analyses of demand data from the 23 hotels, we have concluded that, for any given season and day of the week, the unconstrained total daily arrival transient demand (at the gross level with all market segments and length of stays

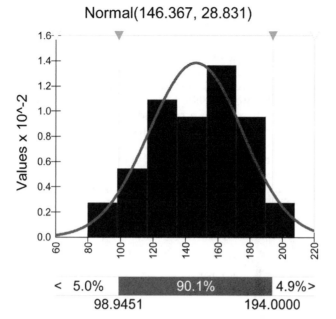

Figure 9.1 Fitting normal distribution to the unconstrained demand data in Example 2

combined) can be well represented by the continuous normal distribution for moderate to larger hotels (say size of hotel > 100 rooms) and by the discrete Poisson distribution with a near symmetric shape for smaller hotels (say size of hotel = 60 to 100 rooms). This result indicates that the normal distribution can fit to the hotel demand for hotels large or small, since a Poisson distribution with a symmetric shape can be very well approximated by the normal distribution. The goodness-of-fit of normal distribution to the unconstrained total daily demand by season and day of the week for hotels H3, H5, H10, H17 and H21 is shown in column 9 of Tables 9.3 to 9.7, where a blank cell indicates that the sample size is too small to fit a distribution. The goodness-of-fit is ranked by 'Excellent', 'Good', 'Fair', or 'Bad', obtained by visual inspection of the fitting of the normal distributions to the demand data similar to Figure 9.1. The fitting in Figure 9.1 is assigned a rank of 'Excellent'.

Let $Z = \sigma/\sqrt{\mu}$, where σ and μ are the standard deviation and the mean of the unconstrained demand distribution. The value of Z measures the demand variability relative to the square root of the average demand for a given season and day of the week in a hotel.

The values of Z for the unconstrained demand data grouped by the arrival day's season (as defined by the hotel) and day of the week for the 23 hotels under study are computed and those in H3, H5, H10, H17 and H21 are shown in column 8 of Tables 9.3 to 9.7. We have also computed the weighted average value $\bar{Z}$ over all seasons and all days of the week for each of the 23 hotels as $\bar{Z} = \bar{\sigma}/\sqrt{\bar{\mu}}$, where $\bar{\mu}$ and $\bar{\sigma}$ are weighted average mean and the weighted average standard deviation defined in the preceding section. The values of $\bar{Z}$ are shown in column 4 of Table 9.8.

Using regression analysis based on the values of $\bar{Z}$ in Table 9.8 and the corresponding size of the hotel measured by the total number of rooms in the hotel, we obtain the following equation

$$\bar{Z} \approx \frac{\text{Hotel size}}{51.1812 + 0.0823 \times \text{Hotel size}}$$

This is slightly different from the one obtained by Liu *et al.* (2002) due to some minor changes in the data set. The usual range for $\bar{Z}$ is between 1 and 10, with larger hotels having larger values of $\bar{Z}$. This conclusion is, in general, consistent with the results of airline demand analysis (Belobaba, 1985; Lee, 1988; Lee, 1990). Based on the size of a hotel, the regression formula provides a rough idea of the value of $\bar{Z}$ and the shape of the total demand distribution (i.e., Poisson versus normal). Recall that for the Poisson distribution, $\sigma = \sqrt{\mu}$, and hence by definition $Z = 1$. Thus, the demand for a 65-room hotel is more likely distributed Poisson and the demand for a 500-room hotel is more likely normally distributed. Figure 9.2 illustrates the year-round unconstrained daily arrival demand for small, moderate, and large sized hotels. The effects of seasonality and day of week on the demand variability are much smaller than that of hotel size as shown in Tables 9.3 to 9.7.

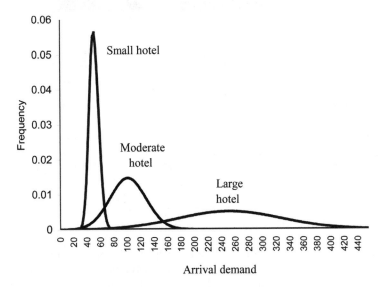

Figure 9.2 Demand distributions by hotel size

ANALYSIS OF HOTEL CANCELLATIONS/NO-SHOWS

Hotels experience cancellations and no-shows when customers cancel their bookings before arrival days (cancellations) or simply do not show up on arrival days (no-shows). Hotel cancellations and no-shows are sometimes also called wash. In this case study, the percentage of wash for a given arrival day is computed based on the actual total daily gross bookings and the actual total daily net bookings obtained from the reservation database. The average wash percentage over the same season (as defined by the hotel) and the day of week for each of the 23 hotels are computed and those in hotels H3, H5, H10, H17 and H21 are shown in column 10 of Tables 9.3 to 9.7. The average wash percentage for each hotel/season/day of week combination can be as low as 0 per cent or as high as over 60 per cent, with airport/roadside hotels having the lowest and business-oriented downtown hotels and resort hotels the highest for obvious reasons. For airport/roadside hotels, where reservations were made much closer to or even on the arrival day or customers simply show up at the front desk, there was a much smaller chance of a customer cancelling the reservation. For business-oriented downtown hotels, frequent changes of schedules by business travellers explains the high cancellation rate, while for resort hotels the long lead-time booking pace provided opportunities for the bargain hunters to switch hotels or packages. We do not see any significant patterns in cancellation rate among different days of the week over all seasons for those 23 hotels.

We find that the cancellation/no-shows distributions have a much lower 'relative variability' calculated as the ratio of the standard deviation over the square root of the mean of the distribution (shown as Z of wash in column 12 of Tables 9.3 to 9.7). The distribution of the cancellation/no-shows percentages tends to be skewed to the right slightly. We have discovered that theoretical distributions, such as the logistic distribution and the extreme-value distribution that can represent right skewness, in general fit the wash percentage data better than the normal distribution. Figure 9.3 shows the extreme-value distribution fitted to the wash data of H5 Monday in regular season (in 8 bins) with a Chi-Square test value 5.60. If a normal distribution were fitted with the same 8 bins, the Chi-Square test value would be 17.20.

We have also computed the weighted average wash percentage over all seasons and day of the week for each of the 23 hotels. The results for hotels H3, H5, H10, H17 and H21 are shown in column 5 of Table 9.8.

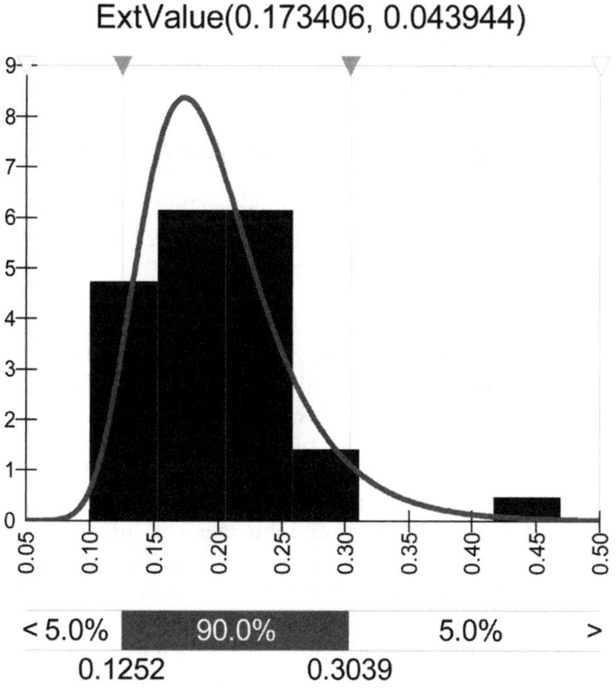

Figure 9.3 Fitting extreme-value distribution to the wash data of H5 Monday in regular season

CONCLUSIONS

In this study we have analysed reservation data for over 8000 arrival days at 23 US hotels, of which about 61 per cent are censored, to answer the three questions outlined in the Introduction.

1. Using the statistical deconstraining methods developed by Liu *et al.* (2002), we have estimated the unconstrained 'lead-time' interval demand over the entire planning horizon (on average 100 intervals for each arrival day) for all the arrival days that were censored (about 5000 days) and then, for each arrival day, added all its unconstrained 'lead-time' interval demand to arrive at the unconstrained total daily demand. These methods are more general and likely to produce more accurate and unbiased estimation than those in previous research in estimating unconstrained hotel/airline demand where only capacity constraints (or booking limits) were considered; other constraints such as prices were never discussed (e.g., Brummer, *et al*, 1988; Hopperstad, 1995; Lee, 1990; McGill, 1995; Pölt, 2000; Skwarek, 1996; Weatherford, 2000; Wickham, 1995; Zeni, 2001). Take peak seasons, for example, where reservation data (both historical and current) are very often heavily (sometimes 100 per cent) censored. While the 'detruncation' methods can do little about the unconstrained demand since there are little or no valid 'historical unconstrained' data, the deconstraining methods by Liu *et al.* (2002) can provide a much better (though not perfect) estimate because extra information such as the parametric form of the demand distribution (e.g., normal, Weibull, Poisson, etc.) as well as the room rates that restricted the demand are fully utilized. The practical significance of these methods for the hotel industry lies in their implementation as a forecasting subsystem in a computerized revenue management (RM) system. By producing more accurate and robust forecasts of future demand for use by underlying optimization routines, the overall reliability and success of RM systems can be significantly enhanced.

2. We have found that, in general, Poisson distribution is not a good fit to the unconstrained arrival day demand, except where the hotel is small (< 100 rooms) and that the normal distribution has a much better fit to the unconstrained demand data for hotels large or small. For the first time, we have obtained a non-linear regression formula that can be used to estimate the value of Z based on the size of hotel. Given the size of a hotel, the regression formula provides a rough idea of the value of $\bar{Z}$ and the shape of the total demand distribution (i.e., Poisson versus normal). Our study shows that the effects of seasonality and day of week on the demand variability are much smaller than that of hotel size.

3. Analysis of the cancellation/no-show data indicates that the cancellation/no-show rates can be as low as 0 per cent or as high as over 60 per cent, with airport/ roadside hotels having the lowest and business-oriented downtown hotels and resort hotels the highest, and the distribution of the cancellation/no-show percentage is skewed to the right. Distributions such as the logistic distribution and the extreme-value distribution that can handle right skewness fit the data better than the normal distribution in general. Accurate information on the cancellation/no-show rates and forms of distributions is crucial to revenue management programmes such as computing the optimal overbooking levels and room allocations.

DISCUSSION QUESTIONS

1. How do you estimate the unconstrained hotel daily demand based on censored booking data?
2. What conclusions can be drawn from this case study about the distributions of unconstrained hotel transient demand (by season, by day of the week, and by hotel type)?
3. What conclusions can be drawn from this case study about the distributions of cancellations/no-shows percentage (by season, by day of the week, and by hotel type)?

REFERENCES

Badinelli, R. D. (2000) 'An optimal, dynamic policy for hotel yield management', *European Journal of Operational Research*, **121**, March, 476–503.

Belobaba, P. P. (1985) 'TWA reservation analysis: demand distribution patterns'. MIT Flight Transportation Lab Report, Massachusetts Institute of Technology.

Bitran, G. R. and Gilbert, S. M. (1996) 'Managing hotel reservations with uncertain arrivals', *Operations Research*, **44**, 35–49.

Bitran, G. R. and Mondschein, S. V. (1995) 'An application of yield management to the hotel industry considering multiple day stays', *Operations Research*, **43**, 427–43.

Brummer, Mark *et al.* (1988) 'Determination of potential load capacity based on observed load factor data: a study for Northwest Airlines.' St Olaf College Undergraduate Practicum Group, Northfield, Minnesota.

Hopperstad, C. (1995) 'An alternative detruncation method'. Boeing Commercial Aircraft Company Internal Document.

Lee, A. O. (1988) 'Airline reservation forecasting'. Proceedings of the 28th Annual AGIFORS Symposium (hosted by American Airlines), New Seabury, MA, USA.

Lee, A. O. (1990) 'Airline reservations forecasting probabilistic and statistical models of the booking process'. PhD thesis, Flight Transportation Laboratory, Massachusetts Institute of Technology.

Liu, P. H., Smith, S., Orkin, E. B. and Carey, G. (2002) 'Estimating unconstrained hotel demand based on censored booking data', *Journal of Revenue and Pricing Management* **1**(2), 121–38.

McGill, J. I. (1995) 'Censored regression analysis of multiclass demand data subject to joint capacity constraints', *Annals of Operations Research*, **60**, 209–40.

Orkin, E. B. (1998) 'Wishful thinking and rocket science: the essential matter of calculating unconstrained demand for revenue management', *The Cornell Hotel and Restaurant Administration Quarterly*, **39**(4), 15–19.

Pölt, S. (2000) 'From Bookings to Demand – The Process of Unconstraining'. Proceedings of the 40th Annual AGIFORS Symposium (downloadable from http://www.agifors.org).

Rothstein, M. (1974) 'Hotel overbooking as a Markovian sequential decision process', *Decision Sciences*, **5**, 389–404.

Skwarek, D. K. (1996) '*Competitive impacts of yield management system components: forecasting and sell-Up models*'. MSc thesis, Flight Transportation Laboratory, Massachusetts Institute of Technology.

Swan, W. M. (1990) 'Revenue management forecasting biases'. Working Paper, Boeing Commercial Aircraft, Seattle.

Weatherford, L. (2000) 'Unconstraining Methods'. Proceedings of the 40th Annual AGIFORS Symposium (downloadable from http://www.agifors.org).

Wickham, R. R. (1995) 'Evaluation of forecasting techniques for short-term demand of air transportation'. MSc thesis, Flight Transportation Laboratory, Massachusetts Institute of Technology.

Zeni, R. (2001) 'Improving Forecast Accuracy by Unconstraining Censored Demand Data'. Proceedings of the 41st Annual AGIFORS Symposium (downloadable from http://www. agifors.org).

Table 9.3 Hotel H3

Season	Day of week	Sample size	Number censored in sample	Censored %	Average bookings	S.D. of bookings	Z of bookings	Fit-to-normal distribution	Average wash %	S.D. of wash %	Z of wash %
Peak	Mon	39	38	97.44	411.10	115.73	5.71	Excellent	39.24	6.43	10.26
	Tue	41	41	100.00	425.59	123.40	5.98	Good	40.20	8.69	13.71
	Wed	39	39	100.00	402.65	108.27	5.40	Good	40.91	7.53	11.78
	Thu	34	31	91.18	367.89	121.09	6.31	Good	41.44	9.52	14.78
	Fri	32	29	90.63	356.84	107.75	5.70	Good	41.84	7.11	10.99
	Sat	35	33	94.29	263.25	84.98	5.24	Fair	40.05	8.67	13.71
	Sun	34	31	91.18	282.88	65.92	3.92	Good	41.07	6.81	10.62
Shoulder	Mon	11	11	100.00	392.19	81.27	4.10	Fair	34.70	4.26	7.23
	Tue	11	11	100.00	381.87	51.28	2.62	Fair	34.33	2.73	4.66
	Wed	12	12	100.00	348.78	45.81	2.45	Fair	35.13	3.30	5.57
	Thu	11	10	90.91	322.72	57.41	3.20	Fair	34.45	3.32	5.66
	Fri	12	10	83.33	361.68	76.35	4.01	Fair	35.63	2.65	4.43
	Sat	10	9	90.00	335.52	159.80	8.72	Fair	39.23	15.46	24.69
	Sun	10	9	90.00	289.26	48.61	2.86	Fair	37.88	5.06	8.23
Slow	Mon	23	18	78.26	268.70	90.39	5.51	Fair	35.06	7.50	12.66
	Tue	20	19	95.00	340.06	165.40	8.97	Fair	41.39	15.87	24.67
	Wed	21	20	95.24	345.44	143.62	7.73	Fair	37.90	12.82	20.82
	Thu	27	20	74.07	237.45	64.00	4.15	Good	34.07	7.71	13.21
	Fri	28	11	39.29	203.13	59.28	4.16	Good	37.29	6.94	11.36
	Sat	27	20	74.07	178.05	115.52	8.66	Fair	38.89	12.02	19.27
	Sun	28	21	75.00	205.93	129.89	9.05	Fair	39.99	13.42	21.23

Table 9.4   Hotel H5

Season	Day of week	Sample size	Number censored in sample	Censored %	Average bookings	S.D. of bookings	Z of bookings	Fit-to-normal distribution	Average wash %	S.D. of wash %	Z of wash %
Regular	Mon	40	5	12.50	135.11	33.70	2.90	Good	19.92	6.15	13.77
	Tue	40	3	7.50	139.11	27.18	2.30	Fair	20.24	5.61	12.48
	Wed	41	6	14.63	173.68	43.63	3.31	Good	20.18	7.59	16.88
	Thu	40	8	20.00	183.72	41.94	3.09	Good	22.52	4.41	9.30
	Fri	39	9	23.08	179.94	38.48	2.87	Excellent	23.00	5.45	11.37
	Sat	40	15	37.50	146.37	28.83	2.38	Excellent	22.00	5.56	11.86
	Sun	40	7	17.50	156.99	30.61	2.44	Good	20.60	7.95	17.52
Summer	Mon	16	2	12.50	148.51	38.82	3.19	Fair	22.73	11.55	24.23
	Tue	16	4	25.00	161.55	48.65	3.83	Fair	22.97	13.38	27.91
	Wed	16	4	25.00	178.50	50.65	3.79	Bad	25.12	13.52	26.97
	Thu	17	3	17.65	173.88	53.43	4.05	Fair	25.79	14.23	28.01
	Fri	17	6	35.29	159.16	44.85	3.55	Fair	22.18	9.30	19.75
	Sat	16	5	31.25	164.13	51.81	4.04	Fair	18.79	9.82	22.67
	Sun	16	2	12.50	154.84	51.77	4.16	Excellent	23.23	11.55	23.96
Convention	Mon	3	0	0.00	142.67	3.51	0.29		10.21	5.17	16.18
	Tue	3	1	33.33	155.40	3.34	0.27		14.85	9.63	25.00
	Wed	2	0	0.00	197.50	13.44	0.96		19.52	6.55	14.82
	Thu	2	0	0.00	125.50	82.73	7.38		12.36	4.81	13.69
	Fri	2	0	0.00	116.00	108.89	10.11		9.04	5.53	18.40
	Sat	3	0	0.00	139.00	79.64	6.76		3.12	2.75	15.59
	Sun	3	0	0.00	120.67	44.64	4.06		9.21	9.38	30.91

Table 9.5 Hotel H10

Season	Day of week	Sample size	Number censored in sample	Censored %	Average bookings	S.D. of bookings	Z of bookings	Fit-to-normal distribution	Average wash %	S.D. of wash %	Z of wash %
Summer	Mon	8	7	87.50	386.37	78.86	4.01	Fair	38.02	6.17	10.01
	Tue	7	5	71.43	318.53	80.33	4.50	Good	35.88	4.68	7.82
	Wed	7	6	85.71	402.86	118.69	5.91	Bad	34.95	4.12	6.96
	Thu	7	6	85.71	421.42	108.98	5.31	Good	36.22	3.19	5.30
	Fri	9	9	100.00	510.64	84.48	3.74	Good	42.48	4.14	6.36
	Sat	9	9	100.00	449.17	135.38	6.39	Fair	44.12	4.84	7.28
	Sun	9	8	88.89	433.80	135.78	6.52	Fair	38.11	2.95	4.78
Open	Mon	6	3	50.00	35.67	11.34	1.90	Fair	26.22	9.02	17.62
	Tue	7	1	14.29	44.26	23.38	3.51	Fair	22.29	8.16	17.28
	Wed	7	1	14.29	53.14	30.26	4.15	Bad	25.78	11.47	22.59
	Thu	7	2	28.57	52.59	44.62	6.15	Bad	25.33	8.56	17.01
	Fri	6	0	0.00	61.17	28.81	3.68	Fair	29.15	8.82	16.33
	Sat	6	0	0.00	80.50	52.49	5.85	Bad	20.62	5.56	12.24
	Sun	6	3	50.00	42.23	26.29	4.05	Fair	23.67	15.49	31.84
Shoulder	Mon	6	3	50.00	61.50	26.21	3.34	Good	38.67	22.77	36.62
	Tue	6	4	66.67	48.04	14.07	2.03	Good	23.30	2.10	4.34
	Wed	6	2	33.33	61.44	33.75	4.31	Fair	25.08	9.59	19.15
	Thu	6	2	33.33	78.08	62.30	7.05	Fair	30.44	8.69	15.75
	Fri	6	2	33.33	71.08	30.68	3.64	Fair	25.66	8.45	16.68
	Sat	6	3	50.00	61.87	17.29	2.20	Fair	30.38	11.03	20.01
	Sun	6	3	50.00	49.31	13.02	1.85	Fair	33.48	15.18	26.23
Slow	Mon	10	7	70.00	131.39	96.84	8.45	Bad	36.35	7.14	11.84
	Tue	10	6	60.00	102.28	61.65	6.10	Fair	30.91	6.82	12.27
	Wed	10	6	60.00	110.05	60.45	5.76	Fair	37.12	6.50	10.68
	Thu	10	9	90.00	148.78	97.84	8.02	Fair	41.14	5.97	9.31
	Fri	9	0	0.00	245.11	192.57	12.30	Bad	46.81	8.83	12.91
	Sat	9	6	66.67	171.57	108.20	8.26	Fair	37.50	8.02	13.09
	Sun	9	3	33.33	161.55	139.77	11.00	Bad	34.14	8.36	14.31

Table 9.6 Hotel H17

Season	Day of week	Sample size	Number censored in sample	Censored %	Average bookings	S.D. of bookings	Z of bookings	Fit-to-normal distribution	Average wash %	S.D. of wash %	Z of wash %
Holiday	Mon	4	0	0.00	34.25	13.70	2.34		14.39	7.62	20.09
	Tue	4	1	25.00	57.77	27.17	3.57		15.73	5.36	13.51
	Wed	4	2	50.00	55.78	18.67	2.50		14.42	5.15	13.56
	Thu	4	1	25.00	50.01	20.51	2.90		17.13	4.10	9.91
	Fri	2	2	100.00	76.05	52.33	6.00		25.86	0.32	0.63
	Sat	2	1	50.00	50.53	6.40	0.90		21.10	0.91	1.98
	Sun	3	1	33.33	29.71	5.57	1.02		19.92	7.40	16.58
Low	Mon	23	0	0.00	51.13	17.24	2.41	Fair	13.69	7.07	19.11
	Tue	23	0	0.00	54.30	16.25	2.21	Fair	10.70	5.54	16.94
	Wed	22	0	0.00	52.09	12.91	1.79	Bad	10.86	7.00	21.24
	Thu	22	0	0.00	44.68	12.19	1.82	Fair	13.08	7.60	21.01
	Fri	23	0	0.00	55.26	19.23	2.59	Good	17.10	10.27	24.84
	Sat	23	0	0.00	50.22	16.99	2.40	Good	12.43	8.13	23.06
	Sun	23	0	0.00	32.65	9.18	1.61	Good	17.30	7.40	17.79
Regular	Mon	65	3	4.62	63.25	14.94	1.88	Good	17.83	9.41	22.29
	Tue	65	6	9.23	58.04	16.07	2.11	Good	16.56	10.69	26.26
	Wed	66	7	10.61	58.19	17.25	2.26	Good	18.40	12.53	29.21
	Thu	65	6	9.23	55.93	15.92	2.13	Good	22.40	15.95	33.70
	Fri	67	10	14.93	69.60	22.43	2.69	Good	26.72	10.32	19.96
	Sat	67	14	20.90	55.88	21.16	2.83	Good	21.66	10.13	21.77
	Sun	66	2	3.03	39.91	13.12	2.08	Good	19.17	12.78	29.19

Table 9.7 Hotel H21

Season	Day of week	Sample size	Number censored in sample	Censored %	Average bookings	S.D. of bookings	Z of bookings	Fit-to-normal distribution	Average wash %	S.D. of wash %	Z of wash %
Leisure	Mon	10	10	100.00	57.37	24.78	3.27	Fair	39.67	8.92	14.16
	Tue	10	9	90.00	51.80	25.10	3.49	Good	43.36	12.78	19.41
	Wed	11	11	100.00	61.38	21.00	2.68	Fair	36.58	12.05	19.92
	Thu	12	12	100.00	71.38	18.15	2.15	Fair	36.03	11.88	19.79
	Fri	12	11	91.67	121.94	28.46	2.58	Fair	41.08	8.25	12.87
	Sat	11	10	90.91	107.44	33.37	3.22	Fair	37.82	9.36	15.22
	Sun	10	6	60.00	68.68	12.23	1.48	Fair	33.73	7.40	12.74
Peak	Mon	10	10	100.00	82.04	49.61	5.48	Fair	39.86	13.68	21.67
	Tue	10	10	100.00	64.14	39.17	4.89	Fair	30.02	11.52	21.03
	Wed	10	9	90.00	78.86	35.34	3.98	Fair	39.00	10.03	16.06
	Thu	8	7	87.50	92.71	59.15	6.14	Fair	38.55	8.13	13.09
	Fri	8	8	100.00	157.59	59.92	4.77	Fair	40.48	7.27	11.43
	Sat	9	9	100.00	111.03	27.39	2.60	Fair	38.58	5.09	8.19
	Sun	10	8	80.00	78.58	36.19	4.08	Bad	43.24	9.73	14.80
Summer	Mon	11	11	100.00	98.01	40.92	4.13	Fair	43.18	11.23	17.09
	Tue	11	11	100.00	57.13	19.52	2.58	Fair	50.11	12.63	17.84
	Wed	11	10	90.91	69.32	27.05	3.25	Fair	45.52	17.00	25.20
	Thu	11	9	81.82	81.76	25.20	2.79	Fair	39.35	5.76	9.18
	Fri	11	11	100.00	136.35	36.72	3.14	Fair	40.70	7.44	11.66
	Sat	11	10	90.91	142.20	88.19	7.40	Fair	40.47	7.08	11.13
	Sun	11	11	100.00	99.74	38.32	3.84	Fair	44.27	6.29	9.45

Table 9.8 Summary statistics of the 23 hotels

Hotel ID	Weighted average bookings	Weighted average S.D. of bookings	$\bar{Z}$ of bookings	Weighted average wash %	Weighted average S.D. of wash %	$\bar{Z}$ of wash %
H1	209.65	70.90	4.90	37.68	9.62	15.67
H2	316.18	119.59	6.73	44.47	9.85	14.76
H3	320.18	105.27	5.88	39.05	8.99	14.38
H4	228.52	74.51	4.93	38.38	7.94	12.81
H5	159.52	40.81	3.23	21.39	8.27	17.88
H6	1016.95	338.40	10.61	38.29	6.91	11.16
H7	31.75	18.33	3.25	26.27	16.96	33.09
H8	99.94	33.71	3.37	31.06	9.49	17.03
H9	118.48	39.48	3.63	35.98	7.83	13.05
H10	184.37	88.51	6.52	37.51	8.71	14.22
H11	63.92	17.15	2.15	24.36	9.07	18.38
H12	63.72	14.83	1.86	29.64	7.85	14.41
H13	65.68	17.60	2.17	24.76	10.57	21.24
H14	41.80	10.28	1.59	32.18	10.02	17.66
H15	57.79	21.65	2.85	21.25	9.46	20.53
H16	212.28	58.95	4.05	45.87	7.73	11.42
H17	54.85	17.27	2.33	18.94	10.80	24.81
H18	187.61	112.63	8.22	49.80	14.59	20.67
H19	39.26	10.67	1.70	38.19	11.38	18.41
H20	54.91	17.10	2.31	44.80	10.90	16.28
H21	89.55	38.78	4.10	40.19	10.20	16.08
H22	121.98	40.27	3.65	42.90	9.42	14.37
H23	112.57	36.77	3.47	42.06	8.59	13.24

10

Bolton Wanderers: A Case of Good Practice in the Football Industry?

Gerald Barlow

INTRODUCTION

In 1997 Bolton Wanderers' new life seemed to begin. It was perhaps not a perfect start, but as with many things today after a delayed start things really came to life. Their new £35 million Reebok Stadium was opened, the team had bounced back into the Premier League and all was going to plan. Within an hour of the opening game at the new stadium the team had lost its second player, but this time they were to lose a player with a double fracture to his leg for the rest of what was to be a long season. This was to be reflected throughout the season with the team returning back to Division One. However, with the new stadium came new life and with it the need for new financial and operational management.

The objectives for this chapter are to help understand how capacity plays a major part in the finances of a football club and how clubs currently manage the variety of issues around capacity and revenue generation.

Crisis in the Football Industry

In March of 2002 the UK football league was thrown into disarray when the television company ITV Digital, operating the football league television programmes and providing financial sponsorship of the league, 'pulled out' of the sponsorship agreement and eventually went into receivership. This led to much speculation about the future of many of the Nationwide Football League clubs. Barry Hearn, chairman of Third Division club Leyton Orient, went on record as saying, 'In my view, a club will go to the wall within a year. In the past, the banks have allowed people to roll up money, roll up interest. But there will be a domino effect this time, when the first one goes, there's no future' (*Guardian*, 22 February 2002). Hearn went on to suggest that 75 per cent of the clubs in Division Three, half of those in the Second Division and 25 per cent of the First Division could easily be lost to the game! The clubs' finances have been developed upon the assurance of television income, and many of the players' wages had been inflated as a result. If many of these clubs are to survive then they will need to start looking much closer at how they operate and their financial management techniques will need to change. Yield or revenue management is one of the techniques that clubs could consider. It is likely that the approach needed in this area will be an adaptation to suit the industry and will be more akin to a form of revenue management, than a complex computer based yield management system.

Is the Football Industry Suited to Yield or Revenue Management?

Kimes (1989a) identified seven key techniques necessary for the success of a yield management system:

- Ability to segment the market
- Perishable inventory
- Product sold in advance
- Fluctuation in demand
- High fixed costs
- Low marginal costs
- High marginal production

Kimes (1989b) also identified five key core requirements for the operation of a yield management system.

- Booking patterns: yield management systems require information on how ticket sales/reservations are made for specific events
- Knowledge of the demand patterns by market segments
- An overbooking policy
- Knowledge of the effect of price changes
- A good information system

HOW DOES THE FOOTBALL INDUSTRY MEET THESE REQUIREMENTS?

- All clubs segment their markets: into season tickets (sold a season in advance), with differing markets dependent on area and price; and tickets for individual games by game tickets.
- Football seats are all perishable; there are very few games per season, for example Bolton Wanderers FC have a guarantee of 19 home league games, and up to a maximum of 29 games a year, and once the game is over that particular game is not repeated for at least a year.
- Tickets are sold in two types, season tickets, sold for the entire season and prior to the commencement of the season, and individual match tickets sold prior to the game or right up to the start of the game.

- The demand for tickets is affected by the success of the team, the opposition, date and timing of the game, the weather, etc.
- The fixed costs are high, based on the costs of the ground, the infrastructure, practice grounds, support services, the players, wages/transfer costs, etc.
- The marginal cost, which is the cost of selling an extra seat in the case of a football match, is very low. For example, what additional costs are incurred in selling either one extra seat for a specific game, or one extra season ticket?
- Marginal production, which relates to the cost of increasing capacity to cope with an excess in demand, in the case of a football club could well be impossible in the short or even medium term, and very expensive in the long term; it could include building a new stand, or as in the case of Bolton Wanderers a new stadium. The option chosen by some small clubs in the past, when extra demand exists for a one off event like the later stages of the FA cup competition, and a small club draws a home game against one of the top clubs and demand for tickets will exceed their ground's capacity, has been to forgo the advantage of a home tie in favour of playing at the larger club's ground and thereby receiving much greater revenue. It is likely that the small club has accepted that they would be unlikely to win the tie either home or away, and the increased income is a much more attractive alternative.

As can be seen, a football club/business meets most of the requirements that apply regarding an organization considering employing yield or revenue management techniques.

BACKGROUND

Bolton Wanderers, one of the original twelve founder members of the Football League, were originally known as Christ Church when they were formed in 1874. Their first really permanent home was to be Burnden Park, which they arrived at after spells at The Park Recreation Ground, Cockles Fields and Pike Lane. Burnden Park became home to Bolton Wanderers in 1895 and was their home for 102 years. Over the years 'The Wanderers' have seen their fair share of fame, fortune and disaster, cup finalists in 1894 and 1904, and the first winners of the FA Cup at Wembley in the famous 1923 'White Horse Final' where an estimated 200,000 fans packed the Empire Stadium with 50,000 left outside. Further success following in 1926 and 1929, cup defeat in another famous final of 1953, 'The Stanley Mathew's Cup Final', and finally the defeat of Manchester United in 1958, where Bolton legend Nat Lofthouse scored both goals in the 2–0 victory.

Since the formation of the Football League, Bolton were to see unbroken spells in the First Division between 1911–33 and 1935–64, the club's best position being third in the years 1892, 1921 and 1925. The lows were being in the Third Division between 1971 and 1973, with the team bouncing up and down from the First to Third Divisions until they dropped into the Fourth Division in 1987, however this was only for the one season. A series of successful promotion winning seasons led to the club gaining Premier League status for the first time at the end of the 1994–5 season; it also saw the team reach Wembley in the final of the Coca-Cola Cup but losing to Liverpool, since when Bolton Wanderers have had a roller-coaster ride between the Premier and First Divisions.

Much has been written during 2002 about the troubles regarding the financial side of the football industry, the problems facing clubs after the collapse of ITV Digital and its sponsorship of the football league. Perhaps a reflection of the problems many clubs face can be seen from a brief look at one club during the 2000–2001 season, Leyton Orient, who started the season as they finished it in Division Three of the football league, but on the whole had a good season. This included playing Tottenham Hotspur in the cup, which provided a full ground; playing Newcastle United (both Tottenham and Newcastle teams being Premier League teams) home and away in the Worthington Cup; and reaching the play-off finals. All of this resulted in a profit of £84,000. In reality, the club estimates that without a cup 'run', they will have a financial deficit of around £600,000 a year. How long can football league clubs find fans/supporters, like Leyton's chairman, Barry Hearn (*Financial Times*, 15 March 2002), who are prepared to cover the club's losses for the occasional good season and the glory? Hearn (*Guardian*, 22 February 2002) estimates that in its current form the football league could see up to 30 of its clubs go; this might be considered excessive but during the 2001–2002 season three clubs got into serious financial difficulties and may not open their gates for the start of the new 2002–2003 season. York City, Bury and Halifax all have deep financial problems (Fifield 2002). York's chairman Douglas Craig and his board are unable to sustain the continual losses and 'will walk away, and lock the gates if they are unable to find a new buyer for the club'. Bury FC, a club with a 117-year history, was taken to court by creditors on 4 March, which resulted in the club being placed in administration and put on the market as a going concern (advertisement in the *Financial Times*, Tuesday, 15 March 2002). Other clubs also currently facing financial problems include Exeter who were reported to be months behind in paying their wages to both on and off the field employees. It is only the apparent generosity, deep pockets and maybe foolhardiness, or even in some cases ego, of the clubs' chairman that keeps many clubs afloat. Barry Hearn estimates that he has ploughed at least £2 million of his own money, money that he accepts he won't see again, into Leyton Orient. Therefore the need for yield management, or something similar, to be used in the operational and financial aspects of a football club cannot be over stressed.

Football Club Income

One of the major sources of income for Premier League clubs comes from television and other sponsorship of the Premiership League, all of which have been negotiated by the League's management and is outside the individual club's management.

Bolton Wanderers – sources of income from club activity, excluding income from transfers of players

Ticket sales
   Season tickets
   Match-day tickets
Sponsorship
   Team sponsorship
   Match-day sponsorship
   Associate match-day sponsorship
   Match ball sponsorship

Advertising
  Ground advertising boards
  Videoscreen advertising
  Match-day programme advertising
  Quarterly magazine 'Extra Time' advertising
Hospitality
  Private executive boxes
  Seasonal membership clubs
  Business club
  Match by match hospitality

Ticket sales

Season tickets
Season 2002: pricing structure (purchased on or before 15 June 2002)

	£
West and East Upper stands	
Adults	377
Senior Citizens	260
Juveniles	134
West and East Stand Lower	
Adults	341
Senior Citizens	238
Juveniles	98
Bolton Evening News Stand Upper	
Adults	341
Senior Citizens	238
Juveniles	98
Bolton Evening News Stand Lower	
Adults	278
Senior Citizens	220
Juveniles	98
Family Stands – West Lower and Bolton Evening News North Upper	
One adult and one child	359
Two adults and two children	629

Lifeline members (purchased on or before 15 June 2002)

	£
West and East Upper stands	
Adults	358
Senior Citizens	247
Juveniles	127
West and East Stand Lower	
Adults	323
Senior Citizens	226
Juveniles	93
Bolton Evening News Stand Upper	
Adults	323
Senior Citizens	209
Juveniles	93
Bolton Evening News Stand Lower	

Adults	264
Senior Citizens	209
Juveniles	93

Family Stands – West Lower and Bolton Evening News North Upper
One adult and one child	341
Two adults and two children	597

Season tickets season 2002: pricing structure (purchased after 15 June 2002)

West and East Upper stands   £
Adults	419
Senior Citizens	289
Juveniles	149

West and East Stand Lower
Adults	379
Senior Citizens	265
Juveniles	109

Bolton Evening News Stand Upper
Adults	379
Senior Citizens	265
Juveniles	109

Bolton Evening News Stand Lower
Adults	309
Senior Citizens	245
Juveniles	109

Family Stands – West Lower and Bolton Evening News North Upper
One adult and one child	399
Two adults and two children	699

Lifeline members (purchased on or before 15 June 2002)

West and East Upper stands   £
Adults	398
Senior Citizens	274
Juveniles	141

West and East Stand Lower
Adults	360
Senior Citizens	251
Juveniles	103

Bolton Evening News Stand Upper
Adults	360
Senior Citizens	251
Juveniles	103

Bolton Evening News Stand Lower
Adults	293
Senior Citizens	232
Juveniles	103

Family Stands – West Lower and Bolton Evening News North Upper
One adult and one child	379
Two adults and two children	664

Matchday tickets
Prices set for season 2001–2002

	£
East and West Upper tier Stands	
Adults	27
Senior Citizens and Students	18
Juniors	14
East and West Upper tier Stands	
Adults	24
Senior Citizens and Students	16
Juniors	10
North Stands (Upper tier)	
Adults	24
Senior Citizens and Students	16
Juniors	10
North Stands Lower	
Adults	20
Senior Citizens and Students	15
Juniors	10
North Stands (Family tickets)	
One adult and one junior	18
Two adults and two juniors	36
Away fans	
South Stands Upper	
Adults	24
Senior Citizens	16
Juniors	10
South Stands Lower	
Adults	20
Senior Citizens	15
Juniors	10

These single match ticket prices are set for all games for that season.

PRICING POLICY

Bolton Wanderers have established a pricing structure based upon achieving a high percentage of prepaid season tickets and prepaid all season advertising. This policy can be seen as successful in that by mid June 2002 of the discount period, the club has sold 15,000 season tickets, almost 54 per cent of the capacity. This provides for a smaller proportion of the ground being offered to the opposition, and the remainder being available to home fans on a match by match basis.

Similarly, the advertising is initially sold on a season by season basis: for example, the shirt or team sponsorship is sold for a minimum of one season, so ensuring that the club will not have any games without sponsorship. Other areas of the ground where permanent or long-term advertising is available, for example pitch side advertising, roof advertising, is on a season by season basis. Larger areas of advertising, for example

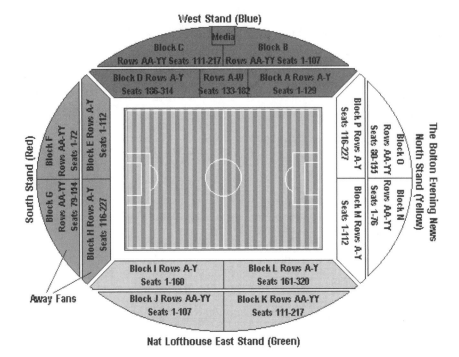

Figure 10.1   Reebok Stadium seating arrangements

seats, or even specific stands, such as the Bolton Evening News Stand or the North Stand are sold for a minimum of one season and preferably longer. The remaining areas, for example programme advertising, are sold like the seating – a mixture of seasons booking, monthly or game by game.

Bolton's aim is to maximize the known revenue, by having as much as possible paid in advance, whilst reducing the risk of losing perishable capacity, seating or advertising. The final area is the hospitality seating, where seats and boxes are sold either for the season as are season tickets, or for specific games, although some games and dates are sold well in advance.

Other Areas of Revenue

These are areas where revenue maximization and sales prices cannot be adjusted in accordance with demand. These include programme pricing, merchandise sales such as team shirts, match-day catering, and promotional events and items like lotteries. None of these items are suitable for price management techniques used in yield management.

Sales Techniques Employed

Season tickets: These are offered in advance, with preference given to the previous seasons ticket holder who can renew their ticket before any new supporter can buy a ticket but there is a cut-off date for doing this (30 June for the 2002–2003 season).

The remainder are then sold until the allocation is taken up. Season tickets are available for sale over the telephone, in person at the ticket office, by post, but not on-line! The club will not permit 100 per cent of their seats to be sold in advance as season tickets, but it is possible for all seats for specific games to be sold in advance. This is achieved initially by the season ticket sales, then the balance of seating is split into two sections: (1) tickets available to home fans, and (2) tickets allocated to away fans. In the case of big games, major teams like Manchester United, or quarter finals of the FA Cup competition, away fans' tickets are allocated to the away club to sell in advance. In the case of a club like Manchester United, this amount will not be adequate to meet the demand of their fans, and so all of these tickets will be sold. The remaining home fans' match-day tickets will all be sold by the club in advance sales, so ensuring 100 per cent capacity prior to the game.

Match-day tickets: Are sold, in person, in advance, the specific time in advance varying depending on the particular game, but generally in person from the ticket office up to ten days in advance, and on the day at the ground entrance. There are no web sales!

Hospitality and Advertising

All corporate hospitality programmes have a pricing structure based upon the opposition of the specific day.

A +	A	B	C
Manchester City	Liverpool	Aston Villa	Fulham
Manchester United	Arsenal	Sunderland	Charlton Athletic
	Leeds United	Tottenham Hotspur	Southampton
	Newcastle United	Middlesbrough	Birmingham City
	Everton	West Ham United	West Brom' Albion
	Blackburn Rovers		
	Chelsea		

The corporate hospitality is provided with eight different options.

Match-day sponsorship: Covers twenty guests with full hospitality services, from car park passes, tours of the stadium, exclusive use of the Hopkinson Suite, complementary bar throughout, cushioned seating on half-way line, meals, refreshments during the game, souvenir and choice of official Man-of-the-Match, post-match presentation and commemorative photographs. The following facilities are provided for the sponsorship company:

- two pitch-side advertising boards;
- full-page advertising in match-day programme plus acknowledgement and welcome on manager's page, advertorial and company logo on the programme cover;
- photographs and acknowledgement in subsequent match-day programme;
- acknowledgement on in-house TV system;
- company logo on stadium videoscreen.

Game category	£
A+	6500
A	6000
B	4500
C	3500

Associate match-day sponsorship: This package is provided for ten guests, and includes a dedicated host, reserved parking (one pass per four guests), stadium tour, use of West Stand executive box, drinks reception, full pay bar throughout, exterior balcony with cushion seating, half-time refreshments, post-match presentation and commemorative photographs, souvenir gift. The following is provided for the company:

- half-page advertising in match-day programme and advertorial featuring company logo, photographs and acknowledgement in subsequent match-day programme;
- acknowledgement on in-house TV system;
- company logo on stadium videoscreen.

Game category	£
A+	3000
A	2800
B	2300
C	1800

Match ball sponsorship (six guests): This is a unique opportunity for one person to present the match ball to the officials on the pitch prior to kick-off. All guests receive:

- dedicated host, reserved car parking (one pass per four guests), stadium tour, three-course pre-match meal, full pay bar throughout the day, cushioned match seating on the half-way line, match-day programme, half-time refreshments, full-time coffee, post-match presentation, commemorative photographs, souvenir gifts.

The company will receive:

- half-page advertising in match-day programme and advertorial featuring company logo;
- photographs and acknowledgement in subsequent match-day programme;
- acknowledgement on in-house TV system;
- company logo on stadium videoscreen.

Game Category	£
A+	1500
A	1300
B	1000
C	800

Match-day hospitality: Private executive box (eight or ten guests) offer, which can be hired on a match-by-match basis, including:

- reserved car parking (one pass per four guests);
- Buck's Fizz reception, three-course pre-match meal with wine, full pay bar facility,

exterior cushioned balcony seating, half-time refreshments, match-day programme, colour television showing action replays, free stadium tour.

Game category	£ per (8)	£ per (6)
A+	1900	1500
A	1800	1400
B	1600	1200
C	1300	1000

The Party Suite (twenty guests): Similar to the Executive boxes but for twenty guests.

Game category	£ per (8)
A+	2800
A	2600
B	2300
C	2000

Hospitality Suites: This is an interesting package providing many of the features of other packages but also a compère and guest speaker. There are two packages within the range:

VIP match-day package: Reserved car parking (one pass per four guests), Buck's Fizz reception, three-course pre-match meal with wine, full pay bar facility, cushioned balcony seating, half-time refreshments, match-day programme, full-time coffee, souvenir gift.

Executive match-day package: Reserved car parking (one pass per four guests), three-course pre-match meal with wine, full pay bar facility, cushioned match seating on the half-way line, half-time refreshments, match-day programme, full-time coffee.

Game category	VIP package (10) £	Executive package (per person) £
A+	1700	120
A	1600	110
B	1400	100
C	1100	90

Premier Suite: Special feature, only available for the following fixtures: Blackburn Rovers (A), Everton (A), Liverpool (A), Manchester City (A+) and Manchester United (A+). The package includes, three-course pre-match meal, match ticket and match-day programme.

Game category	£
A+	95
A	95
B	n.a.
C	n.a.

Corporate Season Executive Boxes: These boxes are situated in the East and West Stands, enjoy superb views and include the following benefits:

Ten person box: Exclusive use of the box for every first team home league and cup game, 10 feet of advertising signage over the box, videoscreen advertising, drinks service from full pay bar, exterior cushioned seating for ten guests, use of corporate bar area, company name on the door plate, match-day programmes, two reserved car parking spaces, teamsheets delivered to the box, colour TV with action replay and post-match analysis, free stadium tour on match days (must be pre-booked), quarterly newsletter, and membership to Club De Vere with offers for De Vere Hotels nationwide. Price from £14,500; catering package 10 people £3985 per person.

Eight person box: Exclusive use of the box for every first team home league, drinks service from full pay bar, exterior cushioned seating for eight guests, match-day programmes, two reserved car parking spaces, teamsheets delivered to the box, colour TV with action replay and post-match analysis, free stadium tour on match days (must be pre-booked), videoscreen advertising, use of hotel bar area, quarterly newsletter, and membership to Club De Vere with offers for De Vere Hotels nationwide. Price from £11,000; catering package 8 people £3180 per person.

Advertising

Match-day programme: A newly designed 68-page programme on sale throughout the stadium on match days, delivered to all boxes, which provides news and views direct from the club. In addition to the traditional page or half page adverts, it is possible to sponsor a regular page or feature and special issues.

Match-day Programme Advertising

	Full season (minimum 19 issues)	Single issue insertion A+	A	B	C
Outside back cover	£8500	n.a.	n.a.	n.a.	n.a.
Inside back cover	£7000	n.a.	n.a.	n.a.	n.a.
Full page	£5000	£1500	£1250	£1000	£750
Half page	£3000	£1000	£750	£500	£400
Page/feature page sponsorship	£1500	n.a.	n.a.	n.a.	n.a.

'Extra time' magazine: A new quarterly 48-page magazine, with a current subscription of over 20,000 sold through club Superstore and circulated to all season ticket holders. Full colour and design prices:

Game category	VIP package (10)	Executive package (per person)
Full page	£4000	£1250
Half page	£2500	£750

Videoscreen sponsorship and advertising: As a focal point on match days the LED videoscreen has a 16:9 wide screen with a format of 20mm pixel pitch and 5600 Nits of brightness. The screen can accommodate a succession of still frames or full video commercials and the club offers a design service to help set the adverts.

	Season	A +	A	B	C
3 × 10 second impact (still frame)	P.O.A.	£650	£500	£350	£200
3 × 10 second video commercial	P.O.A.	£900	£550	£550	£400
3 × 10 second full commercial	P.O.A.	£1000	£750	£750	£600

Other options on the videoscreen are:

Videoscreen clock sponsorship: The clock is visible for the full 90 minutes and is available as another area for advertising.

Action replays sponsorship: A minimum of eight action replays take place per game, each last approximately 10 seconds, guaranteeing full crowd attention. Again, advertising is available.

Corner/bookings/substitutions 'Magic Sponge' sponsorship: Quick instant impact advertising at the important high profile points of a game

	Season price
Videoscreen clock	P.O.A.
Action replays	£5000
Corners	£3500
Bookings	£3500
'Magic Sponge'	£3500

Pricing Strategy Concessions

In the pricing strategy at Bolton Wanderers, the only concession to revenue management for the ordinary fan's tickets is found in the season tickets where there is a discount for previous season ticket holders who buy their tickets before a set date. There is no price difference for the individual game tickets, irrespective of the opposition, day of the week, or period in advance when the ticket is purchased; unlike the corporate sales, where both ticket sales, seasonal or game by game, and sponsorship and advertising have a price variation dependent upon the opposition. Here the club has broken the games into four categories, representing the most popular opposition with the price increasing to reflect expected demand. The only other area of price differentiation, which the club could consider, is the time of week, where evening midweek games may prove less popular than those played during the day at weekends. However, the question must be asked, why is this policy only applied to corporate sales, be they for seats, boxes or advertising, and not for the individual ticket sales. Game by game ticket sales account for over 30 per cent and season tickets for over 50 per cent of all sales.

Market Segmentation

Hospitality and Advertising

In the case of advertising, the market is not in anyway segmented. In the case of hospitality, the market is segmented into clear segments:

A: Those simply watching the match
B: Those using the range of hospitality services, bar, catering, etc.

The two segments are then sub divided into two sectors:

I.   Season ticket customers
II. Game by game customers

Again, the pricing range is based upon these two sectors, i.e., financial benefits offered for season ticket customers.

Supporters

The supporters were in two main segments:

A: Season ticket holders
B: Match ticket supporters

These are separated into the following segments:

I.   Adults
II.   Students holding NUS student cards
III. Senior citizens
IV.   Juveniles, persons under 16, on a specified date
V.   Family

The fans in some ways segment themselves into specific fan types by the ground location they chose.

ISSUES FOR CONSIDERATION

Bolton Wanderers have over the last years of the twentieth century and the first years of this century been a relatively successful football club, somewhat yo-yoing between the Premier League and First Division, but at the same time building a very highly rated new stadium successfully supported by sponsorship as the name implies (The Reebok Stadium), and which includes a commercial hotel, the De Vere White Hotel. This shows some good practices in revenue management when related to their corporate sales, both in the seasonal and game by game approach, but a failure to develop this into their main match-day revenues, either season or match-by-match ticket sales. There is little development here of any form of sophisticated revenue management, despite it being adopted commercially or corporately in the sales. There can be much speculation as to why this may be the case. A quick look around the Premier League and First Division will draw a large number of clubs that manage their fan based sales in the same way. There are some who have started to adopt a revenue management approach (maybe on a small scale) by segmenting the games, in the same way as Bolton Wanderers have with their corporate and advertising sales (view the web sites of Birmingham City and Norwich City for examples).

Perhaps one of the factors that helps this management style to exist and survive is that in today's football business the income generated through the sale of match tickets to the fans is only a small proportion of the income the club/business generates per year when one looks at the income received from television sponsorship, which is provided to the clubs through the leagues' governing body. However, with the demise of the ITV Digital income in the Football League divisions, for how long can the football clubs continue to ignore the value of a technique like yield or revenue management?

DISCUSSION QUESTIONS

1. With the demise of ITV Digital and the associated revenue to the FA football league clubs, the income derived directly from the clubs' activities has become increasingly important. How might these football clubs use revenue/yield management to help manage these problems?
2. The income generated by Premiership clubs like Bolton Wanders from gate income is such a small percentage of their total income that developing a revenue management programme will have no or little value. Discuss.
3. If Bolton Wanders were to decide to operate a yield/revenue management programme, in which areas of revenue do you consider they should employ revenue management techniques, and why?

REFERENCES

Fifield, D. (2002) 'League prepares for last stand', *Guardian*, 22 March.
Financial Times (2002) Classified business for sale section, 15 March.
Guardian (2002) 'We could soon lose 30 clubs claims Hearn', 22 February.
Kimes, S. E. (1989a) 'The basics of yield management', *Cornell Hotel Restaurant HRA Quarterly*, **29**, November, 14–16.
Kimes, S. E. (1989b) 'Yield management: a tool for capacity-constrained service firms', *Journal of Operations Management* **11**(4), 348–63.
Mitchell, K. (2002) 'When the going gets tough', *The Observer*, 3 March.

Other sources of information
Harding, J. and Smith, A. (2002) 'Companies & Finance UK' 'Tough times put Carlton 179m in the red', *Financial Times*, 29 May.
Mott, S. (2002) *Daily Telegraph*, 4 March.
Speck, I. (2002) *We could soon lose 30 clubs claims Hearn http://www.soccernet.com*, 22 June.
http://www.bwfc.co.uk
http://www.leytonorient.com

11

Unconstraining Demand Data at US Airways

Richard H. Zeni and Kenneth D. Lawrence

INTRODUCTION

US Airways is an international airline operating a bid price, origin and destination revenue management system that the company implemented in late 1998. During the two years following implementation, forecast accuracy studies indicated that the system consistently underestimated demand. Further investigation revealed the cause of this negative bias: censoring of the historical data hampered the forecasting models.

Optimization systems can only produce good results if the underlying data is good. For US Airways, the output of the revenue management optimizer is a bid price that determines seat availability at a particular fare. In other words, if the fare a passenger is willing to pay is above the bid price, the seat is available; otherwise, the system denies the request. Inaccurate demand forecasts lead to inaccurate bid prices and the wrong accept/reject decision at the time of sale.

Similar to optimization systems, forecasting systems can accurately predict future demand only if the underlying data accurately represents historical demand. An accurate historical demand figure, however, is difficult to obtain. Actual bookings often understate true demand because of the booking limits the revenue management system imposes. Consequently, even if the forecast models function correctly, the resulting forecast underestimates demand because of the censored (or constrained) data. Lawrence Weatherford estimates that companies can lose up to 3 per cent of potential revenue if revenue management system forecasts have a negative bias (Weatherford, 1997: 120–42). There is clearly a need to unconstrain the historical data before inputting it to the forecasting models.

CASE STUDY AIMS AND OBJECTIVES

The airline concluded that incorporating a method for unconstraining the data would enhance demand forecast accuracy and significantly improve revenue. One of the chief objectives of this study was to quantify the results for various unconstraining methods. The project team tested several heuristic and statistical models using the airline's historical data, analyzed the results from each test, and recommended implementation of the method with the best cost-to-benefit ratio. The goal was not necessarily to achieve the most accurate demand forecasts possible, but to determine which unconstraining method provided the best revenue improvement relative to its increased costs.

DEFINING THE CENSORED DATA PROBLEM

The US Airways revenue management system determines the number of seats available at a particular fare on a specific flight – the booking limit – based on its calculation of the bid price. The airline accepts reservations in a fare class until demand equals the booking limit. At that point, the system stops selling seats in that fare class and also stops collecting valuable data. Although demand for travel in that fare class may exceed the booking limit, the data does not reflect this demand. Consequently, the data is censored, or constrained, at the booking limit, as illustrated in Figure 11.1. Censored data is endemic to revenue management systems because the systems' booking limits cause the constraining.

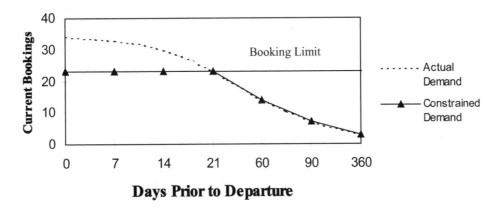

Figure 11.1   Censoring caused by the booking limit

As illustrated in Figure 11.2, the demand profile defines demand for a particular fare class at various time points. The system estimates demand at each of these points by taking snapshots of the current booking information. The instance of each snapshot is called a *review point*. If the data is not constrained, demand is simply a measure of how many bookings exist in the given fare class at each review point. On the other hand,

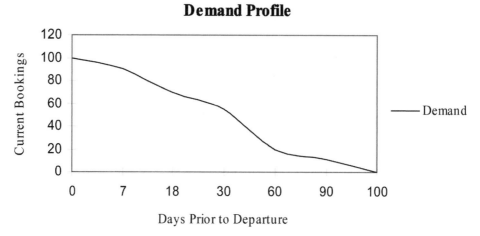

Figure 11.2   Demand profile

constrained observations reflect the booking limits rather than the true demand at each review point.

MODELLING THE CENSORED DATA PROBLEM

Developing a reliable set of test data was one of the project team's principal testing obstacles. The ideal data set consists of true demand observations for the entire booking history of a flight, including the underlying data observations censored at the booking limits. With such a data set, the project team could apply the various unconstraining techniques to the censored data and compare the results to the true demand. Because this ideal data set does not exist, the project team had to work with the available data to develop a viable test set.

One alternative is to gather data from flights in which the observations are censored and apply different methods for unconstraining the data to this data set. The obvious drawback to this method is the difficulty of determining how well the unconstrained values approximate true demand because no comparison data set exists.

Another approach is to first gather data from flights in which no data censoring occurred so that the data represents the true demand, and then to artificially constrain the data so it simulates the censored observations. Unfortunately, determining the best method for artificially constraining the data can be as daunting a problem as developing the unconstraining method itself. The constraining technique must simulate typical airline and passenger behaviour. Otherwise, the outcome of the unconstraining methods will be misleading and unreliable.

The project team decided to adopt a modified simulation approach (Zeni, 2001: 107–15). They first collected uncensored demand from US Airways flights in which demand did not reach the booking limits throughout the flights' entire booking periods. Their next step was to simulate censoring by artificially reducing the capacities of the aircraft.

Working with a large data set of US Airways flights that departed during 1997 and 1998, the team selected flights with no data censoring throughout their entire booking histories, thereby creating a data set that represented the true demand profiles for the flights in the sample. For the censoring simulation, they artificially reduced the capacity of the flights and then calculated the booking limits for the different review points. The capacity reduction constrained the original demand data at various points and produced a censored data set.

The project team now had a workable data set containing the actual true demand and censored data. After applying various unconstraining methods to the data set's censored observations, they could compare the results to the actual demand and analyze the results.

EVALUATING METHODS FOR UNCONSTRAINING THE DATA

The goal of an unconstraining method is to estimate an accurate demand profile from the observable data, some of which may be censored. US Airways considered several alternatives for handling the censored data, ranging from simple heuristics to complex statistical methods. The project team considered a variety of methods because of concerns over the trade-off between the cost of implementing a particular method and its benefits. The project team considered and evaluated the following unconstraining methods:

- Direct data capture
- Ignore and discard methods
- Mean imputation method
- Multiplicative booking profile method
- Expectation–Maximization algorithm method
- Projection detruncation method

Direct Data Capture

The most obvious way for US Airways to determine true demand is to simply collect the data. Instead of merely informing passengers that the seats they have requested are unavailable, the airline could record these unfulfilled requests and add them to the accepted reservations, resulting in an accurate demand figure.

This method is impractical for a number of reasons. Most customers make their reservations through traditional and on-line travel agencies rather than directly with the airline. US Airways could not expect these agencies to collect additional data unless the airline was willing to provide some incentive for the additional work. However, even if the airline could devise an appropriate arrangement, the data collected from multiple sources with no oversight might not be considered reliable.

Alternatively, the airline could track requests made through its own reservations offices. With this approach, US Airways would have much better control of the data collection process and could scale the numbers by the appropriate amounts. However, airline managers are reluctant to add additional burdens to already busy reservations agents, reasoning that the agents' efforts should be focused on providing good service, and not on collecting data. An equally important consideration is determining the best method to record the data. Under such circumstances, the cost of collecting the data would quite likely exceed the benefits.

Even if the airline decided that direct data capture was a viable option, obtaining reliable demand data is an ongoing process. The airline could not simply develop one formula that converts the censored data into true demand because unconstraining demand is not a one-time process. Consumer behaviour changes over time for reasons that are too difficult to model. Demand for airline travel is extremely sensitive to economic conditions and consumer confidence and requires a more systematic approach. The project team therefore rejected direct data capture as a viable solution to the unconstraining problem.

Ignore and Discard Methods

Two common approaches for handling censored data is to simply ignore (*ignore method*) the data censoring or to discard (*discard method*) cases in which the censoring occurs and base estimations on the remaining data as if the censoring never existed. Analysts then use complete-data techniques without any consideration for the nature of the data. These two simple methods do not attempt to deal with the censoring problem, but can be useful in certain circumstances. For example, if censoring affects only a small portion of the data, ignore or discard procedures may be appropriate. The additional accuracy resulting from the use of more sophisticated techniques may not be worth the implementation and maintenance costs of the models.

Ignoring or discarding censored data almost certainly produces a forecast with a negative bias. In the airline's case, the mechanism that leads to the censoring of the data is the booking limit set by the revenue management system. If the booking limit is reached and this information is ignored, the observed value will likely be an under-estimate of demand. If these cases are discarded, the remaining uncensored observations will be those where the number of bookings was never high enough to reach the booking limit, again underestimating average demand.

Mean Imputation Method

Imputation is a generic term for filling in missing data with plausible values. Practitioners often use imputation to transform incomplete data sets into complete data sets and then proceed with their analyses as if the imputed values are real data. Various methods for imputing missing values include *hot deck* imputation, in which recorded units in the sample are substituted for the missing data; *mean* imputation, in which the mean from a set of recorded values is substituted; and *regression* imputation, in which the missing values are predicted from a regression model using the known variables for that case (Little, 1982: 237–50).

The US Airways project team evaluated mean imputation as an unconstraining method because it is a commonly used method for filling in missing values and represents a compromise between discarding the censored observations and ignoring the censoring altogether (Little and Rubin, 1987: 44).

The method compares the number of reservations at particular time points of a flight's history with the corresponding booking limits. Depending on the circumstances, analysts either consider the censored observations missing (discarded) and replace them with the mean of the historical uncensored observations or ignore the censoring and use the observations as is.

If the number of bookings is at or above the booking limit, the data is censored and an indicator is *closed.* Otherwise, the indicator is *open.* The indicator's status determines the demand estimate at each time point:

- If the indicator is open, no constraining has occurred and the observation stands as is because it represents the true demand.
- If the indicator is closed, the first step is to compare bookings with the average number of bookings for similar flights that were open at this point. If a censored observation is greater than this mean, the censored observation stands as a representation of the true demand. Otherwise, the mean replaces the censored observation.

The two principal advantages of the mean imputation method are its ease of implementation and its ability to provide some unconstraining of the data. The weakness of the method is that the unconstrained observations will still likely underestimate the true demand because the mean itself is constrained. Even though the mean is computed from uncensored observations, the reason those observations are not censored is because of low demand. If the demand were high, the observation would have been censored and not included in the average. Consequently, using the average as an imputed value for the censored observation will more closely approach true demand, but the result will still be an underestimation.

Multiplicative Booking Profile Method

The US Airways project team also evaluated the multiplicative booking profile method as a way to unconstrain demand data. This method first estimates the shape of the booking profile from uncensored data and then uses that shape to predict the true demand from censored data. The method's underlying assumption is that the shape of the true booking profile is independent of the demand level. In other words, for a given fare class and flight, the shape of the booking profile is the same, regardless of the booking activity level. Stated another way, the percentage increase in demand between review points is constant for a group of similar flights, such as those serving the same market or those departing on a certain day of week. Accepting the underlying assumption as true, analysts can accurately estimate the booking profile by averaging the demand at each review point from similar uncensored flights in a group. They can then unconstrain censored observations by multiplying the last uncensored observation by the percentage increase. This model is adapted from Wickham's thesis (Wickham, 1995: 60–2).

The following example illustrates the model. Table 11.1 lists average demand for a group of similar flights. These are uncensored observations. The Table also shows the percentage increase in bookings for each day prior (DP) to departure.

The percentage increases become the bases for predicting the actual demand from the censored observations, as illustrated in Table 11.2. For example, at DP 90 the data are

Table 11.1 Uncensored observations

	DP 0	DP 7	DP 18	DP 30	DP 60	DP 90	DP 360
Average uncensored demand	50	47	35	30	17	10	0
Average increase (%)	6	34	16	76	70	–	–

Table 11.2 Unconstrained demand (shaded area indicates censored observations)

	DP 0	DP 7	DP 18	DP 30	DP 60	DP 90	DP 360
Average increase (%)	6	34	16	76	70	–	–
Observed data	33	33	33	32	15	12	0
Estimated unconstrained demand	53	50	37	32	15	12	0

not constrained, so the observed value is equal to the actual demand. However, at DP 18, the number of seats was restricted by the booking limit. The estimate of demand at DP 18 is determined by multiplying the previous uncensored observation of 32 by the average percentage increase of 1.16 to arrive at 37. Similarly, the unconstrained demand at DP 7 is 37 × 1.34 = 50, and so on.

Expectation-Maximization (EM) Algorithm Method

US Airways also considered statistical models as a way to avoid the ad hoc nature of the imputation methods. Statistical model advantages, however, come with the cost of additional complexity and involve validation of the model assumptions.

A common statistics-based model is the expectation-maximization algorithm which iteratively calculates the maximum likelihood estimates of parameters in incomplete data problems (Dempster et al., 1977: 1–38). Mathematicians usually apply the EM algorithm to problems in which model estimation is difficult because some part of the data is missing.

The EM algorithm is a two-step iterative process, consisting of the expectation step, or E-step, and the maximization step, or M-step. Based on an initial guess of the model parameter values the E-step predicts the values of the missing data. In the M-step, the E-step predicted values are the basis for re-estimates of the parameters. The process continues until convergence.

The EM algorithm estimates the incremental demand between adjacent review points. Given data that is normally distributed $N(\mu, \sigma^2)$ and an observed constrained observation C, the best estimate of the unconstrained value is $E[X \mid X > C]$ as illustrated in Figure 11.3 (Salch, 1997).

The EM algorithm computes the initial mean and variance of the sample from uncensored observations at the flight number/market origin and destination (O&D)/

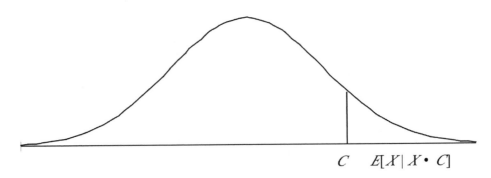

$$C \qquad E[X \mid X \cdot C]$$

Figure 11.3 Expectation of censored observations

fare class/review point level. The EM algorithm examines the open/closed indicator at each review point and then unconstrains demand according to the following procedure:

1. Examine the open/closed indicator.
    a. If the fare class was open to bookings at this review point, use the observation to represent true demand.
    b. If the fare class was closed to bookings at this review point, unconstrain the censored data using the EM algorithm.
2. Obtain initial estimates of μ and σ^2.
    a. Compute the initial estimates of the mean and variance of the distribution for each review point from the uncensored history of n similar flights.
    b. Computation of the mean and variance is not possible if all of the observations in the sample are censored. If all of the data is censored, the initial estimate of unconstrained demand is equal to the observed incremental bookings.
3. In the E-step, replace the censored observation with its expected value.
4. In the M-step, re-estimate μ and σ^2 at each iteration, given the new unconstrained data.
5. Repeat steps 3 and 4 until convergence.

As indicated in step 2, a limitation of the EM algorithm is that it does not work when *all* the observations in a sample are censored. An extension to the EM algorithm developed by the author addresses this situation (Zeni, 2001: 217–20). The extension is somewhat of a hybrid approach that takes advantage of the strengths of both the EM algorithm and the mean imputation method.

The extension uses data one level higher, at the market O&D/fare class/review point level. By dropping the flight number from the aggregate, more data is available from which to calculate the mean. After computing the mean, the next step is to compare the mean to the value of the censored observations. If the mean exceeds the value of the censored observations, then the mean is used instead of the value. Otherwise, the value is not adjusted.

One of the advantages of the extended EM algorithm approach is that it is likely to improve the demand estimates and unlikely to produce a deleterious effect. As previously established, if all observations are censored, the resulting EM estimate will almost certainly be an underestimate. With the EM extension, if the calculated mean is less than this estimate, no changes occur. Because the estimate remains the same, use of the EM extension has no negative impact on the demand estimate. The estimate is replaced only if the EM extension mean is greater than the EM estimate. Because the EM extension mean is higher than the estimate and the estimate is too low, the value will likely be improved. A deleterious effect would occur only if the mean were higher than the true demand for that observation. Additionally, the average would need to be greater than the true demand by at least the same amount as the original estimate was lower than the true demand. Because such a situation will seldom occur, using the extended EM algorithm carries little associated risk.

Projection-Detruncation Method

Craig Hopperstad at Boeing developed the projection-detruncation (PD) method (Hopperstad, 1997). The PD method is similar to the EM algorithm in that it iteratively replaces censored observations with expected values and uses an E-step and an M-step.

The PD method differs from the EM algorithm primarily in the calculation method for expected values of the constrained observations. An additional parameter, τ, also affects the aggressiveness of the unconstraining.

The idea underlying the PD method is that the probability of underestimating the true demand from a censored observation is known and constant. This probability becomes the parameter τ. Given a value for τ, analysts can calculate the expected value of the constrained observation.

Figure 11.4 illustrates the logic. Based on a sample of historical data from a particular flight, calculation of the mean (μ) and variance (σ^2) of the incremental bookings between adjacent review points is based on the uncensored observations only. After making the distribution assumption, the next step is to draw the distribution curve based on the estimated parameters and draw a line to represent the booking-limit restriction.

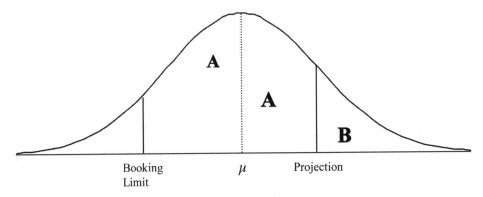

Figure 11.4   Projection-detruncation method

Observations that fall to the right of the booking limit line in areas A and B represent censored data. Area B indicates an underestimate of the projected value for those observations. The probability τ is the ratio of area B to areas A plus B or

$$\tau = \frac{B}{A + B}.$$

Given an estimate for τ, analysts can calculate a solution for B because they can find the A + B area from the booking limit. Once they know the value of B, they can determine the projected values of unconstrained demand. These values replace the constrained observations in the data set, and the parameters of the distribution, μ and σ^2, are calculated from the complete sample. The projected values are then re-estimated given this new distribution. The process continues until convergence (Zickus, 1998: 37–9).

MEASURING PERFORMANCE

After the project team performed the experiments, they analyzed the results and measured the accuracy of each of the unconstraining methods. One effective approach for evaluating the accuracy of a forecasting method is to first produce results from a simple, naive method. These results provide a basis for comparison of more formal methods. For example, after calculating the mean absolute deviation (MAD) for two forecasting methods – a simple one and a more sophisticated method – the difference between the two statistics provides a measure of the improvement attainable through the use of the more formal method. Because it provides a basis for evaluating the relative accuracy of results, this approach is preferable to simply computing the performance statistics for the method of interest (Makridakis *et al.*, 1983: 64).

Another useful measure of forecast accuracy is to compare the performance of a given method with the results from an optimal forecast. Such a comparison provides a measure of the minimal attainable error achieved from the model of interest.

In this study, the project team used both of these approaches to evaluate the performance of the unconstraining methods. They used the ignore method for the baseline naive forecast. Because this method simply ignores the presence of censored data and makes no attempt to correct it, any unconstraining method that attempts to explicitly estimate the actual demand from the censored data should provide more accurate results.

The best estimate of unconstrained demand occurs if the uncensored data values are observable. In that case, the optimal forecast is the actual demand value with an error of zero. Therefore, the team evaluated unconstraining methods based on the reduction of the forecast error relative to the ignore method. This approach provided a convenient range in which to evaluate the performance of the methods. A 100 per cent decrease in forecast error is the best possible performance.

The team used the MAD to evaluate the accuracy of demand estimates from each of the unconstraining methods. This statistic provided an effective way to measure the error from estimating the actual mean and variance of remaining demand at a particular review point.

COMPARING PERFORMANCE

Table 11.3 and Figure 11.5 show the performance results (reduction of MAD) for all of the unconstraining methods evaluated in this study.

The worst-performing method was the discard method because it actually increased the error versus the ignore method. The reason is due to the fact that the discarded data contains a great deal of information about the true level of demand. Demand tended to be the highest in the censored, discarded observations. In the remaining uncensored

Table 11.3 Error reduction comparison for all methods

	MAD reduction	
Method	Mean estimate (%)	Variance estimate (%)
Discard	−38.54	−28.00
Mean imputation	11.51	12.41
Booking profile	9.75	9.97
Expectation-maximization	31.44	33.86
Extended EM	48.93	53.62
Projection detruncation	15.05	16.25

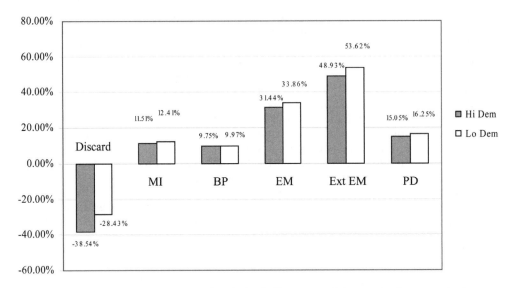

Figure 11.5   Performance (reduction of MAD) of all unconstraining methods versus the ignore method

observations, demand was not high enough to reach the booking limits. When only the uncensored observations form the basis of the mean's calculation, the mean will be lower than if all the data were included in the calculation, as in the ignore method.

The mean imputation method did a good job of providing some unconstraining at a limited cost. Implementation is relatively straightforward and requires a fraction of the computer time that the statistical methods require. The mean imputation method shares a weakness with the ignore method, however, in that the parameters used to unconstrain demand are estimated from only the uncensored observations in the sample. This sample bias inevitably leads to an underestimate of demand. The multiplicative booking profile method does not suffer as much from sample bias as the other methods and outperformed the other heuristics. While the percentage increases are calculated only from uncensored observations, the estimate of unconstrained demand is not limited. However, this strength of the multiplicative booking profile method may also be a weakness. Its performance is erratic at times, producing unrealistically high values of demand. Implementation of this method would necessitate placement of sanity bounds on the estimates.

The PD method performed better than the heuristics, producing results equivalent to the EM algorithm. However, the PD method required nearly twice as many iterations as the EM algorithm to converge. One advantage of the PD method is the ability to adjust – based on feedback from the system – the degree of unconstraining with the value of τ. If evidence shows that the method is unconstraining too aggressively, then the level may be decreased. In theory, it is possible to adjust the range of unconstraining from zero to infinity by setting τ from one to zero respectively. During experimentation, however, the method was very unstable at the extremes of the range. Reliable results were obtained with $0.40 < \tau < 0.60$.

The EM algorithm performed well, recovering approximately 33 per cent of the demand lost to censoring by making good use of all available information. Although the initial parameter estimates come from uncensored observations only, the algorithm quickly incorporates the censored observations and uses all the data to produce an estimate of demand. However, the increased cost of this method is a consideration. Requiring an average of eleven iterations to converge, the EM algorithm uses considerable processing time compared to the heuristic methods. Nevertheless, the improved accuracy would seem to justify the cost.

The extended EM algorithm produced the best performance. Built upon a solid foundation, the extension addresses a weakness with the EM algorithm without introducing much risk. Additionally, this one-step process adds little to the overall processing time. The extended EM algorithm reduced the error from estimating the mean of the distribution with censored data by an average of 51 per cent.

US AIRWAYS CASE STUDY RESULTS

The use of real airline data and the simulation of censoring from a revenue management system lend credibility to the study results. Based on these findings, it is reasonable to expect that the airline will receive similar results from implementing one of the methods in its production environment. Of course, validating the actual performance would be difficult because the true demand values are not available and error statistics cannot be accurately calculated. Thus, while it is not possible to claim that the same improvement in forecast accuracy obtained in this study will be achieved in production, it is reasonable to expect that the relative performance among the methods is accurately represented.

Based on the findings of this study, US Airways is in the process of investigating the implementation of some version of the EM algorithm to unconstrain its demand data. The company believes that it can improve its forecast accuracy by 5–10 per cent from better estimates of historical demand. According to an industry rule-of-thumb, each 10 per cent increase in forecast accuracy increases revenue by half of 1 per cent. Given US Airway's high revenue base, the improved revenue would more than compensate for the cost of implementing the EM algorithm.

CONCLUSION

This case is highlighted by the thoroughness and innovation of the project team. Faced with several challenges, they correctly identified that the most crucial obstacle to clear was the lack of a reliable set of test data. They spent as much effort developing a model for creating this data as they did testing the unconstraining methods. Once the test data was created, the team had a solid foundation to begin testing and devising various methods. This was important from a scientific as well as a business perspective. Any results that were not supported by reliable test data would be suspect and flawed. Since the airline was preparing to make a substantial financial investment in an unconstraining process, the consequences of a poor decision would not only be the initial cost of the system, but the unrealized future revenue that might have been obtained from better revenue management controls.

DISCUSSION QUESTIONS

1. If there was little or no censoring in an airline's historical demand data, what would that indicate about the revenue management system, or the level of demand?
2. Under what conditions would an airline decide not to unconstrain its demand data?
3. After US Airways implements its choice of unconstraining methods, how will the project team be able to measure its success?

REFERENCES

Dempster, A. P., Laird, N. M. and Rubin, D. B. (1977) 'Maximum likelihood from incomplete data via the EM algorithm', *Journal of Royal Statistical Society*, **B39**, 1–38.

Hopperstad, C. (1977) 'PODS modelling update'. Presented at AGIFORS Yield Management Study Group, Montreal, Canada.

Little, R. J. A. (1982) 'Models for nonresponse in sample surveys', *Journal of American Statistical Association*, **77**, 237–50.

Little, R. J. A., and Rubin, D. B. (1987) *Statistical Analysis with Missing Data*, p. 44. New York: John Wiley & Sons, Inc.

Makridakis, S., Wheelwright, S. and McGee, V. (1983) *Forecasting: Methods and Applications*, p. 64. New York: John Wiley & Sons, Inc.

Salch, J. (1997) 'Unconstraining passenger demand using the EM algorithm'. Presented at INFORMS Conference, Dallas, Texas.

Weatherford, L. (1997) 'A review of optimization modeling assumptions in revenue management situations', *AGIFORS Reservations & Yield Management Study Group Proceedings*, 120–42.

Wickham, R. R. (1995) 'Evaluation of forecasting techniques for short-term demand of air transportation'. *MIT Flight Transportation Laboratory Report* R95–7, 60–2.

Zeni, R. (2001) 'Improved Forecast Accuracy in Airline Revenue Management by unconstraining censored demand estimates'. PhD Dissertation, Rutgers University.

Zickus, M. (1998) 'Forecasting for airline network revenue management: revenue and competitive impacts' *MIT Flight Transportation Laboratory Report* R98–4, 37–9.

12

Revenue Management in the
Health Care Industry

Warren Lieberman

INTRODUCTION

At first glance, a medical centre might seem an unlikely candidate for revenue management. To many, establishing prices or access to doctors that provide preferential
health services treatment based on an ability to pay isn't fair or appropriate. To be sure,
institutions do have different fee structures. A public hospital will treat more indigent
or uninsured patients than a private hospital. Doctors have varying fees. But
appointments for a doctor in a private health care facility are typically made on a first-
come first-served basis. The ability to make an appointment with a doctor is not
governed by how much a patient can afford to pay.

Yet health care facilities must also balance their revenues and expenses. Medical and
administrative staff must be paid. Greater revenues and profits enable more money to
be reinvested in upgraded facilities and equipment, enabling better medical treatment to
be offered. To the extent that revenue management principles can enable a medical
centre to increase its revenues and profitability in a manner that is consistent with fair
and ethical treatment of its patients, there is an opportunity worthy of exploration. This
case focuses on how one medical centre used revenue management principles to do just
that.

AIMS AND OBJECTIVES

One of the core principles of revenue management is to find ways to expand the range
of customer segments using a product or service. Typically, this involves designing a
pricing structure that permits sales to be made to those with a lesser willingness or

ability to pay. The pricing structure must be designed so that the revenues of the company are not *diluted* because those customers who are willing and able to pay more modify their purchasing habits in order to obtain the item at the lower price. This enables the company to sell its products to a broader base of customers, while at the same time earning greater revenues and profits. Designing and implementing such a pricing structure typically requires a strong understanding of the company's current and prospective customers.

The purpose of this case study is to ask you to think creatively about customer segmentation. Can a medical centre use revenue management principles to offer its services to individuals that are not currently using the centre for their primary health care needs? If so, how can this be done in a way that is profitable for the medical centre and is fair to its patients?

CASE STUDY

Mid-Peninsula Medical Center (MMC) is a high quality primary care health centre. Located in Foster City, California, MMC is approximately halfway between the cities of San Francisco and San Jose. MMC has a staff of twelve, including five doctors. MMC's hours are from Monday to Friday, 9 a.m. to 6 p.m., Saturday from 9 a.m. to 5 p.m., and Sunday from 9 a.m. to 1 p.m. In 1998, MMC expanded to include a small on-site physical therapy facility for its patients to use. The physical therapy facility contains a variety of equipment, including a treadmill, stationary bicycle, stair climber and weights. MMC patients are able to use the physical therapy equipment, with or without supervision, during MMC's normal business hours. When using the facility without a physical therapist, patients are entitled to free use of the equipment.

Although it wasn't always the case, MMC enjoys a strong reputation for providing high quality health care. Doctors have access to state-of-the-art equipment. Virtually all of MMC's patients live within 5 miles of the facility. The patients who do not live within 5 miles of the health centre work for companies located near the health centre.

Foster City is primarily residential, but also contains many small businesses. More recently, larger businesses have located there as well. There are approximately 500 small businesses with fewer than twenty employees, about 100 businesses with 20 to 250 employees, and several dozen larger businesses with more than 250 employees, including retail stores and other businesses that employ temporary workers for several months per year on a regular basis. Such part-time workers are generally hired to handle increased business during holidays and to meet seasonal needs.

Unemployment levels in the San Francisco Bay Area and the surrounding geographic region all the way to San Jose have been relatively low for the past decade. Companies fiercely compete for employees. At times, retail companies have experienced difficulties in hiring sufficient part-time and seasonal staff to meet their needs during holiday seasons.

Approximately 90 per cent of MMC's patients carry health care insurance. Many of the smaller companies either do not provide their employees with health insurance or provide very limited coverage. Larger companies usually offer health insurance as a benefit to their employees either six months or a year after they are hired. Only a few companies offer health insurance to their employees at the time they are hired. Larger companies generally do not provide health care benefits to part-time and seasonal workers. These individuals, as well as those that are unemployed, usually do not carry health insurance, as health insurance premiums can be several hundred dollars per month or more. Such individuals often 'take their chances' and use health care facilities less frequently than those who carry health insurance.

Recently, companies have begun to offer flexible benefits plans to their employees. Under such plans, employees are given a certain number of 'points' to allocate to their total health insurance needs on an annual basis. Employees have discretion in how they allocate these points among alternative health care levels. An employee's decision remains in effect for a year, after which they can reallocate their points. This enables employees to customize their health insurance plan to their specific needs. For example, employees who need glasses tend to allocate more points to vision programmes. When employees elect to allocate fewer points than the company gives to them, they receive additional compensation for each unallocated point. This has led many younger employees to 'under-insure' themselves so that they receive additional compensation. Younger employees are often willing to take greater risks with health insurance as they do not think they will have a strong need for health care.

Depending on the specific type of medical treatment provided and the type of insurance carried, health insurance enables individuals to obtain primary care health services for much lower costs than are otherwise possible. Health insurance generally pays for 80 to 100 per cent of the fee charged to a patient. Many patients carry health insurance that requires them to pay a $5 or $10 'co-payment', while their insurance company pays for the balance of the fee. When a patient has primary and secondary health insurance, a patient will often have no out-of-pocket expense for typical primary health care services. The secondary insurance will pay for whatever costs are not paid for by the primary insurance, including the co-payment. Patients who are married and have working spouses frequently have primary and secondary health insurance.

Because of their size, health insurance providers are able to negotiate lower fees for primary care services with medical centres. For example, a visit to a doctor due to an illness or for a routine check-up might normally cost an uninsured patient $165. If the patient has health insurance, however, the medical centre's contracts with insurance companies generally stipulate that the centre will charge only $75 for its services. Some of this fee might be paid for by the patient as a co-payment, or all of the fee might be paid for through the patient's insurance company (or companies).

Table 12.1 contains a list of the most common types of services provided by MMC, the cost of these services to uninsured patients, and the payment received by MMC from patients possessing health insurance (as noted above, this fee may consist of a patient's portion plus an insurance company payment).

MMC had been a marginally profitable business for a number of years. In 1997, MMC came under new ownership. Formerly with United Airlines, the medical centre's

Table 12.1 List of MMC's services and fees

Service	Fee for uninsured patients ($)	Fee received by MMC from insured patients ($)
Routine physical examination	165	75
Care for acute illness	85	50
Returning patient visit	105	50
Lab tests	65	25
Office procedures	100	60

new Director believed that by upgrading the centre's equipment and providing added services the medical centre would attract new patients and increase its revenues and profits. The medical centre was in strong competition with other health care facilities in the area and the new Director believed a large and diverse patient base was crucial for the medical centre to have long-term success. It was also important for the health centre to be financially strong so that it could retain its doctors by providing them with compensation that was competitive with what the doctors could earn at other health centres.

The centre's doctors divided their time among multiple health centres. Some of the doctors worked at MMC five days per week while others worked at MMC for two or three days per week. In addition, a doctor might be on duty for as little as four hours or as much as eight hours. Because they work at multiple health centres, doctors prefer to have the same weekly schedule for at least six months.

The Director has sought to schedule the number of doctors who were on duty to match the level of demand for the centre's services. Fluctuations and uncertainty in demand, combined with minimum scheduling requirements (e.g., a doctor could not be scheduled to be at the centre for only one hour), result in wide variations in doctor and equipment utilization. Consequently, utilization of doctor time was consistently high during certain time periods such as Monday mornings, and consistently low during other periods, such as mid-day on Tuesdays and Thursdays.

When the utilization of doctor time approaches or exceeds 85 per cent, keeping appointments on schedule becomes a significant challenge. Some patients arrive late and some require more time than expected. When patients are required to wait more than 10 or 15 minutes, they often get upset. In addition, MMC has a rather small waiting area, so having several patients waiting at the same time can lead to uncomfortable situations for patients as well as for MMC's administrative staff.

Table 12.2 contains estimates of how much doctor time was utilized during the past month at various times of the day for each day of the week. During the weekends, doctor utilization runs very high, generally over 90 per cent during the centre's hours. Table 12.3 contains the average number of doctors that were on duty during these time periods during the past month. On weekends, there are two doctors on duty throughout the day.

Table 12.2 Utilization of doctor availability at MMC (%)

Time of day	Monday	Tuesday	Wednesday	Thursday	Friday
8–10 a.m.	85	75	90	80	85
10–12 p.m.	75	55	72	52	83
12–3 p.m.	72	45	83	38	78
3–6 p.m.	81	90	81	68	74

Table 12.3. Number of doctors on duty at MMC

Time of day	Monday	Tuesday	Wednesday	Thursday	Friday
8–10 a.m.	3	3	3	5	4
10–12 p.m.	3	3	3	5	4
12–3 p.m.	3	2	4	3	3
3–6 p.m.	3	2	4	3	3

During the first two years of his leadership, the medical centre's new Director made significant investments in equipment and improving its facilities. As the centre expanded its capabilities, including adding a Physical Therapy facility, the centre's reputation grew and the centre attracted additional patients. The centre's revenues grew, but its profitability remained relatively flat as the centre's operating expenses also increased.

As the Director continued to look for ways to increase the centre's profitability, one of the leading options being considered was expanding the centre's hours. The Director believed that keeping the centre open longer during evening hours from Monday to Friday would attract additional patients – in particular, parents with sick children who had a difficult time coming to the centre during normal business hours. Keeping the centre open longer would increase the centre's expenses, as doctors and staff would need to be paid for the extra time, but the Director believed that the additional revenues received from patient visits would more than compensate for the incremental expenses.

As the Director considered the available options for generating additional revenues, including advertising and other non-traditional alternatives, he also wondered whether revenue management principles might be applied to his new business. He was well aware that revenue management had proven to be very successful in the airline industry as a means to increase revenues and profits. Although he was not sure that revenue management was applicable to his new business, he thought it was worth exploring.

As he considered the application of revenue management in the airline industry, he recognized that if revenue management principles could be applied, their implementation would be very different. Most insurance companies required that the rates they paid to the medical centre were the lowest rates charged by the medical centre for the same level of service. If the medical centre set up a differentiated rate structure for a particular type of procedure, the insurance companies would pay the lowest rate charged. So, charging a discounted rate when an appointment was made more than some number of days in advance would result in insurance companies paying no more than that discounted rate, regardless of when the appointment was made by one of their members. Placing a restriction on when an appointment was made was not considered as a differentiated service.

Different rates could be charged for services that were viewed as being different. For example, the medical centre could charge a lower fee for patients making appointments for a particular time. So, if the centre chose to charge only $55 for a basic check-up when a patient made an appointment for Tuesday morning between 10 a.m. and noon, this would not affect the rates paid by insurance companies for appointments made outside these hours. As he considered such an option, however, the Director didn't think that providing such a discount would increase the centre's revenues and profits. Also, he was concerned that making the fee structure too complex might ultimately confuse and anger patients.

The Director of MMC has just contacted a local revenue management expert to see if it is worth pursuing this direction. It is now Monday afternoon and they have agreed to have lunch on Wednesday.

DISCUSSION QUESTIONS

1. If you were the revenue management expert meeting with the Director of MMC, how would you advise the Director on whether revenue management principles could be used to improve the medical centre's profitability?
2. If you believe revenue management could be beneficial for MMC, what actions would you recommend?
3. How would you estimate the potential benefits and risks of your recommendations? If possible, quantify your estimates.

13

Revenue Management in Visitor Attractions: A Case Study of the EcoTech Centre, Swaffham, Norfolk

Julian Hoseason

INTRODUCTION

Visitor attractions form an integral part of the total tourism product for both the domestic and incoming visitors to a region. Attractions cover a broad spectrum of activities based upon the natural or man-made environment ranging from heritage sites through to purpose built centres usually devoted to leisure and recreational activities (Getz, 1993; Swarbrooke, 1999; Hall and Page, 1999). The attractions sector is complex in definition and provides different levels of engagement with the visitor when the 'encounter' takes place (Crouch, 1999). While visitors enjoy this variety, attractions offer an intangible experience (Yeoman and Leask, 1999), which makes visitor management and marketing complex (Prentice *et al.*, 1998) since seasonality and a spatial element enter into the pricing strategy.

In the mid-1990s Norfolk was experiencing a decline in its agricultural base and indicators suggested alternative strategies needed implementation to avoid unemployment and social blight in the community of Swaffham. Regional funding from the European Union enabled an imaginative proposal for the development of a sustainable attraction to act as a growth-pole for inward investment. The EcoTech Centre was to be an experimental showcase in design and construction techniques with the emphasis upon environmental management and education. As an attraction, the EcoTech Centre would need to reach a critical mass of around 50,000 visitors per annum to be viable. The centre would be competing against the region's existing attractions, the coast and an area of wetland known as the 'Norfolk Broads'.

As the implementation of revenue management matures across the travel and tourism industry, the resultant benefits must make the implementation or adoption a basic management strategy. Research indicates that the attractions sector has yet to extensively adopt revenue management as a management technique, therefore this sector produces lower financial performance figures compared to other sectors. Research by Yeoman and Leask (1999) into heritage visitor attractions indicated that the highly seasonal nature of the market necessitated revenue management techniques being applied to main season activities with more specialist activities being introduced during low or out of season periods for maximization of revenue. However, major capital projects funded by the UK's National Lottery, may have caused distortion to the attractions sector at local, regional and national level where sudden increases in market capacity cannot be met by corresponding increases in visitor activity. Over £1.2 billion has been awarded to over 180 major projects with an additional £2.8 billion being awarded through European funded grants for projects (Anon, 2000). Key projects like the Royal Armouries in Leeds, and the Earth Centre, failed to live up to projections not only of visitor numbers but also in revenue management where overestimates and losses threatened their future (McClarence, 2000). For the EcoTech Centre, its future success may not simply lie in developing a highly innovative attraction, but consideration of micro-market behaviour in relation to the capacity of the 'ideal market' or catchment area characteristics.

AIMS AND OBJECTIVES

The aim of this case study is to demonstrate how simple revenue management techniques encourage visitors spend in higher profit earning centres within an attraction. The objectives are to:

1. Evaluate the impact of a high profile attraction in the attractions market.
2. Evaluate the relationship between pricing and revenue strategies.
3. Analyze the relationship between attractions design and critical mass in attracting visitor numbers.

BACKGROUND

The EcoTech Centre has been built on a brownfield site on the edge of Swaffham, a market town in the centre of Norfolk. Sited on a former derelict firework factory, the project aimed at cleaning up a polluted site for the benefit of the community. The original proposal envisaged an experimental building in terms of design and construction techniques, attracting 50,000 visitors annually, and providing an interactive learning centre based on environmental education. By targeting the enhancement of leisure and tourism facilities it was hoped to attract high inward investment to a showcase project. Regeneration would provide a high profile attraction to bolster the regional tourism and leisure product base. An experimental building would provide an opportunity to be innovative in not only design but also construction techniques, where fusion between designers and the construction industry could present alternatives to current building practices and where visitors and the community would be engaged with the project. The 'environmentally friendly' experimental building was designed to embrace energy efficiency, ecological waste treatment and provide a centre for environmental education, with facilities in skills training for the local community. The management and marketing of a multi-faceted project requires a full understanding of site development and site management, with market segment behaviour and pricing strategies for the management of revenue being effectively implemented.

The EcoTech Centre would form part of an economic growth pole (Higgins, 1983) where a group of 'propulsive enterprises' would produce widespread effects within the region. D'Hauteserre (1997) highlighted the positive economic impacts this technique brought to the Marne Valley since the establishment of Disneyland, Paris. The EcoTech Centre was planned by the partnership between Breckland District Council and the EcoTech Centre Trustees to be a high profile EU funded capital project to optimize benefits to the community. Offering an eco-based experience would attract additional investment into the region and alter the public perception of the attractions sector profile. Provision of a sustainable resource was seen as critical to the project. As part of the site development programme, a wind turbine with viewing platform was built by Ecotricity and opened to visitors in May 1999. This massive structure instantly provided a focal point and Unique Selling Point (USP) for the site since there were no similar attractions in the UK. The decision to construct a viewing platform had been based upon visitor experiences of a similar attraction in Europe. The opening of the wind turbine has pushed visitor numbers up to 28,500 despite a revised target of 32,000 which reflects current performance more accurately.

It was recognized within the first year of operation that further development plans could not be indefinitely postponed and were critical to the attraction reaching its critical mass to ensure a sustainable and viable future. Ongoing projects to secure funding for the development of an experimental eco-house and an environmental management/energy advice centre remain core to the attraction's development. Through the use of COPIS funding, the attraction is to build an interactive walk-through compostor to enhance the attraction's coverage of future techniques in sustainability of resources. Other developments have included rainwater recycling systems and the construction of a Viking round tower using traditional techniques which acts as a counterbalance and is in contrast to the high tech design and materials used elsewhere on the site. As EcoTech matures as an attraction and the novelty factor diminishes the need for revenue management will increase. The reliance upon programmes of exhibitions, and improving the aids to interpreting exhibits, will form only part of the revenue management strategy and the shift towards more specialist and community-based micro-markets will need to be addressed (Johns and Hoseason, 2001).

THE ECONOMICS OF VISITOR ATTRACTIONS

The visitor attractions sector is highly fragmented and diverse (Bull, 1995). The very diversity of the market dictates the economic conditions which impact upon the market and the operators or suppliers within it. At one end of the product continuum, natural heritage sites are often free to visitors and managed either by government agencies, for example English Heritage or organizations like the National Trust that has charity status. At the other end of the continuum, there are commercially based organizations providing built attractions that require profit or revenue maximization (Bull, 1995; Tribe, 1995; Yeoman and Leask, 1999). Since alteration to public funding in the 1990s, many organizations, irrespective of organizational structure and status, have increasingly used commercial, i.e. revenue maximization, techniques to support an attraction's viability. Similar to the accommodation sector, visitor attractions (Yeoman and Leask,

1999) are capital intensive or are high in capital value, as in the case of built heritage sites. However, there is also an 'unpriced' value (Bull, 1995) within the economic structure of attractions. These include social cost/benefit pricing and tourist values that are elements included within the tourist product. They may be inseparable from the experience, but cannot be given a market value (Sinden and Worrell, 1979) and this particularly applies to the natural environment. Managers of visitor attractions subsequently manage revenue through profit maximization, break-even pricing or social cost/benefit pricing. As Bull (1995) points out, it makes comparison of economic or financial performance almost impossible, particularly where the local authority assists by providing financial support, or donations are made. A number of high profile projects funded through the National Lottery, for example the Millennium Dome or the Armouries in Sheffield, have foundered where altruism and social cost/benefit pricing has tried to defy gravity models along with economic modelling in demand and supply. The result is a distorted picture in terms of visitor numbers and ultimately the financial viability. A massive influx in major projects funded by the National Lottery has caused management problems for a number of existing attractions on national, regional and local scales.

Wanhill (1998) identified attractions having high fixed costs either through the capital investment required to establish or to expand the development of an attraction. Operational and variable costs are impacted upon by the seasonality of the attraction and may force operators to use cost-orientated pricing to ensure contribution margins are met. While admissions prices form the core of income generation (Swarbrooke, 1999), each attraction suffers from an element of price discretion to cover short run operational costs (Bull, 1995; Wanhill, 1998). Low marginal costs may enable a greater range in price discretion. However, pricing strategies often include an element of the visitor's perception of 'value for money'. Hendon (1982) identified the heritage sector as being highly segmented and relatively inelastic, where changes in admission prices caused little negative impact upon revenue. Reliance on measuring admission prices based upon a general rule of market knowledge and visitor perception increases risks (Rogers, 1995). High visitor numbers are usually required to meet break-even points and this makes attractions susceptible to the vagaries of weather, which effect visitor numbers and the ability to effectively manage revenue.

Yeoman and Leask (1999) demonstrated that heritage based attractions exhibit operational and financial seasonal dependency characteristics that increases the need for stronger revenue management to maximize revenue during peak periods. Swarbrooke (1999) suggested success must not be measured by visitor volume, but through visitor spend. Pricing strategies may target market segments and be used effectively to discriminate against visitors as a technique in visitor management particularly where a heritage attraction has reached its carrying capacity. Research by Prentice *et al.* (1998) indicates there should be a shift away from viewing visitors purely upon socio-economic profiling and move towards a model of benefit segmentation, as it may be a truer reflection of consumer behaviour and willingness to pay. Targeting 'baby-boomers', whose experience and preferences as consumers are different from those of previous generations, make marketing of attractions such as EcoTech for older age groups more challenging and breaks stereotype moulds of the 'over 55s' market, thus providing even greater opportunity for application of revenue management techniques (Johns and Hoseason, 2001).

MARKETING AND IDEAL MARKETS

It has now been firmly established that tourist products are offered to highly segmented consumer markets either through behavioural (Cohen, 1979; Plog, 1973) or archetypal characteristics (Holloway and Robinson, 1995). Middleton (1996) suggested that culturally there was uniformity in drawing on a basic range of segments to visitor attractions irrespective of destination. These segments are broken down into:

1. Local residents living within half an hour's drive.
2. Regional residents making day visits and travelling up to two hours depending upon the motivating power of the site.
3. Visitors staying with friends and family within about an hour from the site.
4. Visitors staying in serviced or non-serviced accommodation within about an hour.
5. Group travel.
6. School and educational visits.

Prentice *et al.* (1998) recognized the importance of benefit segmentation rather than follow a too generalized socio-economic analysis and ignored the geographic nature of 'ideal markets', which Middleton indicated were important. Getz (1993) modelled the 'tourist business district' in terms of attractions being mutually surrounded and interacting with tourism services (i.e., accommodation and transport) and the central functions of government, the retail sector, offices and meetings, where the access and movement of people were important. However, this does not fully explain the 'ideal market'. Attractions display spatial characteristics that cannot be simply analysed through distance decay models (Bull, 1995), consumer profiles or destination 'branding' of image or consumer lifestyle preference (Morgan and Pritchard, 2002). Distance decay assumes the level of activity decreases with distance measured either in time or absolute measurement and therefore enables a geographic market to be delineated.

For spatial interaction to take place, there needs to be 'perfect' complementarity, i.e., demand in one place has to be matched with supply in another (Ullman, 1956), and other stimulators such as fashionability and positioning of the destination as a brand (de Chernatony, 1993; Kotler *et al.*, 1999). By using gravity models, marketers of visitor attractions should consider not only market segmentation processes, but also consider the attractions 'mass' as a pulling power. Where an intervening opportunity exists (i.e., alternative supply), an alternative attraction would only be visited by tourists if there were a criteria match. Empirical evidence suggests marketing managers tend to mismatch the degree of competition with other attractions without analyzing their own customer base to check behavioural characteristics. In terms of pricing strategies, there may be greater emphasis upon consumer perception in 'value for money' and the tourist values than maximization in revenue opportunities through value added processes. Christaller (1966) modelled location in terms of service hierarchy and matched these to distance and sizes of population to produce theoretical ideal markets. In reality, 'ideal markets' or catchment area, will produce not a rigid circle or hexagon on a map, but fluid lines based upon the attraction's 'mass' and the efficiency of flows within transport systems and networks.

The key to recent growth in many attractions has been matching product development with demographic and lifestyle changes (Fry, 1997). Numerous attractions mirror the experience of the hospitality sector by implementing pricing structures to attract the over 55s (Ananth *et al.*, 1992), particularly those with grandchildren. Changes in service provision has aimed at higher quality and more personalized service, e.g., membership schemes, timed tickets or restrictions in access to use retail or hospitality services. Attractions have increasingly recognized the importance of a growing secondary role in providing a meeting place where the emphasis is on hospitality or retail provision rather than a repeat visit to the core area of the attraction, whether it is an ecclesiastical site, museum, zoo or a themed site.

REVENUE MANAGEMENT

As the implementation of revenue management nears maturity as a management tool, published research now covers airlines (Larsen, 1988; Smith *et al.*, 1992; Daudel and Vialle, 1994; Belobaba and Wilson, 1997; Ingold and Huyton, 1997), hotels (Orkin, 1988; Donaghy *et al.*, 1995), tour operations (Hoseason and Johns, 1998; Laws, 1997), cruise (Hoseason, 2000) and car rental operations (Cross, 1998). These studies range from technology impact and implementation studies to marketing, human resource management, revenue and inventory management. Few studies have been made on built visitor attractions, whether they are heritage based or theme parks.

The built visitor attractions industry shares a number of common characteristics with other travel and tourism sectors. Both heritage and purpose built visitor attraction sites have capacity relatively constrained either through the carrying capacity of the site or through other factors, e.g., planning permission or car parking facilities. Demand is both seasonal and highly segmented (Cross, 1998; Wanhill, 1998; Yeoman and Leask, 1999). Supply may also be constrained through seasonality or, in the case of heritage visitor attractions, through conservation policies. Subsequently, the different nature of managing organizations where they straddle the public/private and charity divide requires fundamentally different strategies for managing revenue even though they may emulate revenue techniques from the private sector. While public sector organizations have to give greater consideration to social cost, the use of revenue maximization techniques may have impact upon funding through central and local government budgetary control. However, shifts in government funding have placed greater dependence on public sector organizations to re-evaluate revenue management and become more empowered and independent in control, making the implementation of revenue management techniques even more appropriate in their strategies for revenue management.

Research by Yeoman and Leask (1999) into heritage visitor attractions in Scotland indicated that visitor attractions match to a greater or lesser extent the core necessary conditions and ingredients identified by Kimes (1989) in order to implement revenue maximizing techniques. Unlike the accommodation sector, visitor attractions are dedicated more specifically to a particular tourist market (Bull, 1995). Clearly, this indicates a more customized approach to implementation where careful consideration to the site and local conditions must be made. Cross (1998) suggested that where markets are mature, over-supplied and showing signs of congestion, organizations need to refocus on micro-markets for the benefits of effective revenue management to take place and it is here that visitor attractions now need to concentrate.

Schwartz (1998) suggests that the perishability of the product and the customer's willingness to pay are in fact the key elements in revenue management and not the necessary conditions and ingredients identified by Kimes and Cross. These were felt to be overstated and may be contributing factors but embody misconceptions and misunderstandings of price demand elasticity and consumer behaviour.

The Millennium Commission supported a £4 billion programme covering over 180 capital projects to celebrate the millennium. In the visitor attractions market, impact studies tended to focus on individual projects at the time of funding bids being made, rather than a more holistic approach. While these projects have upgraded and enabled greater diversity in choice, this type of product development may impact upon pricing strategies (Middleton, 1996; Edgar, 1997; Poon, 1993) in order for new sites to reach critical mass in visitor numbers. Established visitor attractions have altered pricing strategies to counter any destabilization and lowering of revenue due to lower visitor numbers. Market capacity should therefore be given far higher visibility and inclusion in revenue management strategies.

REVENUE MANAGEMENT AT ECOTECH

As a new attraction, both the management team and trustees had been aware of the need to reach critical mass for visitor numbers within the first year of operations. Competition within an established market would be fierce, and any 'launch campaigns' would have to shift from media hype to delivery of an 'experience'. A key factor in the performance of any new attraction is being ready for the main tourism season. Although the EcoTech Centre opened in the spring of 1999, delays to building and site completion coupled with poor weather did not turn the opening into a recipe for a disaster but did impact upon visitor targets that were downscaled to 32,000 per annum.

Core concepts of revenue management were established within the business plan and focused upon:

(a) pricing strategies;
(b) main market segments;
(c) trends in micro-markets;
(d) incentives for repeat business;
(e) booking lead-time trends for specialist groups and schools.

Pricing strategies were set well within the range of local attractions and were thought to be 'about right'. Quite early, qualitative research indicated that the first wave of visitors were environmentalists or organizations associated with environmental issues who would turn out to be quite critical of the centre. These groups had a high socio-economic profile of A, B, C1/2, who found the centrepiece exhibition 'Doomsday' reiterating environmental issues as a core theme, but not offering solutions. The interpretation boards would not be fully in place until July 1999 which meant that the full impact of exhibition material could not be appreciated. Also, without the construction of the eco-house and the setting up of the advice centres for energy and environmental waste management for businesses, the EcoTech Centre will not be able to fulfil this role and will remain susceptible to criticism.

Operationally, the centre suffered from similar tourist behaviour patterns experienced by other attractions within the area. Themed attractions and heritage properties see falls in attendance when hot weather conditions exist and they compete head-on with the beach or zoos. The EcoTech Centre was perceived to be an indoor attraction best suited to colder weather, which has brought to the front the need for continued site development to counteract this factor. The centre's design incorporated a passive solar collection system. On hot days visitors and staff found the experimental building too efficient in heat retention and this has caused modification work to be carried out to improve temperature and ventilation.

Ecotricity's agreement to build a wind turbine with a viewing platform provided the EcoTech Centre with an additional showcase exhibit and provided a much-needed value-added element to the visit. Due for completion in May 1999, delays in construction and granting of Health & Safety Executive approval forced re-evaluation of visitor targets and the management of revenue as the turbine finally opened during the month of August. Between April and October 28,500 visitors were attracted to Eco-Tech, a reduction of 36 per cent from estimates made in the feasibility study. Despite delays and coping with a 'learning curve', the number of visitors was comparable to other visitor centres within Norfolk and enabled the centre to become more established within the attractions sector.

In 2000, pricing strategies (see Appendix 1 at the end of this case study) were altered and the principles of revenue management (Cross, 1997) were applied even though they were not directly recognized as such. The wind turbine was priced separately with main entrance prices significantly reduced in order to focus on revenue generation from family or single adults with children. Research indicated the over 55s with grand-children also formed a significant segment of visitors. Their usage of the site would differ from other visitors and the pricing strategy ensured this group's requirements were being met. With a full programme of activities and exhibitions planned for the year, the wind turbine now provided the Unique Selling Point. New marketing and pricing strategies could now provide a more dynamic management plan with the shift in focus to micro-market segments. With a broadened base, the attraction could now effectively use pricing strategies based upon clear segmentation processes to allow sufficient price discrimination to improve revenue. A bold decision was made to close the centre on Saturdays during the off-peak period. Market-day in Swaffham and 'change-over day' for the regions' holiday homes and boats on the Norfolk Broads produced very low visitor numbers. In conjunction with new pricing strategies, a more defined marketing strategy towards a more formalized programme of educational visits for staff and school children was put together with a target of 6,000 visitors per annum.

The impact of the new strategy saw a significant shift in relationships within revenue centres. Figure 13.1 shows there are clear indications that the new pricing strategy saw a significant improvement in secondary spend, which almost doubled the on-site spend. By implementing micro-marketing and pricing strategies, the enhanced on-site spend will begin to compensate for lower visitor numbers through improvement in visitor spend and value. As the attraction became established, the year-on-year spend made a major contribution to the attraction's revenue.

Since the opening of EcoTech, an emergent pattern between seasonal visitor arrivals and the shop revenue ratios has become established. During peak periods of visitor arrivals, the value of secondary spend falls but remains a relatively stable constant ratio, whereas during the out of season period, the value of visitor spend is almost four times the main season's average. While this phenomena may be part explained by gift shopping and school holiday activities, it is also possible that poorer weather encourages a longer than planned visit to an indoor attraction as a 'change of scene'. Since gross profit margins are typically between 40 to 60 per cent, this revenue centre is making an active contribution to overall revenue management and smoothes the seasonality effect upon income fluctuations.

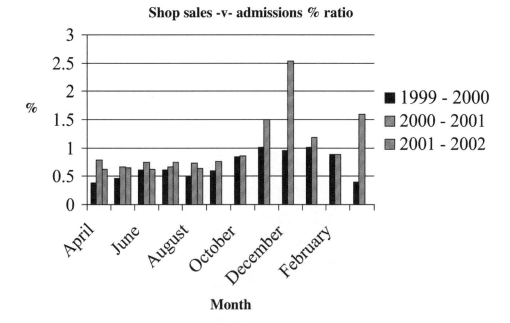

Figure 13.1   New pricing strategy: impact of secondary spend

REVENUE MANAGEMENT CONSTRAINTS

The East of England Tourist Board (2000) estimated there were 4.18 million trips to Norfolk in 1998, and visitors spent £603 million on tourism related services; 4.5 per cent were overseas visitors who spent £54.5 million. In 1998 Norfolk had around half a million visits spread across 69 major visitor attractions (EETB, 2000, and see Figure 13.2). Recent trends indicate many attractions within the region have either remained stable or seen a reduction of between 3 and 7.5 per cent, depending upon year and the type of attraction. These figures broadly follow known national trends (Hanna, 1999; Howell, 2000). Many attractions within the region have a core geographic market representing up to 40 per cent of the visitors, which demonstrates that proximity to major towns influences visitor behaviour and should be factored into marketing and revenue strategies. Consideration must also be given to a number of constraints that impact upon the EcoTech Centre and similar attractions in Norfolk. Empirical evidence suggests that the following factors need to be included within the revenue management system:

1. Timing or planning of visits
2. The size of the ideal market and its capacity
3. Seasonality.

Day-trippers do not pre-plan trips in the same way as other tourists use cognitive decision making models (Chen, 1997; Prideaux and Kininmont, 1999). Recent research from different locations within Norfolk indicate that between 20 to 30 per cent decided

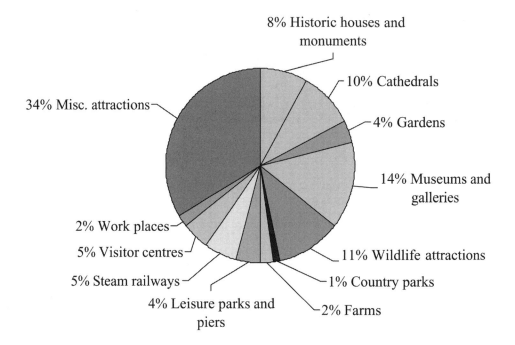

**Market share of Norfolk
visitor attractions 1998**

8% Historic houses and
monuments

10% Cathedrals

4% Gardens

34% Misc. attractions

14% Museums and
galleries

2% Work places

5% Visitor centres

5% Steam railways

11% Wildlife attractions

1% Country parks

4% Leisure parks and
piers

2% Farms

Figure 13.2   Market share of Norfolk visitor attractions 1998, per cent (*Source*: East of England
Tourist Board (2000))

to visit an attraction on the 'spur of the moment' and between 16 to 35 per cent on the
day of visit. Between 15 and 21 per cent would make a decision two days prior to the
visit and between 8 and 25 per cent would plan a visit up to a week before. Less than 23
per cent would make trip plans more than a week ahead. While weather is a significant
element in the planning process, responses across all segments indicated the decision-
making process was subject to an emotional response within the decision group. No
amount of advertising or promotions can fully exploit variance and change influences
within these groups.

   The second constraint is the concept of the 'ideal market' and threshold population
sizes needed to support services (Christaller, 1966). Norfolk has a population of 772,000
and a density of 144 people per square kilometre where 80 per cent of land use is
agriculture. In economic location modelling there is insufficient local population to
support any of the major attractions within the county and therefore relies heavily upon
the 4 million visitors to compensate and enable attractions to reach threshold figures.

While many major Lottery projects have been located within major urban areas within the UK, any expansion in capacity or shortfall in visitor numbers leaves all attractions exposed to a lowering of revenue performance. Clearly, the development plans for the EcoTech Centre will broaden its base as an attraction, but as the capacity within the visitor attractions market increases, the exposure to lower performance remains. This constriction in opportunity for revenue management needs careful consideration prior to reshaping marketing strategies. Empirical evidence also indicates that visitor attractions may be an anomaly within gravity models devised by Ullman (1956). Gravity modelling assumes the larger the function of place or level in service, human behaviour would follow Reilly's Law, i.e., the larger the attraction, the larger the 'pull factor'. Research indicates that local residents within 15 miles of an attraction may not visit it due to a combination of experience or poor perception of the attraction or by what constitutes a 'day out'.

Between 20 and 42 per cent had not visited an attraction adjacent to where they resided and yet between 50 and 70 per cent would travel more than 20 miles to an attraction. Fewer than 15 per cent would travel less than 15 miles to an attraction and this creates a 'doughnut' effect around an attraction. Clearly, visitors do not see a local attraction as a 'day out' and this has major implications in marketing (Kotler *et al.*, 1999) and in revenue management. To regain local resident/visitor confidence in the attraction, highly targeted marketing campaigns with additional concessions will be needed to improve revenue performance from this segment. Capacity management has been identified by Kimes (1989, 1997) and Cross (1997, 1998) as an essential element for revenue management to be effective. Should there be capacity increases within the region's visitor attractions, then revenue must be expected to fall, unless the volume of visitors into the region has increased, as thresholds may not have been reached.

The third constraint is seasonality (Cross, 1998; Wanhill, 1998; Yeoman and Leask, 1999). EETB figures show that 35 per cent of visitors to Norfolk arrive in the period July to September. An additional 26 per cent visit between April to June. However, the statistics do not show that the peak in activity spans only a six to eight week period across July and August, when operational efficiency is at its peak. Yeoman and Leask (1999) suggested seasonality increased the need for revenue maximizing techniques to be implemented to offset low season performance. The implementation of a programme for educational visits and specialist activities, particularly during half term and school holidays, has eased seasonal variance. Revenue figures show these activities have boosted out of seasonal revenue and attracted higher secondary spend (Figure 13.1).

CONCLUSIONS

Revenue management is designed to optimize revenue. Institutional change and less reliance upon public sector or European Union funding will force a greater need for effective revenue management. The EcoTech Centre is severely constrained by the economic thresholds that operate within the ideal market locally. There is insufficient population to support the region's attractions without the seasonal influx of visitors. The 'doughnut effect' which surrounds the attractions has major implications towards revenue management. Marketing and revenue management strategies need to refocus their attention on this segment as local residents within 15 miles of an attraction form the threshold for survival. Add an element of seasonality together with performance in weather and all of the attractions then become very exposed to marginalized revenue performance. Too little attention has been paid at national and regional level in terms of the changes in capacity through Lottery funded projects. The impact is not segment selective and can hit the educational sector as sharply as any other. As the EcoTech Centre matures as a visitor attraction, the plans to build an experimental house together with the business advice centre will become critical to the long-term success of the centre. The behaviour of the micro-market segments is the essence of successful revenue management implementation. Without a continued programme of innovative exhibitions and site development, the EcoTech Centre will fail one of its original objectives, that of experimentation and innovation.

DISCUSSION QUESTIONS

1. Identify and describe factors which might act as constraints upon revenue management at an attraction.
2. Define capacity management and propose what strategies could be adopted to improve revenue management.
3. Analyse market segmentation of attractions and devise a strategy for improving revenue from one major and one niche segment.

APPENDIX 1

EcoTech Discovery Admission Prices 2000 (Centre Only)

Category	£	Percentage change since opening
Adults	4.00	−20
Children (up to 15 years)	3.25	−7.14
Concessions (senior citizens, etc.)	3.50	−17.6
Family tickets		
2 adults + 2 children	11.00	N/A
2 adults + 3 children	11.00	N/A
2 adults + 1 child	9.00	N/A
1 adults + 2 children	9.00	N/A
1 adult + 3 children	9.00	N/A
Grandparents		
2 grandparents + 2 children	8.00	N/A
2 grandparents + 3 children	8.00	N/A

Note: Access to wind turbine an additional £1.90 per adult and £1.30 per child.
Source: The EcoTech Centre

REFERENCES

Ananth, M., DeMicco, F. and Howey, R. (1992) 'Marketplace lodging needs of mature travellers', *Cornell Hotel and Restaurant Administration Quarterly*, **33**(4), 12–24.

Anon (2000) *Marking the close of the second millennium and celebrating the start of the third millennium*. The annual accounts of the Millennium Commission, 1998–1999, The Stationary Office.

Belobaba, P. P. and Wilson, J. L. (1997) 'Impacts of yield management in competitive airline markets', *Journal of Air Transport Management*, **3** (1), 3–10.

Bull, A. (1995) *The Economics of Travel and Tourism*, 2nd edn. Harlow: Longman.

Chen, J. (1997) 'The tourists' cognitive decision making model', *The Tourist Review*, 4, 4–9.

Chernatony, L. de (1993) 'Categorizing brands: evolutionary processes underpinned by two key dimensions', *Journal of Marketing Management*, **9** (2).

Christaller, W. (1966) *Central Places in Southern Germany*, translated C. W. Baskin, Englewood Cliffs, NJ: Prentice-Hall.

Cohen, E. (1979) 'A phenomenology of tourist experiences', *Sociology*, **13**, 179–201.

Cross, R. G. (1997) 'Launching the rocket: how revenue management can work for your business', *Cornell Hotel and Restaurant Administration Quarterly*, April, 32–43.

Cross, R. G. (1998) *Revenue Management*: Orion Business Books.

Crouch, D. I. (1999) 'Encounters with leisure/tourism', in D. I. Crouch (ed.) *Leisure/Tourism Geographies: practices and geographic knowledge*. London: Routledge.

Daudel, S. and Vialle, G. (1994) *Revenue Management: Applications to air transport and other service industries*. Paris: Institut du Transport Aerien.

D'Hauteserre, A. M. (1997) 'Disneyland Paris: a permanent growth pole in the Francilian landscape', *Progress in Tourism and Hospitality Research*, **3**, 17–33.

Donaghy, K. and McMahon-Beattie, U. (1995) 'Managing yield: a marketing perspective', *Journal of Vacation Marketing*, **2**(1), 55–62.

Donaghy, K. McMahon, U. and McDowell, D. (1995) 'Managing yield: an overview', *International Journal Hospitality Management*, **14** (2), 139–50.

East of England Tourist Board (2000) *Facts of Tourism, 1998*. Hadleigh: EETB.

Edgar, D. A. (1997) 'Economic aspects', in I. Yeoman and A. Ingold (eds) *Yield Management: Strategies for the Service Industry*. London: Cassell. pp. 12–28.

Edgar, D. A. (1998) 'Yielding: giants v's minnows, is there a difference?', *Progress in Tourism and Hospitality Research*, **4** (3), 255–65.

Fry, A. (1997) 'Shades of grey', *Marketing*, 24 April, 23–4.

Getz, D. (1993) 'Planning for tourism business districts', *Annals of Tourism Research*, **20**, 583–600.

Hall, C. M. and Page, S. J. (1999) *The Geography of Tourism and Recreation, Environment, Place and Space*. London: Routledge.

Hanna, M. (1999) 'Visitor trends at attractions', *Insights*, ETC, London.

Hendon, W. (1982) *The Economics of Historic Houses: The Sources of Admission Income*. The Historic Houses Project, Akron, Ohio: Centre for Urban Studies, University Akron.

Higgins, B. (1983) 'From growth poles to systems of interactions in space', *Journal of Growth and Change*, **14** (4), 3–13.

Holloway, J. C. and Robinson, P. (1995) *Marketing for Tourism*, 3rd edn. Harlow: Longman.

Hoseason, J. M. (2000) 'Capacity management in the cruise industry', in Ingold, A., McMahon-Beattie, U. and Yeoman, I. (eds) *Yield Management: Strategies for the Service Industry*, 2nd edn. London: Continuum.

Hoseason, J. M. and Johns, N. (1998) 'The numbers game: the role of yield management in the tour operations industry', *Progress in Tourism and Hospitality Research*, **4** (3), 197–206.

Howell, D. (2000) 'The role of leisure and theme parks in the new Millennium', *Insights*, ETC, London.

Ingold, A. and Huyton, J. R. (1997) 'Yield management in the airline industry', in I. Yeoman and

A. Ingold (eds) *Yield Management: Strategies for the Service Industry.* pp. 143–59. London: Cassell.

Johns, N. and Hoseason, J. M. (2001) 'Which way for the visitor heritage attractions?', in S. Drummond and I. Yeoman *Quality Issues in Heritage Visitor Attractions.* Oxford: Butterworth-Heinemann.

Kimes, S. (1989) 'The basics of yield management', *The Cornell HRA Quarterly*, **3** (3), 14–19.

Kimes, S. (1997) 'Yield management: an overview', in I. Yeoman and A. Ingold (eds) *Yield Management: Strategies for the Service Industry*, pp. 3–11. London: Cassell.

Kotler, P., Asplund, C., Rein, I. and Haider, D. H. (1999) *Marketing Places in Europe. How to attract investments, industries, residents and visitors to cities, communities, regions and nations in Europe.* London: *Financial Times*-Prentice Hall.

Larsen, T. D. (1988) 'Revenue management and your passengers,' *ASTA Agency Magazine*, June, 46–8.

Laws, E. (1997) 'Perspectives on pricing decisions in the inclusive holiday industry', in I. Yeoman and A. Ingold (eds) *Yield Management: Strategies for the Service Industry*, pp. 67–82. London: Cassell.

McClarence, S. (2000) 'Look on my works, ye mighty … ?', *Times Weekend*, 20 April.

Middleton, V. T. C. (1996) *Marketing in Travel and Tourism*, 2nd edn. Oxford: Heinemann.

Morgan, N. and Pritchard, A. (2002) 'Contextualizing destination branding', in N. Morgan, et al. (eds) *Destination Branding: Creating the unique destination proposition.* Oxford: Butterworth-Heinemann.

Orkin, E. B. (1988) 'Yield management makes forecasting fact not fiction', *Hotel and Motel Management*, 15 August, 112–18.

Plog, S. C. (1973) *Why Destinations Rise and Fall in Popularity.* Los Angeles: Unpublished manuscript of the Travel Research Association. This has subsequently appeared in the public domain as: Plog, S. C. (1977) *Why Destination Areas Rise and Fall in Popularity in Domestic and International Tourism* E. M. Kelly (ed.). Wellesley, MA: Institute of Certified Travel Agents.

Poon, A. (1993) *Tourism, Technology and Competitive Strategies.* Wallingford: CAB International Press.

Prentice, R. C., Witt, S. F. and Hamer, C. (1998) 'Tourism experience: the case of heritage parks', *Annals of Tourism Research*, **25** (1), 1–24.

Prideaux, B. R. and Kininmont, L. J. (1999) 'Tourism and heritage are not strangers: a study of opportunities for rural heritage museums to maximise tourist visitation', *Journal of Travel Research*, **37**, 299–303.

Rogers, H. A. (1995) 'Pricing practices in tourist attractions: an investigation into how pricing decisions are made in the UK', *Tourism Management*, **16** (3), 21–24.

Schwartz, Z. (1998) 'The confusing side of yield management: myths, errors and misconceptions', *Journal of Hospitality and Tourism Research*, **4**, 413–30.

Sinden, J. A. and Worrell, A. C. (1979) *Unpriced Values.* New York: Wiley.

Smith, B. C., Leimkuhler, J. F. and Darrow, R. M. (1992) 'Yield management at American Airlines', *Interfaces*, **22** (1), 8–31.

Swarbrooke, J. (1999) *The Development and Management of Visitor Attractions*, Oxford: Butterworth-Heinemann.

Tribe, J. (1999) *The Economics of Leisure and Tourism.* London: Butterworth-Heinemann.

Ullman, E. (1956) 'The role of transport and the bases for interaction', in W. L. Thomas (ed.) *Man's Role in Changing the face of the Earth.* University of Chicago Press.

Wanhill, S. (1998) 'Attractions', in C. Cooper et al. (eds) *Tourism: Principles and Practice*, 2nd edn. Harlow: Longman.

Yeomans, I. and Leask, A. (1999) 'Yield management', in Leask, A. and Yeomans, I. (eds) *Heritage Visitor Attractions: An Operations Management Perspective.* London: Cassell.

14

To Trust or Not to Trust:
Variable Pricing and the Consumer

Una McMahon-Beattie, Adrian Palmer and Ian Yeoman

The following complaint was received by www.complaints.com on 5 August 2002:

*RE: Sky Broadcasting – paid too much for Premiership Plus Subscription – unfair pricing. I have been a Sky subscriber from the very beginning, and have always thought their service to be excellent. However, I feel cheated and conned by them. It has, in my opinion, always been their marketing policy to increase their subscription prices as any pay per view event gets closer. BUT NOT THIS TIME. I subscribed paying £50.00 in July 2002, the fee earlier being £40.00. I feel conned because contrary to all previous marketing policies the fee has now been reduced to £40.00! This is not acceptable and Sky's customer services were adamant that despite being a very loyal customer no recompense would be made. I shall consider very carefully whether or not I subscribe [to] Sky's Premiership Plus or any other events as I no longer **TRUST** them.'*

This type of complaint is indicative of the reaction of many customers to the variable pricing practices employed by many service companies. Indeed, one of the key elements in revenue management is the variable pricing. However, the perception of trust and its effect on variable pricing decisions is an undervalued and under-researched area. Therefore, in the following cases, we will examine customer perceptions of pricing and the concept of trust by examining the interactions of revenue, pricing and trust through investigating the ongoing buyer–seller relationship in service industries. We will first investigate the impact of variable pricing on customers through a simulation case of two dining clubs. Then, we will examine the actual reactions to attempts by Amazon.com in September 2000 to implement a differential pricing structure that would track on-line purchasing behaviours in order to charge loyal customers higher prices for the same product. The aim of these cases is to help you understand how variable pricing can severely undermine trust in a service provider and to help you consider how to manage a long-term buyer–seller relationship if you actively engage in variable pricing and revenue management.

WHAT IS TRUST?

Trust is a complex concept that has been seen as a crucial precursor to and outcome of buyer–seller relationship development. Indeed, in the business field there has been an increasing number of studies undertaken into the concept of trust, particularly its role in cooperative behaviour in distribution channels (e.g., Morgan and Hunt, 1994; Chow and Holden, 1997; Garbirino and Johnson, 1999). There is a distinct difference between manifesting trust in a discrete transaction and trust earned over an extended set of encounters or purchases. There are also differences between physical, person to person trust and digital trust as experienced with on-line transactions.

Using the findings of interpersonal research (Larzelere and Huston, 1980), most studies define trust as the extent to which a firm believes that its exchange partner (e.g., organization) is honest and/or benevolent. Trust in a partner's honesty is a person's belief that a partner is reliable, stands by their word, fulfils their promises and role obligations, and is sincere (Anderson and Narus, 1990). Trust in the partner's benevolence is a person's belief that a partner is genuinely interested in one's interest and is motivated to seek joint gains. A benevolent partner subordinates immediate self-interest for long-term group gain (Crosby *et al.*, 1990) and will not take unexpected actions that would have a negative impact on the organization (Anderson and Narus, 1990). In marketing terms, trust is important in channels of distribution, and indeed is a prerequisite to most buyer–seller relations requiring long-term commitments (Larzelere and Huston, 1980).

Three characteristics of trust make it vitally important for further examination of the impact of variable pricing on customers. First, it is risky (Swan and Nolan, 1985; Gambetta, 1988) and therefore has significant implications for customer purchase decisions. To trust someone or indeed something involves a rational decision-making process. It also involves taking a risk. Trust, in other words is not 'blind faith', but can be calculative, and by this very definition, involves risk. Indeed risk and trust are inseparable components in decision-making. Second, you cannot substitute it completely (Shapiro, 1987) making a reliance on trust almost a necessary condition of purchase exchange. Third, where a trusting relationship develops, it represents an intangible value (Granovetter, 1985) which, from a transaction cost economics perspective, may help explain exchange relationships better. Furthermore, research has suggested that whilst traditional aspects of the marketing mix, namely price and reliable delivery, actually make a sale, trust operates as an 'order qualifier', not as an 'order winner' (Doney and Cannon, 1997). As such, trust, like product quality, must be at a satisfactory level for the product or service to even be included in a buyer's consideration set. This has significant implications for revenue managers both in establishing a satisfactory level of trust and in the implementation of strategies that maintain it.

THE IMPACT OF INFORMATION TECHNOLOGY ON TRUST

Information technology is allowing revenue management inventory organizations to set their prices in very much the same way as traditionally practised in eastern bazaars – by individual bargaining and haggling. 'The price list' is not typical of small businesses dealing with small numbers of buyers. It has no part in the business methods of traders in many eastern countries for whom bartering on a one-to-one basis is the norm. Price lists emerged in response to the industrialization of economies and the growth in the size of markets served by individual firms. Price lists became a method of simplifying transactions between a large organization and large numbers of its customers.

Over time, there has been a tendency for societies to fragment in their motivations to make purchases, which has been reflected in companies developing increasingly fine methods of segmenting markets (Kotler *et al.*, 1996). In the move from mass marketing to target marketing, firms subtly developed multiple price lists, based on slightly differentiated product offers aimed at different market segments. Today, the process of market segmentation has proceeded to the point where companies can realistically deal with individual market segments (Peppers and Rogers, 1995). Intriguingly, the conditions for pricing by suppliers of consumer goods and services would appear to be reverting to those that apply in eastern bazaars, in which the seller seeks to apply a price that is uniquely appropriate to each individual buyer. There is plenty of evidence of this move towards unique one-to-one pricing in the Internet-based auction sites which have grown in number during the late 1990s (Wisse, 1999; Palmer and McCole, 1999).

On-line auctions represent an extreme case of one-to-one pricing which is being facilitated by information technology. Much more pervasive is the ability of firms to subtly adjust prices offered to individual customers. Rather than having a fixed price list, an enquirer for a specified product may receive different quotations at different times of enquiry. Similarly, two different enquirers may simultaneously receive different price quotations.

The theory and practice of relationship marketing has been based on an assumption that companies are able and willing to enter a dialogue through which additional value is generated (Gummesson, 1998). A seller may learn more about the needs and motivations of individual customers and develop product offers that are unique in satisfying those needs. In this two-way relationship a seller should be able to assess the value which each individual buyer (or potential buyer) puts on its product, and price its offer uniquely. To an economist, the supplier would seek to appropriate the consumer surplus, which arises as a result of individuals being prepared to pay a price which is higher than a ruling and uniform market price.

There is now considerable evidence of companies who adjust prices according to the unique circumstances of individual buyers. National newspapers for example, typically charge low annual subscriptions to encourage uptake among potential customers, but reduce their discounts as customers show increasing levels of loyalty. Travel related companies have become sophisticated in finely adjusting their prices according to their availability of capacity and the travel motivations of the buyer. However, variable pricing of this nature would appear to undermine a central thesis of the relationship marketing argument, that trust is an essential antecedent of successful long-term buyer–seller relationships (Morgan and Hunt, 1994). It has been noted that trust is a particularly important factor early in a relationship and an essential precondition for the relationship to move to more committed stages of development (Grayson and Ambler, 1999). As such it could be argued that trust may be undermined where a buyer of consumer goods or services perceives that the price that they are being offered for a specified product is less equitable than a similar bundle of benefits offered to another buyer, or offered to that customer on a different occasion.

Traditional haggling over prices in open markets was visible for all to see. With many modern (and particularly on-line) IT-based systems of individual pricing, the results are less visible and can typically only be compared indirectly. The lack of openness in pricing creates conditions for mistrust. Indeed, several recent pricing studies suggest that consumers' reactions to a price change depend not just on the magnitude and direction of the change, but on buyers' perceptions of the seller's circumstances and motivations that led to it (Bobinski *et al.*, 1996). For example, Kahneman *et al.* (1986) have examined how consumers' perceptions of the 'fairness' of price increases were influenced by the circumstances that led to them. They found that buyers typically perceive a given price increase as 'fair' if it is a reaction to an increase in seller costs, but as unfair if it is a reaction to increased consumer demand. This has obvious direct implications for revenue management pricing systems. Similarly, Lichtenstein, *et al.* (1989) examined how consumers' attributions regarding a retailer's motives for discounting a product influenced their attitudes toward the deal. They found, for example, that consumers had more negative attitudes toward the deal when they attributed it to the retailer's desire to unload a difficult-to-sell offering.

Customer perception is therefore important, especially in relation to the use of IT, since there is a greater opportunity to offer price differentials to consumers on a one-to-one basis. Trust and mistrust are at bipolar opposites (Pearce, 1974), and consumers who perceive that suppliers are untrustworthy through various pricing differentials consider them to be practising malfeasance, and not having their best interests at heart. Therefore, consumers risk that the price they pay at a particular moment in time is the best price that they will get.

TRUST AND EQUITY

Trust is at the heart of relationship marketing and revenue management. It is a fundamental element in a successful long-term relationship with our customers. It is also reasonable to assume that trust is related to equity. Can a buyer trust a seller when there is a suspicion that the seller is providing a lower price to other buyers for an identical bundle of benefits? Likewise, if a new customer is targeted and is rewarded with low prices, what does this say about loyal customers' trust in the supplier? Should it encourage individual buyers to disloyalty? These are the types of questions that you will consider in the following cases.

DINING CLUBS CASE

In order to test the effect of variable pricing on consumer trust, the authors set up a simulation involving two hypothetical dining clubs. A dining club, as defined here, offered discounts at a selection of restaurants. Each dining club offered facilities for club 'members' to obtain membership prices at a selection of five local restaurants. The restaurants themselves were real and were known by respondents. The management of the restaurants was aware of the simulation exercise. The two dining clubs differed only in respect of the pattern of discounting employed – the average price charged was similar for the two clubs. Restaurants were chosen as the product in question since they were typical of products with a cost structure which typically allows for wide variability in prices; as a product they should be fairly low in involvement; and most consumers should be reasonably familiar with prices of the type of product. As a simulation approach was adopted, no transactions were actually completed. However, the ability to vary prices was considered to be typical of what currently happens in large organizations.

The members were presented with a series of flyers relating to offers at the various restaurants. The price of the offers varied over the period of the simulation. In addition, members of each dining club were divided into two communication groups. One group received communication by means of a printed flyer; the other group received messages by email. They understood that this was a simulation exercise and were encouraged to participate by the offer of a number of prizes of free meals. The sample comprised 104 respondents who were self-selecting. Their demographic characteristics were felt to be representative of diners in general.

The dining clubs were positioned as offering a discount to the normal prices charged by the sample of restaurants. The mean discount was pitched at 10 per cent below normal prices. However, the dining clubs differed in their variation of prices around this mean.

- Dining Club A1: The same discounted prices were offered at all times. A weekly newsletter by email reminded customers of the offer.
- Dining Club A2: As dining club A1, but communication was by printed flyer.
- Dining Club B1: Some deep discounts were offered. At other times the price was higher than what would have been obtainable by dealing directly with the restaurant. A weekly newsletter by email gave special offers.
- Dining Club B2: As dining club B1, but communication was by printed flyer.

Each dining club was given a distinctive name to improve memorability. The series of messages was communicated to potential and actual customers of the product and were differentiated only by price. Six messages were sent to members over a period of six weeks. Trust by respondents in each product was measured at the conclusion of the simulation. The dining clubs were 'new' to respondents, so it was assumed that trust at the outset was equal for the two clubs.

How was Trust Measured?

Trust was measured using a multiple item scale based on those developed by Butler (1991). This has been tested for validation and standardisation in many studies (e.g., Chow and Holden, 1997). Butler identified ten conditions of trust: (1) availability, (2) competence, (3) consistency, (4) discreteness, (5) fairness, (6) integrity, (7) loyalty, (8) openness, (9) promise fulfilment, and (10) receptivity. Butler also developed an eleventh scale, 'overall trust', which tests the relationships between the conditions and overall trust in an individual. Butler's scales were adapted for this simulation on the basis of the inputs of focus groups. Basic demographic and behavioural variables were also recorded and analysed.

Outcomes

The trust survey achieved a response rate of 47 per cent, with 43.8 per cent of these having received communications by means of a printed flyer and 56.2 per cent by email. Notably, results recorded on the scales measuring the conditions of 'overall trust', 'integrity' and 'loyalty' indicated that the respondents' level of trust was lower in the club offering variable discounts. For example, the recorded responses to one of the statements measuring *overall trust* ('This company is basically honest') effectively highlighted the lower level of overall trust in the club offering variable discounts. Fifty-five per cent of respondents agreed with this statement in relation to the club offering a steady 10 per cent discount, while only 39 per cent of respondents agreed with it in relation to the variable discount club. Similarly, lower levels of trust were recorded in the club offering a variation of prices in responses to a statement regarding the 'integrity' of the two dining clubs ('This club would not make false claims to me about any offer'). The uniform discount club recorded 47 per cent of respondents in agreement with this statement whilst the variable discount club only registered 39 per cent in agreement. As such it may be assumed that respondents tended to be less trusting of the variable pricing club. With regard to the medium of communication, the use of email appeared to lower the proportion of respondents who would join the club offering a uniform discount but increased slightly the proportion of those wanting to join the variable discount club.

There are strong theoretical reasons for supposing that a consumer's trust in an organization may be undermined where there is a perception that they might not have obtained the best deal available from the supplier. This basic simulation has provided some evidence of this effect. Despite the advantages of the longitudinal simulation approach adopted in this simulation, its limitation should be recognized, especially the absence of a significant level of risk on the part of participants. Nor could the simulation develop trust on the basis of tangible property qualities since there were no actual interaction with the service on which trust could be based. However, it did allow trust to focus on messages, how these were manipulated and how they affected customers' perceptions of trust in a service provider.

AMAZON.COM: VARIABLE PRICING IN PRACTICE

In September 2000, Amazon.com attempted to implement a differential pricing structure that would track on-line purchasing behaviours to charge loyal customer higher prices for DVDs. Consumers were quick to discover the price differences and complaints followed. Amazon customers on DVDTalk.com, an on-line forum, reported that certain DVDs had three different prices, depending on the so-called cookie a customer received from Amazon (Wolverton, 2000). Cookies are small files that web sites transfer to customers' hard drives through the browsers they use. These files allow sites to recognize customers and track their purchase patterns. Depending on previous purchases a DVD such as *Men in Black* could cost $33.97, $27.97 or $25.97. The list price was $39.95. Streitfeld (2000) also cites the example of one customer who ordered the DVD of Julie Taymour's *Titus* paying $24.49. The next week he went back to Amazon and saw the price had jumped to $26.24. As an experiment, he stripped his computer of the electronic tags that identified him to Amazon as a regular customer and the price fell to $22.74. One angry poster on DVDTalk.com stated, 'Amazon apparently offers good discounts to new users, then once they get the person hooked and coming back to their site again and again, they play with the prices to make more money' (cited in Bicknell, 2000). Loyal, repeat customers were particularly incensed. One such customer on DVDTalk.com stated:

> *This is a very strange business model, to charge customers more when they buy or come back to the site more. I have no problem with coupons for first-time customers as marketing enticements, but I thought the idea was to attract first and then work hard to keep them. This is definitely not going to earn customer loyalty.* (Cited in Streitfeld, 2000)

Amazon.com quickly issued reports claiming that it had been presenting different prices to different customers but denied that it had done so on the basis of any past purchasing behaviour at Amazon. As spokesman Bill Curry stated:

> *It was done to determine consumer responses to different discount levels. This was a pure and simple price test. This is not dynamic pricing. We don't do that and have no plans ever to do that.* (Cited in Streitfeld, 2000)

However an Amazon customer service representative claimed in an email to a DVDTalk member that the company had been engaged in a dynamic price test:

> *I would like to send along my most sincere apology for any confusion or frustration caused by our dynamic price test. Dynamic testing of a customer base is a common practice among both brick and mortar and Internet companies.* (Cited in Streitfeld, 2002)

Amazon.com quickly cancelled its differential pricing and refunded the difference to customers who had paid the higher prices (Adamy, 2000).

We are well aware that Amazon's experience with different prices is not new. Airlines, hotels, car rental companies and cruise lines have been charging different prices for the same service for years. Even physical retail outlets charge customers different prices for the same product depending on the store's location and the time of year (Cox, 2001). The problem with on-line variable pricing is that the customer is an unwilling participant. As Streitfeld (2002), a *Washington Post* staff writer, points out:

> *... traditional methods used to calculate prices are sledgehammers compared with the Internet's scalpel. For one thing, the Web provides a continuous feedback loop: The more the consumer buys from a Web site, the more the site knows about him and the weaker his bargaining position is. It's as if the corner drugstore could see you coming down the sidewalk, clutching your fevered brow, and then double the price of aspirin.*

Adverse customer reaction resulted in a speedy end to Amazon's experiment with differential pricing. Customers were disillusioned by the company's attempts to 'punish' loyal consumers. As John Dziak, a Los Angeles-based actor, summarized it, 'you trust a company, then you hear they're doing this kind of stuff, your trust wavers and you go somewhere else.' (cited in Wolverton, 2000). Trust is an essential component of long-term buyer–seller relationships and is one of a company's biggest assets. Yet, the paradox is emerging that one-to-one pricing on the Internet may severely undermine trust in a service provider.

DISCUSSION QUESTIONS

1. Why is the maintenance of trust particularly important with on-line transactions where the price charged to the consumer by a particular company may vary considerably overtime?
2. What strategies would you advise a revenue manager to adopt in order to maintain consumer trust whilst employing differential pricing?
3. How would you avoid the appearance of punishing regular, loyal customers with higher prices?

REFERENCES

Adamy, J. (2000) 'E-tailer price tailoring may be a wave of the future', *Chicago Tribune*, Section 4, 25 September, 4.

Anderson, J. C. and Narus, J. A.(1990) 'A model of distributor firm and manufacturing firm working partnerships', *Journal of Marketing*, **54**, January, 42–58.

Bicknell, C. (2000) 'Online prices not created equal', *Wired News*, available from http://wired.com/news/business/0,1367,38622,00.html. Accessed on 7 November 2002.

Bobinski, G., Cox, D. and Cox, A. (1996) 'Retail sale advertising, perceived retail credibility and price rationale', *Journal of Retailing*, **72**(3), 291–306.

Butler, J. K. (1991), 'Toward understanding and measuring conditions of trust: evolution of a conditions of trust inventory', *Journal of Management*, **17**(3), 643–63

Chow, S. and Holden, R. (1997) 'Toward an understanding of loyalty: the moderating role of trust', *Journal of Managerial Studies,* **9**(3), 275–98

Cox, J. L. (2001) 'Can differential prices be fair?', *Journal of Product and Brand Management*, **10**(5), 264–75.

Crosby, L. A., Evans, K. R. and Cowles, D. (1990) 'Relationship quality in services selling: an interpersonal influence perspective', *Journal of Marketing*, **54**, July, 68–81.

Doney, P. M. and Cannon, J. P. (1997) 'An examination of the nature of trust in buyer-seller relationships', *Journal of Marketing*, **61**, 35–51.

Gabirino, E. and Johnson, M. (1999) 'The different roles of satisfaction, trust, and commitment in customer relationships', *Journal of Marketing*, **63**, 70–87.

Gambetta, D. (1988) *Trust: Making and Breaking Co-operative Relations.* New York: Basil Blackwell.

Granovetter, M. (1985) 'Economic action and social structure: the problem of embeddedness', *American Journal of Sociology*, **91**, 481–510.

Grayson, K. and Ambler, T. (1999) 'The dark side of long-term relationships in marketing services', *Journal of Marketing Research*, **36**(1), 132.

Gummesson, E. (1998) 'Implementation requires a relationship marketing paradigm', *Academy of Marketing Science*, **26**(3), 242–9.

Kahneman, D., Knetsch, J. and Thaler, R. (1986) 'Fairness as a constraint on profit seeking: entitlements in the market', *The American Economic Review*, **76**, September, 728–41.

Kotler, P., Makens, J. and Bowens, J. (1996) '*Marketing for Hospitality and Tourism.* New Jersey: Prentice-Hall.

Larzelere, R. E. and Huston, T. L. (1980) 'The Dyadic Trust Scale: towards understanding interpersonal trust in close relationships', *Journal of Marriage and the Family,* **42**(3), 595–604.

Lichtenstein, D., Burton, S. and O'Hara, B. S. (1989). 'Marketplace attributions and consumer evaluations of discount claims', *Psychology and Marketing*, **6**, Fall, 163–80.

Morgan, R. M. and Hunt, S. D. (1994), 'The commitment-trust theory of relationship marketing' *Journal of Marketing*, **58**, July, 20–38.

Palmer, A. and McCole, P. (1999) 'The virtual re-intermediation of travel services: a conceptual framework and empirical investigation', *Journal of Vacation Marketing*, **6**(1), 33–47.

Pearce, W. B. (1974) 'Trust and interpersonal communication', *Speech Monographs*, **41**, 236–44.

Peppers, D. and Rogers, M. (1995) 'A new paradigm: share of customer, not market share', *Planning Review*, **5**(3), 48–51.

Shapiro, S. P. (1987) 'The social control of impersonal trust', *American Journal of Sociology*, **93**, 623–58.

Streitfeld, D. (2000) 'On the Web, price tags blur, *Washington Post*, **27** September, A01.

Swan, J. E. and Jones Nolan, J. (1985) 'Gaining customer trust: a conceptual guide for the salesperson', *Journal of Personal Selling and Sales Management*, **5**, 39–48.

Wisse, B. (1999) 'The Internet – The Future of Travel Distribution'. Key Note Speaker at the 1999 European Travel and Tourism Research Association Conference, Dublin, Ireland. http://www.trc.dit.ie/priceline.ppt

Wolverton, T. (2000) 'Some Amazon.com customers are fuming over random discounts on some of the e-tailer's most popular DVD's', News.Com, available at http://news.com.com/2100–1017–245326.html?tag = rn. Accessed on 7 November 2002.

www.complaints.com Complaints of the Day e-Message for 6 August, 2002. Available at http://www.complaints.com/august2002/complaintoftheday.august6.3.htm. Accessed on 3 October 2002.

15

Cases in Legal Aspects

Michael Boella and Thriné Hely

This chapter focuses on the principal legal issues with consequences for revenue management in the hospitality and tourism industries. It contains five case studies. The first is a simple hotel situation which illustrates the legal constraints placed upon hotels wishing to practise capacity management. The second relates to restaurants. The last three look at three examples of problems encountered in the air transport industry.

The cases are based on English law, some of which now derives from European Union law. In addition some of the principles are informed by international treaties so there may be similarities in other jurisdictions. On the other hand, in some jurisdictions, particularly in emerging economies, there may be little or no such legislation.

GENERAL LEARNING OUTCOMES

As a result of working on these case studies readers should have an awareness of the importance of the legal issues affecting revenue management through a knowledge and understanding of the general legal principles concerning revenue management in the tourism and hospitality industries. This includes the law of contract, key legislation and legal measures adopted by operators designed to mitigate their legal liabilities.

The chapter is intended to equip general managers with a knowledge of the scope of the law and related regulatory processes – it is not intended for lawyers or aspiring lawyers whose knowledge necessarily will need to be much greater. Nor should this replace seeking professional legal advice in situations where legal issues of consequence are concerned.

Of course many of the principles may apply right across the sectors illustrated here and even across other sectors of the hospitality, tourism and travel industries so these should be seen as examples rather than a comprehensive treatment of the legal issues to be confronted.

Much of the law concerning capacity management revolves around the law of contract, trade description and misrepresentation. The following cases, together with a variety of scenarios, are designed to address the principal legal issues, conventions and non-statutory schemes which have a bearing on revenue management. These should be read in conjunction with the chapter 'Legal Aspects' in *Yield Management – Strategies for the Service Industries* (Ingold *et al.*, 2000).

Background to Revenue Management in Practice

In order that hotels, carriers and other similar types of business can maximize occupancy, load factors, profits and maybe also to be able to offer lower prices to customers, many argue that overbooking is an essential part of normal business practice. It has been a part of many sectors of the tourist and hospitality industries for so long that few people within these industries question the ethical basis of revenue management. It is argued that when conducted properly, i.e., based on sound knowledge of business patterns, it should not result often in having dissatisfied customers. However there are occasions when the statistical forecasting necessary to underpin an effective capacity management system will not run 'true to form' and more customers will show than predicted.

In such cases the business has to consider its courses of action, firstly to maintain the customer's goodwill and secondly to avoid the risk of legal action. It is argued that where a customer is 'booked out', 'walked' or 'bumped', so long as what the customer gets (e.g., accommodation) is equal to or better than that originally booked the customer will not have grounds for legal action because the contract has been performed. On the other hand, dependent upon the precise nature of the contract, the business may be in breach of contract, at the least. At worst, it may also have breached criminal law.

In the European Union passengers with a valid ticket for a scheduled flight, which they cannot board because it is full, are entitled to a full refund or to a seat on the next available flight. In addition, the airline must also offer immediate cash compensation of 150 ECUs for flights up to 3500 kilometres and 300 ECUs for flights over 3500 kilometres. This compensation is halved if the airline can get the passenger to the final destination within two hours for flights under 3500 kilometres and four hours for flights over that. Passengers are also entitled to a free telephone call, meals and accommodation, if needed (EU Regulation, 295/91).

What the business therefore needs to do is to set out to persuade the customers concerned to modify the contract. In law effectively, this means that a new contract has to be negotiated. Airlines may do this by 'buying off' or compensating the 'bumped' passengers with offers of cash, hotel accommodation or additional tickets for future occasions. Hotels likewise have various practices including finding alternative accommodation and providing transport, paying for telephone calls, offering upgraded or complimentary rooms on subsequent visits.

From a practical point of view the first question to answer is who is it best to 'book-out'? The question of how to choose a particular customer or customers to be booked out should depend both upon future long-term goodwill issues as well as legal issues. From a legal point of view the hotel staff should look firstly for sound legal reasons for their choice. If a customer was asked to confirm by letter or fax and has not done so that may provide a sound reason. If a customer arrives after room release time that provides another reason. On the other hand, where customers have been very specific about their requirements, e.g., type and position of room, it is unwise to book them out as there may be difficulty in matching precisely their specific requests. Where a number of customers have booked in together it may be unwise to split them as a major part of their purpose may be to meet regularly and easily in the particular hotel.

Where an hotelier fails to provide accommodation contracted for the customer may treat the contract as at an end. The customer may book into another hotel of similar standard and sue the first hotel for the costs of the second hotel. If there is available only a hotel of higher standard the customer could sue for the higher cost.

On the other hand, in many cases, it can be the business that suffers, losing revenue because customers do not show up. In some cases, such as airlines, such eventualities are provided for, e.g., by offering restricted tickets (use or lose tickets), whereas restaurants may lose out if customers who have reserved tables fail to arrive.

CASE STUDY 1: BEE'S HOTEL

Bee's Hotel is a city centre hotel adjacent to the town's concert hall, cinemas, art galleries and cinemas. The hotel enjoys a very good weekend trade, with normally a full house on Friday and Saturday nights.

Around Friday mid-day three business people come in and ask for three rooms for that evening, bed and breakfast only. The hotel has the rooms available but knows that on previous history it will sell out by 6.30 p.m. to people wanting rooms, dinner and breakfast for both Friday and Saturday night. The receptionist refuses the request for the three rooms saying that they are fully booked.

One of the customers, suspecting that the hotel does in fact have rooms, later phones the hotel to check if they really are full and discovers that rooms are available but only for the two nights, i.e., Friday and Saturday.

QUESTIONS

1. What is the hotel's legal position?
2. Was it within its right to refuse the rooms?
3. What are the rights of the three travellers?
4. What measures, if any, can they take against the hotel?

CASE STUDY 2: MIKE BEE'S RESTAURANT

Mike Bee's Restaurant is a busy town centre restaurant which is particularly busy on Friday and Saturday nights. The restaurant has experienced a number of problems recently which has caused lost revenue. They open for service at 7.30 p.m. and close the door at 9.30 p.m., expecting to finish service around 11.30 p.m. The restaurant always asked for a telephone number when accepting a booking. As a policy they have only one sitting, although if early diners leave before 9.30 they will resell the table.

Mr Smith phones the restaurant and asks for a table and a special menu for ten people for 9.00 on a Friday evening, to celebrate an anniversary. The price quoted for the meal is £25.00 per person, excluding wines etc. The restaurant confirms the reservation, explaining that 9.30 p.m. is when they close. The restaurant prepares a special table for ten people, as requested, and does not use the tables for earlier diners for fear that the table will not be free when Mr Smith's party arrives.

Scenario 1

That evening Mr Smith arrives apologizing that their party is now only six people. They have the set menu as agreed.

Scenario 2

At 7 p.m. Mr Smith phones to say that two of the party are sick and that he is having to cancel the party.

Scenario 3

Mr Smith's party never arrives.

QUESTION

In each case what legal rights does Mike Bee's Restaurant have?

CASE STUDY 3: MISSED FLIGHTS

This case study contains three different scenarios concerning a missed flight.

Mrs B booked a flight from Gatwick to Montpellier in France. She received tickets sent through the post and on the day went directly to Zone F in the North Terminal of Gatwick airport. She missed the flight and one hour later flew with the same airline to Toulouse instead.

Mr B, in the meantime, already in France was driving from Lyon to meet Mrs B at Montpellier at 6 p.m., the expected time of arrival. He went to Montpellier and after all passengers had disembarked he asked at the airline desk where was Mrs B. He was told after some time that she had boarded the Toulouse flight and should have arrived at 7 p.m.

Mr B then drove for two and half hours on motorways (approximately £15 charges) to collect Mrs B at around 9.30 p.m. They were too tired to drive on to their destination so they booked into a Novotel. This cost around £60.

Scenario 1

Mrs B, who held a fully-flexible ticket, arrived at Zone F two hours before departure. However she was not an experienced traveller and thought the queue would move sufficiently quickly for her to check in on time. However with only a quarter of an hour to go she realized that things were getting late so she approached a member of the airline company, only to be told that boarding had closed for the flight. The airline staff had not 'combed' the queue.

Mrs B was told that it was her fault that she missed the flight, but as she held a fully flexible ticket the company transferred her to the Toulouse flight an hour later.

QUESTIONS

1. Who was responsible for Mrs B missing her flight to Montpellier?
2. If the fault was the airline's, what compensation was Mrs B entitled to?
3. Was the airline responsible for additional costs incurred by Mr B in having to drive from Montpellier to Toulouse?

Scenario 2

Mrs B, because of traffic problems around the airport, arrived at Zone F only half an hour before departure. Mrs B had a restricted ticket (i.e., it could only be used for that specific flight and no other). Mrs B was told that she had arrived too late and that it was her fault in missing the flight.

QUESTION

Who was responsible for Mrs B missing her flight?

Scenario 3

The airline had overbooked. At the check-in desk the agent asked all those who were waiting to check in for volunteers to be booked onto the Toulouse flight leaving one hour later. There were insufficient volunteers so as Mrs B was travelling alone she was amongst a further group of passengers who were 'denied boarding' on the Montpellier flight. She was rebooked on the Toulouse flight and offered the statutory compensation. She was offered a free telephone call but as Mr B had already left for Montpellier she was unable to inform him of her revised travel arrangements.

QUESTIONS

1. Who was responsible for Mrs B missing her flight to Montpellier?
2. If the fault was the airline's, what compensation was Mrs B entitled to?

CASE STUDY 4: THE JONES FAMILY

The Jones family were excited. They were due to go on holiday to Palma in five weeks time – a two week break that they had been planning for the last eighteen months. Dad had made the booking in January to ensure that they returned to the hotel they had stayed in three years ago. Money was tight but they had paid extra and booked with AB Travel and Tours to ensure that they got a flight time that suited them, living as they do a two hour drive from Gatwick Airport they did not wish to leave too early in the morning as it would have meant either leaving home well before dawn or staying in a hotel adjacent to the airport overnight prior to their flight. As it was, they had booked a flight that departed at mid-day and therefore would arrive in Palma in the afternoon with plenty of time to get settled before they put the children to bed.

However, AB Travel and Tours had decided to collapse two flights into one. They normally had two flights to Palma on a Saturday and had made the decision to 'collapse' one of the flights and move the passengers over to the other flight. The two flights were operated on different size aircraft and it was the larger of the two, the 7 a.m. departure, that best suited their needs for this consolidation, which was why the passengers' departure from Gatwick had been moved forward by five hours. This did not constitute a major change within the contract terms and the notification was within the notice period allowed under the small print in their brochure.

On the Wednesday the Jones received the notification that was to change their plans and cost them more money. AB Travel and Tours wrote to inform them that their flight departure time had been changed to 7 a.m., necessitating a 5 a.m. check-in. What they had originally planned to ensure a later departure had now been changed for them, with seemingly no come-back from the tour operator.

AB Travel and Tours gave no explanation as to why they had changed the flight timings, and offered nothing in the way of compensation. Instead it was a 'take it or leave it' situation with the sure knowledge that if they wished to change their booking in any way they would be subjected to extra costs.

Mr Jones rang the help desk at AB Travel and Tours and spoke to Stephanie, who was pleasant and as helpful on the phone as she could be, listening patiently while he explained the situation. Unfortunately Stephanie was unable to help. AB Travel and Tours had cancelled the original flight and transferred all the passengers over to the earlier departure. There seemed to be no way out for the Jones family – they were going to have to pay for overnight accommodation or cancel their holiday and lose a portion of their money.

QUESTION

What rights did the Jones family have and were AB Travel and Tours within their rights to do what they had done?

CASE STUDY 5: FRED SMITH

Fred Smith settled down in his seat on the flight from Heathrow to Toronto. He had carefully loaded his cabin baggage in the overhead rack, taking care to remove everything that he wanted on the flight beforehand. He had the window seat and knew the flight was full, and he did not wish to disturb the person who would be sitting in the seat beside him.

Fred had planned this trip for some time, and had undertaken extensive research before making his booking to ensure that he got the best possible price. He was visiting his sister who lived outside Toronto, and while he could have got a slightly cheaper flight on a charter he wanted a daylight crossing both ways and the only way he could guarantee that was with a schedule service, so he had paid extra. He had also been unlucky that having found a competitive fare he had taken too long to make up his mind on his dates of travel and by the time he went back to the airline to make the booking he had found that the cheaper seats were now sold out and he had to pay slightly more. It was only a matter of £40 but he was cross that he had not taken advantage of the cheaper fare when he had first found it. As it was his ticket was restricted, and while he could change his return date of travel for an additional payment of £100 he had had to pay immediately the full price of the ticket on confirming the booking, which had meant that the airline had taken his money six months before he travelled.

Fred's travelling companion struggled up the aisle with a huge amount of cabin baggage, and proceeded to force it into the overhead locker. Fred groaned inwardly and immediately formed the impression that this man was not going to be the easiest of travelling companions. When he had finally put the baggage into the locker he then realized that his reading material and glasses were still in his bag and he had to return to the locker to retrieve them. He eventually settled into his seat and extended a hand to Fred: 'My name is Joe,' he said in a London accent, and embarked on a lengthy explanation as to why he was so late on board with such a lot of luggage. He had apparently been travelling in Europe prior to this trip and had booked his seat just over three weeks before, on a whim from a bar in Madrid. He had paid on his credit card and had asked to pick up his ticket at the airport. The queue had been lengthy and he had had to wait for nearly forty minutes before he had reached the head of the queue. It had then been another lengthy wait in line for the check-in desk and he had just made the flight with a quick stop in duty free on his way through departures.

He then went on to describe his luck at getting a cheap flight with a schedule airline just three weeks before departure, 'otherwise I would not have been able to afford the trip'. Fred was incensed. Not only was he going to have to put up with this youngster chatting to him all the way across the North Atlantic, but to add insult to injury, he had to endure it knowing that his travelling companion had paid less for his ticket and had booked it just three weeks ago.

QUESTION

Did Fred have any legal rights to a reduction in price?

REFERENCES

Ingold, A., McMahon-Beattie, U. and Yeoman, I. (eds) *Yield Management – Strategies for the Service Industries*. London: Continuum.

Further Reading

Boella, M. J. and Pannett, A. (1999) *Principles of Hospitality Law*, 4th edn. London: Continuum.
Cournoyer, G. N., Marshall, G. A. and Morris, K. L. (1999) *Hotel, Restaurant and Travel Law*, 5th edn. New York: Delmar, Albany.
Downes, J. and Paton, T. (2002) *Travel Agency Law*. London: Pitman Publishing.
Grant, D. and Mason, S. (2003) *Holiday Law*, 3rd edn. London: Sweet and Maxwell.
Jefferies, J. P. (1995) *Understanding Hospitality Law*, 3rd edn. East Lancing, Michigan: American Hotel and Motel Association.

16

Understanding the Bid Price Approach to Revenue Management: A Case of the Revenue Inn

Dietrich Chen and Michael Freimer

INTRODUCTION

In the hotel context, the basic question addressed by revenue management is, 'Which room rates should we make available to which customers in order to maximize revenue?' Hotels employ a variety of controls in order to maximize revenue; these are typically restrictions on available rate classes or lengths of stay. In this chapter we focus on a very common approach, referred to as the bid price method. Our purpose is to describe in simple terms a technique that underlies many sophisticated revenue management systems. We will examine the analytical tools involved and extract the key model parameters and managerial decisions.

The idea of a rate class control is straightforward. The hotel has an ascending scale of rate classes, separated by *rate fences*, or restrictions that make a particular rate available to one segment of customers but not to another. (For example, a particular rate might only be available to automobile club members.) Based on forecasted demand, the revenue management system declares that for a given day, certain rate classes are open and others are closed. If a guest calls the property and wants to arrive on that day, the reservations agent is directed to quote only those rate classes that are designated as open.

The length-of-stay control is a simple extension of this idea; customers are further segmented by the number of days they wish to stay at the property. Now the revenue management system decides which *combinations* of rate class and length-of-stay to declare open. For example, a guest wanting to spend three nights might be quoted a rate of $99, while another guest, arriving on the same date but wanting to stay only one night, may be offered a higher rate.

The bid price approach provides a simple method for determining which rate class/

length-of-stay combinations are open. For each day of the planning horizon, the revenue management system computes a control price, referred to as a *bid price*. We interpret the bid price for a given date as the marginal revenue the hotel would receive if it were to increase its capacity on that date by one room. The calculation is, of course, based on the forecast of demand for that date.

For one-night-stays, the rate classes above the bid price are declared open; those below the bid price are closed. If the hotel is not forecasted to sell out, the bid price is zero since increasing the capacity will not increase the revenue. In this case all rate classes are open; when the hotel is not forecasted to sell out, it should sell any room it can. When the forecast of demand exceeds capacity, the bid price will be greater than zero, and some of the lower rate classes may be closed. For multiple-night-stays, a typical approach is to average the bid prices for the dates involved. Rate classes above the averaged bid price are open, and others are closed.

It is apparent that the bid price approach relies heavily on the forecast of future demand. (This is, of course, true for other revenue management techniques as well.) The forecast must be of *arrivals*, as opposed to occupied rooms, and must be segmented by rate class and length-of-stay. For a large business hotel, this may involve thousands of combinations. In this case, similar rate classes may be aggregated into a smaller number of *rate buckets*, and the revenue management system will declare certain buckets to be open or closed.

Furthermore we require an *unconstrained* demand forecast. We want to forecast the number of customers who would like to arrive on a given date, without considering the limit imposed by the capacity of the hotel. For a discussion of forecasting techniques used by the hotel industry, see Kimes and Weatherford (1999).

In addition, we assume that the pricing structure is predetermined and static. Consequently, dynamic changes in pricing due to competitive reasons for example, are not considered. Differing pricing structures for the same room type often occur in a competitive environment in order to seize market share. The effect of competitor action in a revenue management environment is difficult to assess and has not been studied in depth so far. For a discussion of revenue management in a competitive environment, refer to Chen (2000).

OBJECTIVES

The objectives of this chapter are the following:

- Appreciate the complexity of determining revenue-maximizing inventory control mechanisms for hotels.
- Understand a common mathematical technique that underlies many modern revenue management systems.
- Illustrate how to extend the basic model to incorporate other features such as overbooking, group reservations, and multiple properties.
- Point out limitations and difficulties of any technical solution methodology and of the bid price method in particular.

THE REVENUE MANAGEMENT MODEL

In order to illustrate the bid price approach, we refer to a fictitious property called the Revenue Inn. Suppose our property has ten rooms, and offers a corporate rate of $129 and a leisure rate of $99. Further assume that hotel guests do not stay more than three days, and the hotel revenue manager's planning horizon is one week. We restrict the number of rooms and rate classes at the Revenue Inn in order to keep the description of the problem manageable; however, the essential nature of the revenue management problem described here is the same as that faced by actual properties.

Suppose the Revenue Inn's manager has generated a demand forecast for the coming week. This forecast is summarized in Tables 16.1 and 16.2. We use the following notation when referring to the forecast: $d_{i,j,1}$ denotes the forecast of corporate demand for guests arriving on day i and leaving on day j, and $d_{i,j,2}$ denotes the forecast of leisure demand for guests arriving on day i and leaving on day j. We refer to the first day of the planning period as day 1, so i can vary from 1 to 6, and j can vary from 2 to 7.

Table 16.1 Forecast of corporate demand

				Departure date, j			
	$d_{i,j,1}$	2	3	4	5	6	7
	1	1	2	3			
	2		2	4	1		
	3			2	3	1	
Arrival date, i	4				1	1	1
	5					1	1
	6						1

Table 16.2 Forecast of leisure demand

				Departure date, j			
	$d_{i,j,1}$	2	3	4	5	6	7
	1	1	2	3			
	2		1	1	1		
	3			1	1	1	
Arrival date, i	4				1	4	5
	5					4	6
	6						5

Once again, the forecast reflects the unconstrained demand for each rate class and length-of-stay combination. This is the number of customers who wish to arrive on a particular date, for a given number of days, at a given rate class. The decision faced by the revenue manager is how many customers of each type to accept. We cast this problem as a *linear programme*.

The term *linear programming* refers to a set of mathematical tools used for making resource allocation decisions. The word 'programme' refers to the idea that we will develop a plan, or programme, for a course of action. The word 'linear' reflects the fact that the equations involved in the problem formulation each take the form of a straight line. It is useful to write the problem as a linear programme since there are powerful techniques available for solving very large-scale linear programming problems, involving hundreds of thousands of variables. Many of these tools were first developed by the US military during the Second World War. For an introduction to linear programming, refer to Bradley *et al.* (1977).

The first step is to identify the set of *decision variables*. These are the elements of the problem under the control of the decision-maker, whose values determine the solution to the problem. The output of the model will be the optimal value for each of the decision variables. In the revenue management problem, this is the number of customers to accept on each date from each rate class/length-of-stay combination, based on the unconstrained demand forecast. We refer to the decision variables as the set $\{X_{i,j,k}, i=1,\dots,6; j=i+1,\dots,\min(i+3,7); k=1,2\}$, where $X_{i,j,k}$ refers to the number of customers to accept who wish to arrive on date i, leave on day j, and pay rate class k. (Note that j must be greater than i.) For the Revenue Inn there are 30 decision variables, one for each of the unshaded boxes in Tables 16.1 and 16.2.

We next determine the *objective function*. This is the performance measure that the decision-maker wishes to optimize; in our case we wish to maximize revenue. Since the model will find values for the decision variables that make the revenue as large as possible, we write this objective function in terms of the decision variables. First, the revenue generated from corporate customers who arrive on date i and stay until date j is $X_{i,j,1} \times (j - i) \times 129$. The revenue generated from leisure customers who arrive on date i and stay until date j is $X_{i,j,2} \times (j - i) \times 99$. To compute the overall revenue, we sum over all possible values for i and j:

$$\textit{Maximize revenue} = \sum_{i=1}^{6} \sum_{j=i+1}^{\min\{7,i+3\}} [\{X_{i,j,1} \times (j\text{-}i) \times 129\} + \{X_{i,j,2} \times (j - i) \times 99\}]$$

The final step is to identify the problem's *constraints*. These are restrictions on the values that the decision variables can assume. For example, the number of reservations we accept for a particular rate class and length-of-stay combination cannot be higher than the forecasted demand; in other words the value of $X_{i,j,k}$ cannot be higher than $d_{i,j,k}$. This is true for all possible values of i, j, and k; therefore we have 30 demand constraints:

$$X_{i,j,k} \leq d_{i,j,k}, \text{ for } i = 1,\dots 6; j = i + 1\dots\min\{i + 3,7\}; k = 1,2.$$

Of course, $X_{i,j,k}$ can also not be negative; hence, we have a similar set of non-negativity constraints:

$$X_{i,j,k} \geq 0 \text{ for } i = 1,\dots6; j = i + 1\dots\min\{i + 3,7\}; k = 1,2$$

Furthermore, for each day of the planning horizon, the total number of guests in the hotel cannot exceed the property's capacity. Therefore we have six capacity constraints:

$$\text{day 1: } \sum_{j=2}^{4} (X_{1,j,1} + X_{1,j,2}) \le 10 \qquad \text{day 4: } \sum_{i=2}^{4} \sum_{j=5}^{i+3} (X_{i,j,1} + X_{i,j,2}) \le 10$$

$$\text{day 2: } \sum_{i=1}^{2} \sum_{j=3}^{i+3} (X_{i,j,1} + X_{i,j,2}) \le 10 \qquad \text{day 5: } \sum_{i=3}^{5} \sum_{j=6}^{\min\{i+3,7\}} (X_{i,j,1} + X_{i,j,2}) \le 10$$

$$\text{day 3: } \sum_{i=1}^{3} \sum_{j=4}^{i+3} (X_{i,j,1} + X_{i,j,2}) \le 10 \qquad \text{day 6: } \sum_{i=4}^{6} (X_{i,7,1} + X_{i,7,2}) \le 10$$

Note that the objective function and constraints are linear functions of the decision variables; therefore, we have defined a linear programme. As stated before, there are powerful tools available for solving large-scale linear programmes efficiently. However, the current problem is small enough that it can be solved easily using the Solver add-on to Microsoft Excel. The solution is displayed in Table 16.3a and b, and yields a total revenue of $7080 over the seven-day planning horizon.

Table 16.3a Optimal decision variables for the corporate rate

		Departure date, j					
	$X_{i,j,1}$	2	3	4	5	6	7
Arrival date, i	1	1	2	3			
	2		0	1	1		
	3			0	3	1	
	4				1	1	1
	5					1	1
	6						1

Table 16.3b Optimal decision variables for the leisure rate

		Departure date, j					
	$X_{i,j,2}$	2	3	4	5	6	7
Arrival date, i	1	1	2	1			
	2		0	0	0		
	3			0	0	0	
	4				0	0	2
	5					0	3
	6						2

It should be noted that the decision variables $X_{i,j,k}$ should always be integer-valued since they are not selling fractional rooms. When decision variables are restricted to be integer-valued, we call the mathematical model an *integer programme*. Integer programmes are much harder to solve than linear programmes. For an introduction to integer programmes, see Bradley *et al.* (1977).

Because integer programmes are so much more difficult to solve than ordinary linear programmes, the constraint that the decision variables should be integer-valued is dropped. Fortunately, the specific structure of the hotel revenue management problem guarantees that when the problem is solved without the integrality constraints, the optimal values of the decision variables $X_{i,j,k}$ are still integers. This means that we can solve the hotel revenue management problem with the more powerful linear programming techniques; we do not need special techniques for solving integer programmes. See Chen (1998) for a discussion of this integrality property of the hotel revenue management model.

Although the Revenue Inn has a limited number of rate class/length-of-stay combinations and a short planning horizon, the revenue management problem is formulated in exactly the same way for larger properties. We end this section with a summary of the variables and parameters that are required to model the revenue management problem:

- the number of days in the planning horizon;
- the number of hotel rooms;
- dollar amounts of the various room rates;
- maximum length-of-stay;
- demand for hotel rooms at each individual room rate for all possible combinations of arrival and departure patterns within the planning horizon.

BID PRICES

In the preceding section we formulated a model to decide how many customers from each rate class/length-of-stay combination to accept. This was based on forecasted demand for each combination. In practice, some of this demand will already have been locked in; a certain number of customers will already have made reservations for a particular rate class and length-of-stay. Therefore it may be difficult to implement the results of the linear programming model directly – the model may ask us to accept fewer customers from a particular demand segment than have already booked.

Fortunately, solving the linear programme provides us with more information than just the optimal mix of rooms. The solution technique enables us to compute *shadow prices* for each of the capacity constraints. The shadow prices tell us how much it would be worth to weaken each of the capacity constraints by one unit. In other words, for a given day, how much would an additional room be worth? In revenue management terminology, the shadow prices are referred to as bid prices (see Williamson, 1992).

Suppose we were able to expand the hotel's capacity by one additional room. If we auction this room off to potential customers, we should start off with the bid price to ensure that the price we receive for that room will be profitable for the hotel. Alternatively, one can think of the bid price as the floor of a potential discount that we would be willing to quote a customer. A rate below this threshold value would not be profitable to the hotel. For instance, if a hotel has four different room rates of, say, $200, $160, $130, and $90, and the bid price for a particular day is $100, then all rates on this day should be available except the $90 room rate which is below the bid price of $100. Thus, bid prices provide us with a simple open/close control mechanism for selling rooms in a hotel. Rooms that have a room rate above the bid price are open for reservations; all other rooms are closed.

When a customer asks for a room for consecutive days in the future, the average bid price for the capacity constraints for these dates specifies the minimum profitable rate. Suppose a customer wants to stay for three nights. We compute the bid prices for the particular days as $100, $170, and $150. To remain profitable, the contribution to revenue from that customer should be at least $100 + 170 + 150 = \$420$. In order to quote the customer a uniform room rate for all three nights, we compute the average bid price, $140. Hence, for this particular customer, rates $160 and $200 remain open, and rates $130 and $90 are closed.

Returning to the Revenue Inn, the bid prices for the planning horizon are shown in Table 16.4. Also shown are the available rate classes for arrival on each day.

Table 16.4　Bid prices (dollars) for the revenue Inn

	Arrival date					
	1	2	3	4	5	6
Bid price	39	129	129	99	99	99
Open rate classes, 1-night stay	99 129	129	129	99 129	99 129	99
Open rate classes, 2-night stay	99 129	129	129	99 129	99 129	
Open rate classes, 3-night stay	99 129	129	129	99 129		
Rooms filled	10	10	10	10	10	10

A final, practical concern is how often the bid prices should be updated. Since they are directly tied to the demand forecast, if the bid prices are to be adjusted, the forecast must be updated as well. Since most forecasting techniques are based on the current number of reservations on hand, in principle the forecast can be updated whenever a new reservation is made. In our experience, however, most hotels update their forecasts (and sets of bid prices) once per day, usually at the end of the day.

OVERBOOKING

A limitation of the revenue management formulation of the preceding sections is that it does not yet allow for overbooking. Since some percentage of room reservations will result in no-shows, most properties overbook their capacity by at least a small number of rooms. The linear programming model is easily modified to allow for this.

The first step is to determine the maximum allowable number of rooms to overbook the property for a given night. There are two common approaches for this decision. The first is an economic approach: the revenue manager balances the cost of 'walking' customers with the cost of an empty room. Suppose we consider overbooking the property by one room. We will overbook if the expected revenue from that room is greater than the expected loss. We gain revenue if the number of no-shows is one or more; since we have only overbooked by one room, no customers are walked. We lose revenue if the number of no-shows is zero, since a customer will be walked. Let N refer to the number of no-shows, and let $P[N \geq x]$ refer to the probability that the number of no-shows is greater than or equal to some value x. In order to overbook the room we must have:

Expected revenue from the room $\geq$ Expected loss from the room
(average room rate) $\times$ $P[N \geq 1]$ $\geq$ (cost of walking a customer) $\times$ $P[N < 1]$

This must remain true for each room that we overbook. So we will overbook by the largest value x such that for the last room overbooked:

Expected revenue from the room $\geq$ Expected loss from the room
(average room rate) $\times$ $P[N \geq x]$ $\geq$ (cost of walking a customer) $\times$ $P[N < x]$
(average room rate) $\times$ $P[N \geq x]$ $\geq$ (cost of walking a customer) $\times$ $(1 - P[N \geq x])$

$$P[N \geq x] \geq \frac{\text{(cost of walking a customer)}}{\text{(average room rate)} + \text{(cost of walking a customer)}}$$

This is known as the *critical fractile method*. For a given number of rooms x, the value $P[N \geq x]$ can be estimated from historical data. Alternatively the manager can estimate the probability that any given reservation will be a no-show, p, and use the binomial distribution to compute $P[N \geq x]$ given that we have overbooked the hotel by x:

$$P[N \geq x] = 1 - \sum_{i=0}^{x-1} \frac{(c+x)!}{i!(c+x-i)!} p^i (1-p)^{c+x-i}.$$

Here c is the capacity of the hotel.

To illustrate this computation, let us determine the optimal overbooking level for day 1 of the planning horizon at the Revenue Inn. The first step is to compute the average room rate. If demand is as forecasted, according to Table 16.3 we will have six guests at the corporate rate and four guests at the leisure rate, for an average rate of $117. Suppose the cost of walking a customer is $200, so the critical fractile is $200/(200 + 117)$ $= 0.63$. Now suppose the revenue manager has determined that the average no-show rate for days like the one in question is $p = 0.15$. Table 16.5 shows $P[N \geq x]$ for various values of x; these values were computed using the formula discussed in the last paragraph.

Table 16.5 Probability of not walking a guest for various levels of overbooking

Overbooking limit x	Probability of not walking a guest $P[N \geq x]$
1	0.83
2	0.56
3	0.31
4	0.15
5	0.06
6	0.02

We choose the largest overbooking limit x such that $P[N \geq x] \geq 0.63$, or $x = 1$ room.

One difficulty with the critical fractile method is that it requires the revenue manager to specify the cost of denying a room to a customer. This may include the cost of finding an accommodation at another hotel, compensation for the inconvenience to the customer, and lost future business. Since this value may be difficult to specify accurately, some property managers prefer to use a *service-level* approach to overbooking. The idea is to specify a risk factor; for example, the manager may decide that he wants to walk a guest no more than once every five nights. If the property is overbooked by x rooms, a guest will be walked if the number of no-shows is less than x, i.e., if $N < x$. Therefore, we choose the largest value of x such that the probability we will not have to walk a guest, $P[N \geq x]$, is at least $4/5 = 0.8$. From Table 16.5 we see that the correct overbooking limit is again $x = 1$ room. (Note that a more reasonable service level might be to walk no more than one guest every 100 nights. However if we applied such a service level to the ten-room Revenue Inn, we would not overbook at all.)

Once the overbooking limit has been determined, the revenue management model is adjusted by updating the capacity constraints. In particular, the capacity of the hotel (on the right-hand-side of the constraint) is increased by the level of overbooking. For example, suppose the manager of the Revenue Inn has decided to allow overbooking by one room every night except day 3, when he will allow the hotel to be overbooked by five rooms. The capacity constraints are adjusted as follows:

$$\text{day 1: } \sum_{j=2}^{7} (X_{1,j,1} + X_{1,j,2}) \leq 11 \qquad \text{day 4: } \sum_{i=1}^{4} \sum_{j=5}^{7} (X_{i,j,1} + X_{i,j,2}) \leq 11$$

$$\text{day 2: } \sum_{i=1}^{2} \sum_{j=3}^{7} (X_{i,j,1} + X_{i,j,2}) \leq 11 \qquad \text{day 5: } \sum_{i=1}^{5} \sum_{j=6}^{7} (X_{i,j,1} + X_{i,j,2}) \leq 11$$

$$\text{day 3: } \sum_{i=1}^{3} \sum_{j=4}^{7} (X_{i,j,1} + X_{i,j,2}) \leq 15 \qquad \text{day 6: } \sum_{i=1}^{6} (X_{i,7,1} + X_{i,7,2}) \leq 11$$

Re-solving the updated model, we find the bid prices listed in Table 16.6.

Table 16.6 Bid prices (dollars) for the Revenue Inn with overbooking

	Arrival date					
	1	2	3	4	5	6
Bid price	39	159	99	99	99	99
Open rate classes, 1-night stay	99 129		99 129	99 129	99 129	99 129
Open rate classes, 2-night stay	99 129	129	99 129	99 129	99 129	
Open rate classes, 3-night stay	99 129	129	99 129	99 129		

GROUP RESERVATIONS

The linear programming model described in the preceding sections concerns only transient reservations; it does not account for decisions involving group reservations. In order to account for groups, the revenue manager can 'reserve' a block of rooms for group business by subtracting the block from the right-hand-side of the daily capacity constraint. For example, if the manager of the Revenue Inn decides to reserve three rooms for group reservations on day 1 of the planning horizon, the adjusted capacity constraint is:

$$\text{day 1: } \sum_{j=2}^{7} (X_{1,j,1} + X_{1,j,2}) \leq 7$$

(Note that this does not reflect the adjustment made for overbooking.)

Alternatively, the transient model can be used as a tool for the groups sales manager to determine the minimum profitable rate for a particular group. The manager solves the transient model twice, once with the group's size subtracted from the capacity constraint, and once without. The difference is the loss in transient revenue due to the group. From this quantity we subtract any F&B (Food and Beverage) or other service revenue expected from the group, and divide by the group size to find the minimum profitable rate.

DISCUSSION QUESTIONS

1. Formulate and solve the revenue management problem in Microsoft Excel using the Solver function.
2. How do the bid prices change if we allow for overbooking? Do they tend to go up or down? Why?
3. Suppose the Revenue Inn has a sister property, the Management Inn, directly across the street. How can the linear programming model be extended to manage the rates for both properties simultaneously? What difficulties might you face in implementing such a model?

REFERENCES

Bradley, S. P., Hax, A. C. and Magnanti, T. L. (1977) *Applied Mathematical Programming*. Reading, MA: Addison-Wesley.

Chen, D. (1998) 'Network flows in hotel yield management', Cornell University, TR1225.

Chen, D. (2000) *'Revenue Management – Competition, Monopoly, and Optimization'*. PhD thesis, Cornell University, Ithaca, NY.

Kimes, S. E. and Weatherford, L. R. (1999) 'Forecasting methods for hotel revenue management: an evaluation', Working Series Paper, Cornell University.

Williamson, E. L. (1992) *'Airline Network Seat Inventory Control: Methodologies and Revenue Impacts'*, PhD thesis, Massachusetts Institute of Technology, Cambridge, MA.

Suggested Solutions

CASE 1

REVENUE MANAGEMENT BASICS IN THE CHARTER BOAT INDUSTRY

Raul Bermudez, Tamara Dieck and Warren Lieberman

Q1. *How could The Moorings provide a more flexible charter to boat assignment (rather than assigning charters to boats as requests come in)? Try to find the best matching of charter contracts to boats for a given base and boat type. The best matching comes closest to equalizing revenue across boats.*

There are a number of ways to approach this, from developing a simple algorithm to a more complex integer program.

Simple algorithm. Consider the example provided in Table 1.2 of the case study. In this example, one possible boat assignment for this period, including the new contract 'x' is shown in Table A1 of this Answers Section. This assignment was made by assigning the boats that are at the dock, on the day they are rented (so not in advance of rental date), beginning with 413–1, going down the list, and when 413–9 is assigned, starting at the top again with the first available boat. This assignment algorithm has to work because when a boat has an open date, the boat is available for charter every future day. With day of rental assignment, no available boat has any future obligations, so no future conflicts are possible. So long as boat availability is greater than zero for each day of a requested rental, boats can be assigned to renters. Thus, keeping track of nothing more than the number of available boats makes assignment trivial.

Table A1   Revised bookings to accommodate the 14 March charter

Boat	11th	12th	13th	14th	15th	16th	17th	18th	19th	20th	21st	22nd	23rd	24th
413–1	a	a	a	a	a	a	a	h	h	h	h	h	h	h
413–2	g	g	g	g		m	m	m	m	m	m	m	m	
413–3	k	k		x	x	x	x	x	x	x	x			
413–4	o	o	o	o			p	p	p	p	p	p	p	
413–5		c	c	c	c	c	c	c	b	b	b	b	b	b
413–6		i	i	i	i	i	i	i	i		d	d	d	d
413–7		n	n	n	n	n	n	n	n	n	n	n	f	f
413–8			e	e	e	e	e	e	e	e	j	j	j	j
413–9			l	l	l	l	l	l	l	l				

This method rotates through the boats, but straightforward rotation may prove insufficient to ensure roughly equal revenue to owners. An alternative that assigns the lowest earning boat to the maximum revenue charter that day, or that always assigns the boat that has been out of charter longest, or some similar algorithm, may serve.

Making boat assignments at the dock on the day charters begin would provide The Moorings with much greater flexibility in accepting reservations and assigning boats. For operational reasons, however, this may not be feasible. For example, boat maintenance and other operational considerations such as staff scheduling at the bases may require The Moorings to set the assignments of charters to boats prior to the start dates. In such a situation, charters could be assigned to boats one or two weeks prior to start dates. But accepting and tracking reservations by boat type to determine boat availability, without making any boat assignment at the time of reservation, is the critical business process change that provides great value to The Moorings.

Integer programme. A more complex method, but one which might lead to better revenue equalization among boats, would be to develop an integer programme that seeks to find the best matching of charter contracts to boats for a base and boat type combination. A best matching is one that comes closest to equalizing revenue across the boats.

The algorithm could even be run in two different modes:

(a) Operational mode – this usage takes all charter contracts occurring 7 to 14 days out (the number of days is dependent on how far out The Moorings wants to make the actual assignments) and finds the best boat assignments for those contracts. These runs would likely be performed on a nightly basis.

(b) Strategic mode – this usage takes all charter contracts with start dates beginning after the operational run and up until the next three to six months out. The results from these 'assignments' would be used to ensure that feasible assignments exist, and to view the expected boat utilization, given the current charter contracts. These runs could be performed weekly. This mode could also be used to evaluate the availability impacts of alternative boat maintenance schedules.

Model Formulation

Let:

X_{ij} =   A 1,0 variable indicating the assignment (or lack of assignment) of Charter i to Boat j

R_i =   Revenue from Charter i

D = Number of days in the time period (e.g., solving for a two-week time period, $D = 14$)

$$R_j = \sum_{i=1}^{n} R_i \times X_{ij}$$

The revenue earned by Boat j is the sum of revenues from the charters assigned to that boat.

M = The revenue earned by the boat with the minimum revenue stream assignments (so if there are two boats and one boat's revenue is \$10,000 and the other boat's revenue is \$8,885, then $M = \$8,885$). The objective of the IP is to maximize M, which works to equalize revenues across the boats.

G_k = A grouping of concurrent charters. That is, a new group is created for each date on which a charter starts and the day after a charter ends. In Table A2, we consider a seven-day time period with nine charters, where an 'x' indicates the days spanned by a charter. For this example, we have a set of five groups of concurrent charters. Group 1 consists of charters 1–4, Group 2 consists of charters 1–6, Group 3 consists of charters 1–7, Group 4 consists of charters 2 and 4–9, and Group 5 consists of charters 5–9.

Table A2 Example of concurrent charter groups

	Day 1	Day 2	Day 3	Day 4	Day 5	Day 6	Day 7
Charter 1	x	x	x	x			
Charter 2	x	x	x	x	x		
Charter 3	x	x	x	x			
Charter 4	x	x	x	x	x		
Charter 5		x	x	x	x	x	x
Charter 6		x	x	x	x	x	x
Charter 7				x	x	x	x
Charter 8					x	x	x
Charter 9					x	x	x

Then we want to solve:

Maximize M
  Subject to:

1. $X_{ij} = 1$, if Charter i is assigned to Boat j
    0, otherwise
2. $R_j \geq M$, for each boat $j = 1, 2,\ldots, m$
3. $\sum_j X_{ij} = 1$, for each charter $i = 1, 2, \ldots , n$
4. For each G_k, $\sum_{i \in G_k} X_{ij} \leq 1$, for each boat $j = 1, 2,\ldots, m$

Condition 1 simply states that the variables, X_{ij}, must be 0 or 1, where $X_{ij} = 1$ indicates the assignment of Charter i to Boat j.

Condition 2 states that the revenue from each Boat j, R_j, must be greater than or equal to M. Since the goal of the IP is to maximize M, this condition ensures that no boat receives 'too little' revenue.

Condition 3 states that each charter contract must be assigned to one and only one boat.

Condition 4 states that within each grouping of concurrent charters, at most one of those grouped charters can be assigned to a given boat.

> *Q2. Develop a pricing strategy to improve the utilization of boats between St Lucia and Grenada.*

What we want to do is help The Moorings make pricing changes that will result in a more profitable flow of boats between St Lucia and Grenada. There are several ways this can be done, including:

- Increase the number of one-way rentals from Grenada to St Lucia.
- Decrease the number of one-way transactions from St Lucia to Grenada while maintaining boat utilization.
- Increase the amount received by The Moorings from one-way rentals from St Lucia to Grenada without reducing utilization.

Currently, one-way pricing does not vary by origin – this could change. The Moorings could charge lower rates for charters starting in Grenada since this is the less desirable starting point.

For customers who are somewhat price sensitive, lowering the price of the Grenada to St Lucia one-way relative to the more favoured direction provides an incentive for sailing in the less desirable direction. (Even with the price of the one-ways being the same, some customers preferred to sail in the more difficult direction, so there are some customers who do prefer sailing in this direction). Combining this pricing change with business process changes that eliminates (or at least reduces the frequency of) automatic re-delivery of yachts to their starting bases could also be effective. Delivery costs can be reduced, and utilization improved, if paying customers move some of the yachts back from Grenada to St Lucia. The Moorings would need to train members of its revenue management team to control the inventory levels based on the demand patterns. Some reservation system changes might be necessary to track the number of boats not at their home base.

In addition, the one-way prices could vary by season. During high demand seasons, when demand exceeds supply, higher prices for one-ways would encourage customers to do round-trip charters instead of one-ways, thereby reducing the days lost for re-delivery and increasing utilization.

Since the favoured direction currently attracts 90 per cent of the one-ways, price changes may not create a perfect balance, but the changes described above could reduce the level of the imbalance.

> *Q3. What recommendations would you give The Moorings to improve its pricing?*

There are many directions The Moorings could take to improve its pricing strategy. Recommendations can be made in the following areas:

- Move from discounts to more flexible pricing.
- Develop different rate sheets.

- Smooth out the seasons.
- Use forecasting.
- Redirect or force higher margin packages during high demand.

A central revenue management capability is manipulating prices to maximize income from each sale in periods of high demand, and increase sales in periods of low demand. This can require micro-managing prices, although this management may be concealed by redefining products. Regardless, prices are targeted as conditions require, avoiding discounts where demand is firm, and losing sales where demand is weak.

Flexible pricing may be difficult to implement because it may confuse customers (both direct and indirect) that are accustomed to the current pricing scheme and might require system changes to handle the additional rate complexity. These issues certainly need to be addressed, but the benefits of flexible pricing are often far greater than the costs of migrating to and implementing such capabilities. Note that although The Moorings may want to get rid of rate sheets altogether, there may be a less drastic recommendation that suggests reducing the effective dates of the rate sheets and perhaps eventually phasing them out. Rather than printing one rate per season for example, rate ranges could be printed or rate sheets could be printed more than once each year.

It was noted that demand dips with pricing season changes. The Moorings could train its charter agents to identify customers that seem to be delaying their start time due to pricing reasons. The charter agents should explain the pricing and make sure customers understand how they will be charged if their days are split between two seasons. If this is not enough to smooth out the utilization dips, another suggestion would be to have the charter agents provide special offers to customers with start dates at the beginning of new seasons. For example, if a customer wants to start a vacation at the beginning of Season C, but availability is good at the end of Season B, offer the customer a special rate on the Season B days. This is another justification for changing the rate sheets and moving towards more flexible pricing.

Part of the pricing problem is in predicting when demand is high versus when it is low. Simple forecasts based on historical data can give a good indication of current achievement, all things held equal. Given the small numbers that may apply for certain boat type and base combinations, we would need to determine a methodology to appropriately aggregate the demand numbers. Forecasts of demand would help The Moorings to determine appropriate pricing strategies and when and how it should redirect demand.

Charter agents could be trained to help redirect demand from high to low demand periods and to sell higher margin products during high demand periods. For example, a customer looking for a lower price during high demand seasons could be offered the following instead of a discount:

- Alternatives of the same boat in a lower-priced season.
- Another boat type that's similar in size (e.g., a Club line boat if they asked for Exclusive).
- A different base (if the demand there is low).

Other creative pricing suggestions may include encouraging more direct sales (e.g., over the Internet), offering special promotions on the Internet, and developing special pricing programmes to attract new customers.

CASE 2

EASYJET: AN AIRLINE THAT CHANGED OUR FLYING HABITS

Gerald Barlow

Q1. What are the potential negative effects that yield management can have on customer relations?

Answer. People could view yield management as unfair because different customers pay different prices for identical services. However, when the strategy is communicated properly, customers can appreciate the benefits of yield management, such as reduced prices for early reservations. Providing them complementary benefits can compensate passengers paying regular or full prices. (However, with easyJet this is difficult to identify.) The answer could use possible examples of the type of problems, etc.

Q2. Select one of the easyJet routes (for example Luton–Nice) and track the prices for the 45 days until take-off. Having selected the route, record the price every 5 days for the first 15 days, then every 2 days until 14 days from take-off, then every day. You need to record the prices for three different time slots, say early morning, mid-afternoon, and the last flight. Comment on your observations and the possible reasons for the price variation between days until take-off.

Answer. Take care in selecting the day; do not select a day with external influences, for example any day up to one week prior to the Monaco Grand Prix if using the destination of Nice. The value of the different time take-off slots is to see if the nature of passengers selecting these slots has any effect. For example, few business customers are likely to select the mid-afternoon slot, so will have a different booking pattern resulting in a different price structure.

Q3. What problems do you envisage easyJet may have with the addition of a company like GO? (GO, an ex-BA company, used a BA-type of yield management programme and alternative sales outlets, rather than simply the Internet and phone sales).

Answer. easyJet must have taken this into any consideration prior to the take over, as integration is a major project for any company. They need to take into account timing, for many issues such as when to fully integrate the booking systems. Issues such as the size of the current IT system must be considered, the problems and complexity of the actual web site such as how to fit in all the new destinations. However, any decision regarding integration of the web site cannot be implemented until the two airlines can operate from one yield management programme. Similarly, the decision regarding the actual programme cannot be decided and implemented until a strategic decision has been made regarding the actual combination of routes and operating bases. It must be remembered that yield management is simply an operational tool when viewed from an overall strategy.

CASE 3

THE WEDDING BELL BLUES

Sheryl Kimes

Q1. What is causing the problem?

- The sales force seems to be rewarded on the basis of revenue goals rather than on contribution goals. This can be seen by their sales of high revenue, but unprofitable items (i.e., ice carvings) to reach their revenue targets.
- They seem to be following a 'first-come-first-served' approach to accepting reservations and are not looking at the booking pace or the amount of demand which is turned down. Many of the reservation requests which were turned down are for higher revenue than those accepted.

Q2. What pricing and duration control management strategies do you suggest?

- Pricing
    - Develop a tiered rate system for high, medium and low demand periods for both the full and half ballrooms.
    - Develop rate fences that can be associated with each rate.
    - Reward sales people on the basis of contribution, not revenue.
    - Give preference to weddings that will also provide roomnights to the hotel.

- Duration
    - Institute early booking fees.
    - Require pre-payment for weddings during peak demand periods.
    - Reduce turnover time (time between functions) so multiple weddings can be held on the same day.
    - Offer shorter wedding reception packages.

Q3. What implementation issues will she face? How should she handle them? How will she be able to measure her success with her revenue management programme?

- Implementation issues
    - Sales force resistance.
    - Customer confusion.
    - Adequacy of data.

- How should she handle them?
    - Revise the incentive system and clearly explain it to all sales staff. Sales people should be rewarded for maximizing contribution and for bringing in business during low demand periods.
    - Clearly present the pricing structure to customers with a focus on how they can get a discount at various times of the year and days of the week.

– Ensure that the relevant computer systems are synchronized and that data is accurate and available.

- Measurement of success
  – Contribution per available square foot.

CASE 4

THE RIGHT PRICE CONSULTANTS

Julie Swann

Q1. Why do different product classes exhibit different results (particularly for profit potential, sources of profit potential, etc.)?

Answer. Dynamic pricing performs differently based on product characteristics such as demand variability – both the magnitude of the variability as well as the pattern of seasonality. For example, in the results shown, dynamic pricing had the largest profit potential for Seas2 and DecMean classes. Those scenarios also have demand significantly higher at the beginning of the horizon compared to capacity. Intuitively, a manufacturer does not have the opportunity to build up inventory in those examples, so dynamic pricing provides a significant tool for flexibility.

Similar concepts hold true for the sources of profit potential. For the Seas1 and IncMean classes, Figure 4.5 of the case study indicates that inventory costs are lower under dynamic pricing than fixed pricing, suggesting that price is being used as a tool to match supply and demand, while the fixed pricing strategy uses inventory to buffer variability.

Q2. What would happen if some of the assumptions were relaxed? For instance, what if customers planned their buying strategically, what impact would this have on the pricing strategies and results? Competition from other firms?

Answer. In some cases, customers may have flexibility in when they purchase items, so they may plan their purchases based on their expectations of price changes. If the demand curves are forecasted under strategic behaviour, the demand elasticities are likely to be higher, indicating a greater sensitivity towards price. The likely effect is that the profit potential is reduced from the results obtained in this study.

Competition from other firms is also another important consideration for many firms. A firm experiencing competition is likely to consider only small changes in price. If firms are price matching, then the profit potential may be reduced. However, this does not imply that dynamic pricing will have no benefits. First, the pricing may be matching supply and demand (for multiple competitors), see the airlines for examples of this. Also, if dynamic pricing results in reduced costs to the manufacturer (in decreased production variability for instance), those savings may be returned to the customer in the form of a lower price, which is especially important in the face of competition.

Q3. What are some guidelines on when it might make sense to use dynamic pricing and when it wouldn't make sense? What should JJT think about if the company wanted to implement dynamic pricing?

Answer. The magnitude of demand variability and the nature of the seasonality are two important factors, as seen in Figure 4.4 of the case study for instance. If there is no seasonality, then fixed pricing strategies often work well, with dynamic pricing only used to clear leftover inventory. The profit potential from dynamic pricing may also be affected by parameters such as inventory holding cost (if the cost is 0, strategic pricing is less important). Many factors affecting the performance of dynamic pricing are industry or firm specific.

JJT would want to consider the reactions of customers carefully. For instance, if this pricing strategy is perceived as price-gouging, then it may have a negative impact. However, if by using it a company is able to meet more demand, or able to reduce costs, customers may be willing to accept new strategies.

The company would also need to think about the kinds of data that would be needed for implementation, as well as changes that might need to be made in their organizational structure. For example, they might need to invest in additional information technology to gather demand data from the Internet, or they might need to have teams combining marketing and production experts to make joint decisions.

CASE 5

REVENUE MANAGEMENT IN RESTAURANTS: A CASE EXAMPLE FROM BORNHOLM, DENMARK

Nick Johns and Charlotte Rassing

Q1. How does the restaurant industry compare/contrast with airlines and hotels in terms of capacity and price management?

Answer. In all three cases the aim of revenue management is to optimize revenue yield on limited capacity, and in principle this may generally be achieved by charging more at peak times. However, both airlines and hotels charge their customers by the space occupied and have almost unlimited scope for adjusting prices, within the parameters of what the market will bear. Airlines know the duration of each flight precisely, and even hotels can predict the duration of guest stays to a large extent. Restaurants in contrast have relatively fixed price tariffs, and the duration of customer meals is generally variable and unpredictable. Therefore the concept of revenue management has to be rethought.

Q2. In what ways does menu engineering equate to revenue management in the restaurant industry? In which ways does it not do so?

Answer. Revenue management in the restaurant industry consists of maximizing revenue by seat occupancy. Seat occupancy can be controlled by managing bookings and reducing the time guests take over their meal. However, these aspects assume demand pressure. If this is absent there is no value in rushing customers, and in fact it may become a source of irritation to them. Revenue can be maximized by charging a premium for periods or situations of higher demand. However, this is only possible if customers will accept it. It is dependent upon a culture in which dining is particularly important at certain times and days and in certain situations. In contrast menu engineering is a valid way to increase revenue at most times and in most situations because the premium is related to the actual food chosen.

> *Q3. Is menu engineering an appropriate way to approach revenue management in restaurants of the kind found on Bornholm?*

Answer. Bornholm is a mature market and therefore competition in the restaurant industry is high and most available niches have been filled. This means that capacity is nicely adjusted to demand which is therefore moderate in all sectors. This severely limits the scope for managing meal duration and seat occupancy. In addition the local culture sets a premium upon the food received but not on the circumstances under which it is eaten. It is relatively difficult to use rate fences for particular days as the season is rather short and the number of special dining days are few. In addition the prevailing culture is unwilling to pay a premium for special dining situations. This leaves menu pricing as the most satisfactory option for revenue management in Bornholm at the present time. However, restaurant managers should be continually looking for ways to overcome these limitations so that they can optimize revenue per seat-hour to the full.

CASE 6

DYNAMIC PRICING OF DISTILLATE PRODUCTS AT PETROLEUM TERMINALS

Douglas Harvey, Nicola Secomandi and Theodore V. Valkov

> *Q1. Can margins be increased without sacrificing volume?*

Answer. In the live tests, profit and margin increases were achieved without substantial decreases in volume. In fact, daily liftings increased on average by 3.5 per cent during the periods covered by our optimization. Furthermore, in the course of the live tests, the optimization identified several opportunities to achieve significant additional profit improvements by moving product from locations where performance was weak to locations where demand was strong. It is impossible for a human operator to perform such an allocation optimization in the context of an actual supply network with several terminals and fluctuating market conditions. This is one area where the automation and analytical support offered by the system can create significant additional benefits.

> *Q2. Where does the additional profit come from? Is it from selling more or selling at a higher price?*

Answer. On any given day, the optimal profit that can be generated at a given terminal depends on the customer willingness-to-pay for the product, the competitor pricing and one's rack position, the commodity index moves, the available inventory and several other factors. The incremental profit is not achieved from selling more on average, or selling at an average higher price, but from increased accuracy of pricing at every terminal every day of the year. It is the increased accuracy that yields a higher average margin and slightly higher volume in our tests. This is the main effect behind the performance improvements reported in this case study.

There are a number of additional potential sources of incremental revenue from the application of this technology on an enterprise-wide, fully implemented scale – network effects, optimal planning benefits, real-time price adjustment benefits, and increased productivity of the pricing team. The live pilot discussed herein was not designed to measure these contributions.

Q3. Are the benefits of pricing optimization sustainable in the long term?

Answer. Change is the only thing that is sustainable over the long term. Markets are in dynamic search of an elusive equilibrium point that is constantly shifting due to changing markets, infrastructure, competition, supply and demand patterns. A competitor who may gain a dominant and profitable position in a given market will immediately find this position challenged by new entrants or competitors who have worked hard to catch up.

The only source of sustainable competitive advantage in this industry is the ability to manage this perpetual change optimally. This is what this type of optimization technology offers to its users, owing to the real-time calibration and learning capabilities, dynamic demand models and reliance on live market data.

CASE 7

FREE NELSON MANDELA? THE POLITICS AND PRICING OF CULTURE WITHIN SOCIETY

Elizabeth Carnegie

Q1. Should access to culture in its many forms be related to ability to pay and if not should such activities be subsidized by the public purse? Consider the implications for the withdrawal of public money.

Answer. This question aims to challenge students into thinking about how cultural activities are or could be paid for so that they best reflect and benefit the widest number of people. Every cultural activity carries a price tag, essentially the arguments are about who should and who can pay. If the state is to pay in the number of ways listed in this chapter, i.e., either directly through grants or subsidies or indirectly through taxation, then at some point every tax paying individual has contributed to such activities whether they participate in events or not. This places at least some community value on cultural activities in that they are deemed worthy of some state and therefore public support. However, issues arise to do with quality, i.e., many community activities are dependent on low paid workers or the volunteer movement and this can seen to devalue the product. International orchestras, ballet companies and major art exhibitions cost more to form and maintain and these activities can be viewed as elitist and will have a smaller audience who might define themselves through access to such activities. Museums hold the key to understanding the past through the material evidence. How then can we price access to ensure that physical, and importantly, *emotional* access is possible for all. Should access be determined by ability to pay? Students need to consider where they place access to culture in their own value system. Can the arts ever be profit-making?

> *Q2. Without a sense of the past and an understanding of where we came from people would have no sense of community. Discuss with reference to how your community emphasizes and interprets its unique cultural traits.*

Answer. In this question students are being asked to consider what is a shared cultural identity and how and where it is used to define a people, nation or country through some consideration of the following: All communities define themselves against what they are not as much as what they perceive to be their unique characteristics. For example, Scottish people may define themselves as being culturally different from their English neighbours. People from Liverpool may define themselves as being Northern, from the home of the Beatles, port and city dwellers or working-class at heart. They have a specific term, Liverpudlians, to define themselves, which can be further broken down by region. Language, accents and dialects, objects which define a people such as emblems, flags, national dress and foodstuffs, symbolic landmarks such as the Angel of the North or the Blackpool Tower or the Derry Walls all serve to emphasize a sense of community as well as highlighting cultural, religious, or territorial differences. Communities seek to reinforce this shared heritage and past triumphs and disasters in order to ensure that people have a sense of place in the present. As society has become less hidebound by traditions and families lead more disparate lives, the sense of community within a large conurbation becomes more symbolic than real and in many ways museums provide the link to the past through objects, photographs and buildings, fulfilling a role no longer the province of the church, state and family within clearly discernable and often rural communities. Students should think of ways in which their area reinforces the messages of a shared history through access to cultural activities. Do these reinforce a sense of community and therefore pride, or can they be divisive, racist or sectarian? Lastly, students should consider whether there is a sense of continuity through community or whether the past is interpretable only as history.

> *Q3. The material evidence of human activity is contained within cultural institutions. Sometimes our cultural identity is mixed up with the misfortunes of others and objects contained within state-run museums may be the cultural property of other countries and cultures. Consider the arguments for repatriation of such objects. Is it possible to honestly determine the issues of ownership?*

Answer. In this question students are being asked to think about how cultural activities and objects can be used to define the highest achievements of human activity or else they can be used to define a people from a very subjective or outsiders position, and they may adopt a culturally superior position. Students will need to consider the role of museums and their collections and the right to hold what can be deemed the cultural property of other societies. Museums, galleries, monuments and the materials they are made from all reflect human activity. Western societies are materially driven and as manufacturing nations fuelled by the Industrial Revolution many have been bequeathed an enormous number of objects which highlight progress. Art, made for its own sake to enrich people's lives, whether in praise of God or simply to reflect the highest level of human achievement, has long been a barometer of civilization. Museums, and of course churches, became the temples of learning and reflection but also of curiosity about the material culture of the unknown world. Objects that reflected the material, symbolic or cultural traits of other cultures were bought, stolen or traded and many ended up in museums often viewed as anthropology or ethnology rather than art or craft forms. Hand in hand with the slave trade some objects represent the movements of people, Empires and attitudes to other countries and cultures. Human remains, mummies, body parts, over-modelled skulls (skulls embellished as part of ancestor worship), are contained in most state museums and are now the subject of much discussion about whether it is ethical to keep human remains. In many cases these remains reflect dispossessed or displaced peoples such as aborigines. The Aboriginal High Commissioner of Tasmania believes that sometimes institutions do not want to negotiate their return because they are ashamed to face up to the truth of how these objects came to be in the collections in the first place. Students should think about the arguments for and against the return of cultural property bearing in mind the need for human dignity. They may like to consider how they would feel if their Grandmother's head was on display in a museum and to consider whether their own attitude to human remains reflects cultural attitudes to death, particularly in a post-Christian society.

CASE 8

SEX AND SAUNAS

Ian Yeoman, Catherine Drudy, Ruth Robertson and Una McMahon-Beattie

Q1. What are the characteristics of sex tourism in your destination?

Answer. This question discusses the problems of trying to define sex tourism, which has a wide range of variables including: saunas and massage parlours, escort agencies, red-light districts, independent escorts, strippers, lap-dancers and exotic dancers, gay parades, dating agencies, 18–30 holidays or similar where the main intent is sex, stag and hen parties/weekends, holiday romances and unplanned rendezvous. It is suggested that the student evaluates each of these variables within the context of their own town or destination. By doing this, the student will build up a rich picture of sex tourism in that destination.

Q2. Discuss the morality, ethics and characteristics of Revenue Management for the sex tourism industry.

Answer. What are the ethics and morality issues of revenue management in the sex tourism industry? This is a very topical question, since the construction of an interpretation of an answer will come from different viewpoints. Can we really discuss revenue management in a exploited environment? Are we pushing out the boundaries of revenue management too far? The morality and ethics of revenue management should be constructed around the following points.

Exploitation: Of who, sex worker or punter and how?
Safety: Crime and health, consequences.
Morality: Promoting a crime or reducing sexually transmitted diseases?
Pricing: Variable or fixed?
Duration: Variable or fixed?
Legality: Within each concept of sex tourism.
Viewpoint: Crime or tolerance.
Health: Prevention or ignore?
Risk: Whose behaviour?
Monies: For what purpose, drugs or revenue?

> *Q3. Discuss Edinburgh's sauna and massage parlour business against Robert Cross's core concepts of Revenue Management.*

This case study uses Kimes' (1997, 2001) ingredients and preconditions to discuss revenue management. An alternative platform, draws upon Robert Cross's core concepts of revenue management. These core concepts are as the following:

- Focus on price rather than costs when balancing supply and demand
- Replace cost-based pricing with market-based pricing
- Sell to segmented micro-markets, not to mass markets
- Save your products for your most valuable customers
- Make decisions based upon knowledge, not supposition
- Exploit each product's value cycle
- Continually re-evaluate your revenue opportunities.

These seven 'core concepts' highlight revenue management as a competitive tool and help to show how it can be integrated into the marketing function. They demonstrate the importance of customer-focused marketing.

CASE 9

HOTEL DEMAND/CANCELLATION ANALYSIS AND ESTIMATION OF UNCONSTRAINED DEMAND USING STATISTICAL METHODS

Patrick H. Liu

> *Q1. How do you estimate the unconstrained hotel daily demand based on censored booking data?*

Answer. This is one of the toughest problems in hotel (also airlines) revenue management and has been studied extensively for many years. In this case study we used the statistical deconstraining methods developed by Liu *et al.* (2002) to estimate the unconstrained 'lead-time' interval demand over the entire planning horizon (on average

100 intervals for each arrival day) for all the arrival days that were censored (about 5000 days) and then, for each arrival day, added all its unconstrained 'lead-time' interval demand to arrive at the unconstrained total daily demand. These methods are more general and likely to produce more accurate and unbiased estimation than those in previous research where only capacity constraints (or booking limits) were considered; other constraints such as prices were never discussed. For example, in peak seasons reservation data are often heavily (sometimes 100 per cent) censored. While the 'detruncation' methods can do little about the unconstrained demand since there are little or no valid 'historical unconstrained' data, our methods can provide a much better estimate because extra information such as the parametric form of the demand distribution as well as the room rates that restricted the demand are fully utilized. By producing more accurate and robust forecasts of future demand, the overall reliability and success of revenue management systems can be significantly enhanced.

> *Q2. What conclusions can be drawn from this case study about the distributions of unconstrained hotel transient demand (by season, by day of the week, and by hotel type)?*

Answer. Almost all research work in the hotel revenue management literature has assumed Poisson distributions for the unconstrained hotel transient demand. However, we have found that, in general, Poisson distribution is not a good fit to the unconstrained arrival day transient demand, except where the hotel is small (less than 100 rooms), and that the normal distribution is a much better fit to the unconstrained demand data for hotels large or small for any season. The effects of seasonality and day of the week on the demand variability (i.e., the spread of the demand distributions) are much smaller compared with that of hotel size. For the first time, we have obtained a non-linear regression formula that can be used to estimate the value of Z (defined as $Z = \sigma/\sqrt{\mu}$, where σ and μ are the standard deviation and the mean of the unconstrained demand distribution) based on the size of a hotel. Given the size of a hotel, this regression formula provides a rough idea of the value of $\bar{Z}$ and the shape of the total demand distribution (i.e., Poisson versus normal). Without doubt, this knowledge of the unconstrained hotel transient demand distributions would be very useful to both academic research and hotel revenue management programmes such as demand forecast and outlier detections.

> *Q3. What conclusions can be drawn from this case study about the distributions of cancellations/no-shows percentage (by season, by day of the week, and by hotel type)?*

Answer. Our analysis indicates that the grand average cancellation/no-show rate (or percentage) of those 23 hotels under study is 37.54 per cent, and that the average cancellation/no-show rate for each hotel/season/day of the week combination can be as low as 0 or as high as 60 per cent, with airport/roadside hotels having the lowest and business-oriented downtown hotels and resort hotels the highest. We also found that the cancellation/no-show rates distributions have a much lower 'relative variability' calculated as the ratio of the standard deviation over the square root of the mean of the distribution and that the distribution of the cancellation/no-show rates is skewed to the right. Distributions such as the logistic distribution and the extreme-value distribution that can handle right skewness fit the data better than the normal distribution in general. Note that as the discrete Binomial distribution with parameter $0 < p < 0.50$ is also right skewed, it is also a good choice for fitting the number of cancellations/no-shows out of a fixed number of reservations. We do not see any significant patterns in cancellation rates among different days of the week over all seasons for those 23 hotels. Accurate information on the cancellation/no-show rates and forms of distributions is crucial to revenue management programmes such as computing the optimal over-booking levels and room allocations.

BOLTON WANDERERS: A CASE OF GOOD PRACTICE IN THE FOOTBALL INDUSTRY?

Gerald Barlow

Q1. With the demise of ITV Digital and the associated revenue to the FA football league clubs, the income derived direct from the club's activities has become increasingly important. How might these football clubs use revenue management to help manage these problems?

Answer. The clubs now have to manage their finance from income, which they directly manage and control; therefore any technique available which will help them to manage the levels and flows of income must be considered. Revenue or yield management can help them to initially realize the potential for better management of their match revenue, and then how to maximize the actual income. The areas where this technique can potentially be of benefit include:

- gate/match revenue
- match-day programme revenue
- match-day advertising revenue
- Individual special games, e.g., late rounds of cup competitions, revenues, etc.

Q2. The income generated by Premiership clubs like Bolton Wanders from gate income is such a small percentage of their total income that developing a revenue/ yield management programme will have no or little value. Discuss.

Answer. It may be true that the income generated by the television agreement with the Premier League is a major percentage of their daily income and therefore a very important factor; however all clubs in the Premier division must realize the risk of one season's poor performance and the overall cost were it to be relegated into the First Division. Secondly, even if the income from television is such that the internal club revenue generated via match-day events is only a small percentage of their total revenue, the television income is not within their actual control and can so easily be reduced or lost without the club being able to have any control over or effect on the decisions. Good revenue practice can never be a bad strategy; the effect of actually operating a good/successful revenue management strategy will only have a beneficial effect for the club. By developing a yield/revenue management strategy the club will be able to have more effect and control on its total income and potential profit. It will encourage good management practice, which will benefit the whole operation.

> *Q3. If Bolton Wanders were to decide to operate a yield/revenue management pro-gramme, in which areas of revenue do you consider they should employ revenue management techniques, and why?*

Answer. Answers should go through all the basic areas of potential revenue and discuss whether yield/revenue management can be applied and the potential benefits and risks. For example:

Match ticket sales:
– season tickets
– match-day tickets – spare ticket sales for poor game dates and times, where a large number of tickets may be available
– advertising – areas of specific advertising such as: programmes; specific game pro-grammes; specific game extra boundary advertising (e.g., cup games); additional kit advertising, e.g., shoulder chevrons, for specific TV games like cup ties
– special games

CASE 11

UNCONSTRAINING DEMAND DATA AT US AIRWAYS

Richard H. Zeni and Kenneth D. Lawrence

> *Q1. If there was little or no censoring in an airline's historical demand data, what would that indicate about the revenue management system, or the level of demand?*

Answer. The presence (or absence of) censoring in the data provides key information regarding historical passenger booking activity. If the portion of the data that is cen-sored is small, the revenue management practitioner might conclude that there is no problem to solve. However, this may be an indication of a problem with the revenue management system. While it is possible that demand was simply low during the period observed, it is also likely that the system is setting the booking limits too high. This may be the result of under-forecasting or a flaw in the optimization process. If the forecasts of demand for business fares were too low, too few seats would be protected for high fare passengers. The low fare classes would not be constrained but revenue would be lost. It is important to understand the mechanism that led to the amount of censoring in the data if the real goal is optimal revenue management controls.

> *Q2. Under what conditions would an airline decide not to unconstrain its demand data?*

Answer. Unconstraining censored data can be a costly process. The benefit of more accurate estimates of historical demand must be weighed against the cost of implementing an unconstraining process.

The benefit of better estimates of demand data will only be realized if there is sufficient demand to begin with. In periods of low demand, revenue management controls will tend to set booking limits very high (near aircraft capacity) and little censoring will occur. If the airline also expects future demand to be low, and there is little chance of filling the aircraft, the optimal controls would be to accept unlimited bookings at any fare. In this case there is little benefit in more accurate estimates of historical demand because both accurate and inaccurate estimates would likely result in the same set of revenue management controls.

If the censoring affects only a small portion of the data, the benefit of better forecasting might not exceed the implementation and maintenance costs of unconstraining the data. Rather than explicitly unconstraining the data, the airline might choose to ignore the fact that data is censored.

> *Q3. After US Airways implements its choice of unconstraining methods, how will the project team be able to measure its success?*

Answer. Gauging the performance of an unconstraining method may be as challenging as developing the process itself. While developing the methods, there is the issue of a lack of reliable test data to deal with. After the process is implemented, the lack of actual demand data presents a similar obstacle. Unfortunately, using simulation, as was done to address the test data issue, will not work for estimating actual demand values, since any simulation would necessarily employ one of the unconstraining methods. Instead, the project team will need to rely on forecast accuracy studies and an examination of the inventory controls. If the studies prior to the implementation of the unconstraining method indicated a negative bias in the forecast, the team will look for a change in the direction of the bias. While it might not turn positive, it should at least be less negative. The real test of the benefit of unconstraining is the improvement in the inventory controls that result from better forecasts. This can be difficult to measure as well, but revenue trends, load factors, and the ratio of business versus leisure traffic can all be used to obtain a general indication of the improvement realized.

CASE 12

REVENUE MANAGEMENT IN THE HEALTH CARE INDUSTRY

Warren Lieberman

> *Q1. If you were the revenue management expert meeting with the Director of MMC, how would you advise the Director on whether revenue management principles could be used to improve the medical center's profitability?*

Answer. There are a variety of ways that revenue management might improve MMC's profitability. The meeting with the Director of MMC could be used to explore a variety of issues, including:

- To what extent are there identifiable customer segments that are currently not using MMC's facilities? Could MMC take any actions to attract patients from these customer segments?
- To what extent are some of MMC's resources (other than doctors) fully utilized during certain days of the week or times of day? Are some patients unable to schedule appointments at the times they prefer? Do resource conflicts lead to undesirable wait times? To what extent do these situations lead to customer service problems or to patients obtaining primary care services elsewhere?
- When appointments are cancelled or patients do not show up for a scheduled appointment, to what extent is MMC able to use that time and associated resources (e.g., doctors, lab equipment, etc.) as profitably as planned? How frequently does this occur?
- What types of value-added services could MMC offer?

If the Director's answers to these questions indicates that MMC's performance suffers in any of these areas, or if the Director notes potential for improvement, these answers can be used as preliminary evidence that revenue management principles are applicable.

It is likely that the Director will not know the answers to some of these questions, or his knowledge will be limited. For example, the Director may be aware that patient cancellations can result in non-billable staff and equipment time. But the Director may not be aware of how frequently this occurs or fully understand the amount of revenue that is being lost. In such instances, there is an opportunity to advise the Director of how additional information can be obtained in these areas so quantitative estimates can be made of the revenue management opportunity.

> *Q2. If you believe revenue management could be beneficial for MMC, what actions would you recommend?*

Answer. Based on the information provided in the case study, four observations can be made:

1. Utilization of doctor time is very low on Tuesday and Thursday afternoons from 12 to 3 p.m. On Thursday afternoons, in particular, there is a high degree of slack in the system as three doctors are on duty and utilization is less than 40 per cent.
2. MMC sees relatively few patients who do not carry health insurance.
3. Seasonal workers and employees who have been recently hired by a large company appear to be an underserved customer segment.
4. Larger companies should be very interested in offering benefits that make their companies more attractive to prospective employees, especially when the cost of offering these benefits is low

As noted above, the seasonal and recently hired workforce of large companies provides a market segment that is underserved by MMC. These workers do not typically carry health insurance and are less likely to seek out primary health care because of the cost.

MMC has an opportunity to increase its revenues and profits if it can increase its penetration into this market without diluting the revenue stream it receives from its current patients. Also, because this appears to be a price sensitive market segment, if MMC chooses to attract this market segment to its facilities, it should do this in a way that does not reduce the level of service it provides to its current patients.

One way to do this is to develop a new product offering that allows larger companies the opportunity to enroll in a 'Corporate Select Hour Program' that allows employees of these companies to schedule appointments at a reduced rate when MMC consistently runs low utilization. This would appear to be on Tuesdays and Thursdays from 12 to 3 p.m. MMC could provide Select Hour ID cards for the company to issue to its employees. In return, the company would agree to provide its employees with information about MMC's facilities and capabilities and provide information about the Select Hour Program.

By participating in the Select Hour Program, a company would be able to offer health care benefits that other companies do not offer. For seasonal and part-time workers, this could be viewed as a desirable benefit and provide an added incentive to work for this company rather than somewhere else. MMC, the company, and the worker all benefit.

By limiting the hours during which appointments can be made for reduced fees, in combination with offering participation in the programme to only a few companies, MMC should be able to portray this as a differentiated service. Consequently, the fees it receives from insurance companies should not be affected. The number of companies that MMC allows to participate in the programme should be limited so that utilization during the Select Hour times does not increase to a level beyond which MMC can satisfactorily serve its patients.

MMC might need to experiment with the rates it offers to Select Hour patients. MMC has several options. Conservatively, MMC could initially set Select Hour rates to the same levels of payment it receives from insurance companies. This option ensures that the potential for revenue dilution is minimal. Revenue dilution would only occur if the Select Hour patients are those that would have used MMC's facilities even in the absence of the programme and paid the higher 'uninsured patient' rate.

If these rates are still too high to enable MMC to attract Select Hour patients, the rates could be reduced further. Before doing this, however, it would be prudent for MMC to conduct a revenue dilution analysis. Such an analysis might estimate the number of patients that MMC receives from the companies that participate in, or are candidates to participate in, the Select Hour Program. Sensitivity analyses could be conducted to estimate the potential for revenue dilution assuming varying percentages of these patient visits were to make appointments under the Select Hour Program.

Alternatively, MMC might initiate the programme with much lower promotional rates designed to ensure that employees who are eligible to receive Select Hour care would take advantage of the programme. The promotional rates might only be effective for a limited time. If MMC currently receives few or no patients from the Select Hour companies, this might be an attractive option that risks little or no revenue dilution. Most, if not all the revenue from Select Hour patients would be incremental revenue.

> *Q3. How would you estimate the potential benefits and risks of your recommendations? If possible, quantify your estimates.*

Answer. Answering the second question in different ways leads to alternative types of analyses for this question. For the Corporate Hour Select Program, a spreadsheet model could be designed to estimate the incremental revenue received from new patients. Assumptions will need to be made about length of time required for a patient's visit and the types of services required. Revenue dilution estimates might also be made, if the cost of service is less than the revenues currently received by MMC from insurance companies.

Providing the Director with a systematic ability to review the assumptions driving the benefits analysis would lead to further discussion of the potential risks and benefits of the revenue management opportunity.

CASE 13

REVENUE MANAGEMENT IN VISITOR ATTRACTIONS: A CASE STUDY OF THE ECOTECH CENTRE, SWAFFHAM, NORFOLK

Julian Hoseason

Q1. Identify and describe factors which might act as constraints upon revenue management at an attraction.

Answer. The purpose of this question is to consider the external and internal factors that impact upon revenue management strategies. The case study highlights the issues associated with an expansion of supply within the market-place where poor coordination in development of government-supported projects has altered the nature of the public, private and charity based attractions at national, regional and local levels.

The case study investigates the relationship of a specialist visitor attraction being located in a rural area and how the 'ideal market' may not be able to sustain the project without the seasonal influx of tourists to expand visitor numbers over a financial threshold. Seasonality presents a problem the management of the EcoTech tackled through special events and exhibitions or through site expansion. Publicly funded projects have been high profile and high risk where social cost and benefit pricing have ignored economic modelling.

In terms of marketing, EcoTech has a Unique Selling Point (USP), however location in a rural area of low density in population will impact upon visitor numbers and the marketing of the attraction. While the much-needed seasonal visitors boost the revenue of attractions, research has indicated day trips are an unplanned and almost spontaneous activity dependent upon weather conditions. Conventional marketing and promotions will be rendered almost ineffective within the day trip segment of the market. Marketers must monitor carefully and constantly review the effectiveness in responses to advertising and other media promotions.

Q2. Define capacity management and propose what strategies could be adopted to improve revenue management.

Answer. Capacity management is concerned with matching the capacity of the operational system with demand placed upon it. However, in the visitor attractions industry, this also includes the numbers of visitors and service provision. While visitor attractions need a critical mass or threshold to make the site viable, any additional growth in the sector will impact upon gate numbers and revenue management strategies. As the demand is relatively fixed and highly segmented, planning at national, regional and local levels will avoid product substitution and reduce intervening opportunities. Research indicates visitor attractions are relatively price inelastic, however if growth in supply expands capacity, the competition for a relatively fixed market segment will force visitor attractions managers and custodians to review revenue management techniques.

New strategies will have to focus more upon micro-market behaviour where visitor attraction managers must recognize more than ever before the need to understand tourist motivation and behaviour in terms of choices and demand for products. The tailoring of product and services to micro-markets will enable further differentiation and is dynamic. The consumer is constantly changing even though some behavioural patterns, for example the sensitivity of some segments to price, may be constant. Special rates for the over 55s accompanying grandchildren and friends or a single parent with friends is just one strategy. Restrictions by time or access to certain parts of the site may also be considered. The revenue management strategy adopted will be based upon individual site experience taking into account local market conditions and the focusing of targets set within different revenue areas.

> *Q3. Analyse market segmentation of attractions and devise a strategy for improving revenue from one major and one niche segment.*

Answer. The purpose of this question is for the reader to tackle just one area of revenue and then target a market segment, i.e., 'education' or the 'over 55s' and then delve deeper into the behaviour of niche markets within it. For example, the 'over 55s' can be segmented further by age, level of economic and physical activity within the market-place. There may be behavioural traits, which enable one niche to be proactively targeted because they have a higher disposable income or different interests within the visitor attraction.

CASE 14

TO TRUST OR NOT TO TRUST: VARIABLE PRICING AND THE CONSUMER

Una McMahon-Beattie, Adrian Palmer and Ian Yeoman

> *Q1. Why is the maintenance of trust particularly important with on-line transactions where the price charged to the consumer by a particular company may vary considerably over time?*

Answer. Trust is important in Internet enabled e-commerce. There are particular paradoxes associated with pricing and trust in Internet enabled commerce. If a price exceeds a referential threshold then consumers may conclude that the product or company no longer provides value for money. The company is perceived as taking advantage of the consumer. If a company raises the price of a product or service excessively relative to value, trust will be violated. Also, dynamic pricing allows Internet customers to receive up-to-date price information on demand from product databases. This information changes with time and by user. Dynamic pricing allows further customization, but also consumer confusion and if price exceeds perceived value, then trust can be undermined. This is particularly the case where a consumer uses the Internet to gather information for a flight. One of the most important criteria for decision is price. The price quoted for a particular flight then becomes a reference point for that consumer. There are cases where consumers have been quoted a price by a service provider or travel intermediary at a specific point in time and when consumers have returned to purchase that flight at a later date, the original price has increased or is no longer available. This is also an important consideration in the case of the 'low cost airlines'. Often advertised prices are not available. Consumers then feel as if they have been lied to and this is a very powerful and efficient way to undermine user trust in that particular site.

Q2. What strategies would you advise a revenue manager to adopt in order to maintain consumer trust whilst employing differential pricing?

Answer. Overall, managers should consider whether the benefits of maximizing revenue through variable pricing are sufficient to outweigh the operational costs and the undermining of trust which may be associated with it. Where variable pricing is based on consideration of costs and/or capacity constraints, managers should ensure that these reasons are made clear to consumers. Firms must explain their motives for differential pricing and the customer must find these motives acceptable. Managers should also consider suggesting ways to customers in which they could save money, e.g., by shifting a flight reservation to a quieter period. This will enhance the good reputation of a company and build consumer goodwill.

Q3. How would you avoid the appearance of punishing regular, loyal customers with higher prices?

Answer. In the Amazon case, loyal customers compared themselves to new Amazon buyers and in this instance perceived the practice of charging different prices for the same product as being unfair. They believed that they were entitled to special rewards. As such, companies should avoid the appearance of punishing regular customers for their loyalty with higher prices which are not matched by some other benefit which goes along with that loyalty.

CASE 15

CASES IN LEGAL ASPECTS

Michael Boella and Thriné Hely

Case Study 1: Bee's Hotel

Q1. What is the hotel's legal position?

The hotel's legal position depends upon whether or not it falls within the definition of a hotel. This is:

> *'hotel' means an establishment held out by the proprietor as offering, food, drink and if so required, sleeping accommodation, without special contract, to any traveller presenting himself who appears able and willing to pay a reasonable sum for the services and facilities and who is in a fit state to be received. (section 1(3), Hotel Proprietors Act 1956)*

Bee's Hotel falls within this definition.

Q2. Was it within its right to refuse the rooms?

No, the hotel in question falls within the definition of an hotel according to the 1956 Act. As a consequence it cannot 'pick and choose between travellers to whom they will offer their services' (Boella and Pannett, 1999). However, from a purely commercial point of view, the hotel would probably stick by its practice of holding rooms for guests booking for two nights.

Q3. What are the rights of the three travellers?

The three travellers have the right to 'such reasonable and proper accommodation ... as the innkeeper in fact possesses' (Hotel Proprietors Act 1956).

Q4. What measures, if any, can the travellers take against the hotel?

They could consider instituting 'common law' criminal proceedings. They could also institute civil proceedings for the difference between the cost of a more expensive hotel and the cost of rooms in Bee's Hotel.

Case Study 2: Mike Bee's Restaurant

Q. In each case what legal rights does Mike Bee's Restaurant have?

General answer to all three scenarios
In each of the three scenarios a contract has been entered into – even if no written evidence exists. However, proving a verbal or 'telephone' booking (evidence of a contract) can be very difficult.

Scenario 1
In this case, legally Mr Smith is liable for the lost surplus (i.e., the agreed price, less direct costs) for the four meals not taken. However, the restaurant has to consider the goodwill element and may just have to take the loss.

Scenario 2
In this case also, legally Mr Smith is liable for the lost surplus (i.e., the agreed price, less direct costs) for the ten meals not taken. The restaurant however is expected to mitigate the loss. This would involve, in this case, accepting any chance trade that might come by.

Scenario 3
Again, legally Mr Smith is liable for the lost surplus (i.e., the agreed price, less direct costs) for the ten meals not taken and as there is little likelihood of mitigating the loss the restaurant might consider issuing a bill for the lost surplus (failing payment, suing in the County court (small claims procedure) for breach of contract).

Case Study 3: Missed Flights

Scenario 1

Q1. Who was responsible for Mrs B missing her flight to Montpellier?

Mrs B's.

Q2. If the fault was the airline's, what compensation was Mrs B entitled to?

Under by the EC Denied Boarding Regulations 1991 Mrs B would be entitled to:

A minimum compensation as specified in the regulations
Reimbursement, without penalty, of the cost of the ticket
Re-routing to final destination at the earliest convenience
Re-routing at a later date at the passenger's convenience, either a full refund, or to
a ticket for the next suitable flight plus compensation as specified
A free telephone, fax or telex message to the destination
Meals and refreshments in reasonable relation to the waiting time
Hotel accommodation where necessary

*Q3. Was the airline responsible for additional costs incurred by Mr B in having to
drive from Montpellier to Toulouse?*

No, conditions of travel as available from airlines exclude all consequential liabilities.

Scenario 2

Q. Who was responsible for Mrs B missing her flight?

The fault was Mrs B's and she had no right to any compensation.

Scenario 3

1. Who was responsible for Mrs B missing her flight to Montpellier?

The airline – it had overbooked, as part of its capacity management procedures.

2. If the fault was the airline's, what compensation was Mrs B entitled to?

Under by the EC Denied Boarding Regulations 1991 Mrs B would be entitled to:

A minimum compensation as specified in the regulations
Reimbursement, without penalty, of the cost of the ticket
Re-routing to final destination at the earliest convenience
Re-routing at a later date at the passenger's convenience, either a full refund, or to
a ticket for the next suitable flight plus compensation as specified
A free telephone, fax or telex message to the destination
Meals and refreshments in reasonable relation to the waiting time
Hotel accommodation where necessary.

Case study 4: The Jones Family

*Q. What rights did the Jones family have and were AB Travel and Tours within their
rights to do what they had done?*

According to the small print of the contract AB Travel and Tours were entitled to do what they did and were not liable for the financial consequences to their passengers. It is however important for a company to bring to the attention of customers such 'small print' terms (Unfair Contract Terms Act 1977).

The reasons behind the action taken by AB Travel and Tours were that they were in a difficult position. There had been poor weather in the Balearics during the spring and unfortunately this had resulted in a lack of bookings for their departures later in the year to Palma. Despite heavy discounting they had been unable to fill all their flight and bed capacity. Many of the hotels were contracted on an allocation basis, upon which the tour operators pay more for the rooms but if they are not sold within a certain time before they are due to be used they can hand them back to the hoteliers with no cost to themselves. However, the flight seats were a different matter. They had two flights to Palma on the day in question and had made the decision to 'collapse' one of the flights and move the passengers over to the other flight. One consequence was that for some passengers the departure from Gatwick had been moved forward by five hours. This did not constitute a major change (which would have been a twelve hour difference in departure times), and therefore they were not liable to compensate the passengers. This was also reinforced by the amount of notice they had given their passengers. It was within the notice period allowed under the small print in their brochure and so the Jones had no way of gaining compensation to help them with their additional expenses.

The other aircraft would now be used on their Alicante route, all their Costa Blanca holidays had sold out and they were busy contracting extra beds to put together additional holidays for the Alicante gateway. It is by undertaking such yield management techniques that tour operators ensure their continuing success, particularly in a flat market such as AB Tours and Travel were experiencing this particular year.

Case Study 5: Fred Smith

Q. Did Fred have any legal rights to a reduction in price?

No, Fred had no such rights – he had entered into perfectly legally enforceable contract.

The airline had undertaken some rigorous yield management in as much as they had kept a continuous check on the way the flight was selling. Six months prior to the flight departure it seemed that sales were buoyant and they had taken the cheapest seats out of the system, which is why Fred had only been able to book the next cheapest seat. Although it had less restrictions on it than the very cheapest seats (which cannot be changed under any circumstances – use it or lose it), there had been a rapid downturn in North Atlantic traffic and the airline was under pressure to fill their seats. Eventually they bowed to the inevitable and released the cheapest seats back into the system much nearer the date of departure.

This is a recognized form of yield management. Teams of staff keep an eye on all flight/routes to ensure that they take advantage of times when the market is hardening (i.e., demand is increasing) by restricting or removing totally the cheap seats from the systems, and when the market softens releasing the cheaper seats back into the system. This does not just happen in economy class but can also take effect in Business and First Class, with deals and offers being made at the front of the aircraft to encourage sales. Such revenue management systems operate through the whole tourism and hospitality businesses.

CASE 16

UNDERSTANDING THE BID PRICE APPROACH TO REVENUE MANAGEMENT: A CASE OF THE REVENUE INN

Dietrich Chen and Michael Freimer

Q1. This chapter has described a revenue management problem for the Revenue Inn. Formulate and solve the revenue management problem in Microsoft Excel using the Solver function.

Answer. The purpose of this question is to provide the reader with some experience in making simple revenue management calculations. A solution to this question is provided in the accompanying printout of an EXCEL file. The tables labelled 'Demand Forecast, Corporate' and 'Demand Forecast, Leisure' contain the data from the problem. The tables labelled 'Decisions Variables, Corporate' and 'Decision Variables, Leisure' contain the cells whose values Solver will attempt to optimize. The cell labelled 'Overall Revenue' contains the objective function, which is calculated from the tables labelled 'Revenue, Corporate' and 'Revenue, Leisure'. Finally, the table labelled 'Capacity Constraints' is used by Solver to be sure that the property is not overfilled. The bid prices derived using EXCEL's SOLVER function are shown in the sensitivity report.

Q2. How do the bid prices change if we allow for overbooking? Do they tend to go up or down? Why?

Answer. The purpose of this question is to test the reader's understanding of the key parameters of the model. The solution requires the reader to correctly interpret changes in certain parameters and their impact on the solution.

Since the overbooking policy is an internal decision, it is reasonable to assume that the demand for hotel rooms stays the same regardless of whether we overbook or not. On the other hand, allowing overbooking artificially increases the capacity of the hotel. As a resource, rooms are less scarce and hence less valuable. Since the bid price specifies the amount an additional room in the hotel is worth, bid prices tend to decrease when we allow overbooking. Potentially more rate classes will be open.

Q3. Suppose the Revenue Inn has a sister property, the Management Inn, directly across the street. How can the linear programming model be extended to manage the rates for both properties simultaneously? What difficulties might you face in implementing such a model?

Answer. The purpose of this question is to test the reader's understanding of the model's assumptions and limitations when applied to a different environment.

To extend the basic linear programming technique to manage rates for the two properties simultaneously, add the capacities of both hotels, add the demand forecasts for arrivals in common rate classes, and retain the demand forecasts and rate structure for the remaining classes to construct a super-hotel. With the newly constructed information on capacity and demand, run the linear programme to determine bid prices for inventory control purposes.

This approach assumes customers will be indifferent between staying at the Revenue Inn and the Management Inn. Another limitation is that the general managers for each hotel may have separate profit and loss responsibilities, and each may seek to maximize their own property's revenue instead of maximizing the revenue for the combined entity. Other factors impeding an implementation of a joint inventory control mechanism may include: differences in cost of service, critical load-balancing for staffing, and incompatible reservation and system platforms. Furthermore, cannibalization may occur if pricing structures are not revisited in light of the room types and services offered in each hotel.

The Excel model:

	A	B	C	D	E	F	G
1	Demand Forecast, Corporate						
2	d(i,j,1)	2	3	4	5	6	7
3	1	1	2	3			
4	2		2	4	1		
5	3			2	3	1	
6	4				1	1	1
7	5					1	1
8	6						1
9	Demand Forecast, Leisure						
10	d(i,j,2)	2	3	4	5	6	7
11	1	1	2	3			
12	2		1	1	1		
13	3			1	1	1	
14	4				1	4	5
15	5					4	6
16	6						5
17							
18	Decision Variables, Corporate						
19	X(i,j,1)	2	3	4	5	6	7
20	1	1	2	3	0	0	0
21	2	0	0	1	1	0	0
22	3	0	0	0	3	1	0
23	4	0	0	0	1	1	1
24	5	0	0	0	0	1	1
25	6	0	0	0	0	0	1
26	Decision Variables, Leisure						
27	X(i,j,2)	2	3	4	5	6	7
28	1	1	2	1	0	0	0
29	2	0	0	0	0	0	0
30	3	0	0	0	0	0	0
31	4	0	0	0	0	0	2
32	5	0	0	0	0	0	3
33	6	0	0	0	0	0	2

	A	B	C	D	E	F	G	H
35			Revenue, Corporate					
36		2	3	4	5	6	7	Total
37	1	=B20*129	=C20*129*2	=D20*129*3				=SUM(B37:G37)
38	2		=C21*129	=D21*129*2	=E21*129*3			=SUM(B38:G38)
39	3			=D22*129	=E22*129*2	=F22*129*3		=SUM(B39:G39)
40	4				=E23*129	=F23*129*2	=G23*129*3	=SUM(B40:G40)
41	5					=F24*129	=G24*129*2	=SUM(B41:G41)
42	6						=G25*129	=SUM(B42:G42)
43			Revenue, Leisure					
44		2	3	4	5	6	7	Total
45	1	=B28*99	=C28*99*2	=D28*99*3				=SUM(B45:G45)
46	2		=C29*99	=D29*99*2	=E29*99*3			=SUM(B46:G46)
47	3			=D30*99	=E30*99*2	=F30*99*3		=SUM(B47:G47)
48	4				=E31*99	=F31*99*2	=G31*99*3	=SUM(B48:G48)
49	5					=F32*99	=G32*99*2	=SUM(B49:G49)
50	6						=G33*99	=SUM(B50:G50)
51								
52		Overall Revenue:	=SUM(H37:H50)					
53								
54		Capacity Constraints						
55	Day	# Guests in the Hotel	Hotel Capacity					
56	1	=SUM(B20,C20,B28,C28)	10					
57	2	=SUM(C20,D20,C21,E21,C28,D28,C29,E29)	10					
58	3	=SUM(D20,D21,E21,D22,F22,D28,D29,E29,D30,F30)	10					
59	4	=SUM(E21,E22,F22,E23,G23,E29,E30,F30,E31,G31)	10					
60	5	=SUM(F22,F23,G23,F24,F30,F31,G31,F32,G32)	10					
61	6	=SUM(G23,G24,G25,G31,G32,G33)	10					

The Solver window:

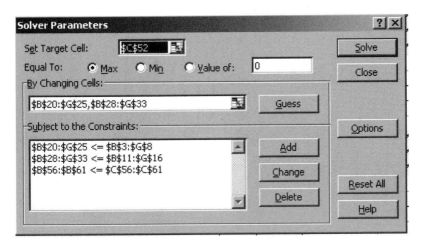

The sensitivity report:

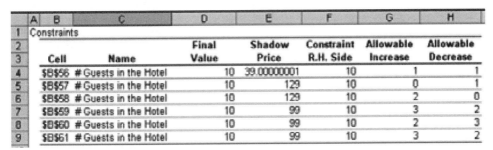

Cell	Name	Final Value	Shadow Price	Constraint R.H. Side	Allowable Increase	Allowable Decrease
Constraints						
B56	# Guests in the Hotel	10	39.00000001	10	1	1
B57	# Guests in the Hotel	10	129	10	0	1
B58	# Guests in the Hotel	10	129	10	2	0
B59	# Guests in the Hotel	10	99	10	3	2
B60	# Guests in the Hotel	10	99	10	2	3
B61	# Guests in the Hotel	10	99	10	3	2

Endnote

Simply put, revenue management (RM) is the science of applied microeconomics with regard to perishable products. It began in the airline industry and quickly grew to other travel-related industries and eventually took in new industries like broadcasting, energy and health care, to name a few. Perhaps the most significant note is not necessarily where it is currently being practised, but how the science of revenue management is expanding. That which started as a scientific approach to an allocation problem has evolved into a complex science that encompasses a systematic approach to dynamic pricing, price elasticity, marketing, inventory optimization and many other economic characteristics relating to the desire for companies to maximize profits. So the traditional saying of 'selling the right product to the right customer at the right time' should include the flexibilities around supply, and the importance of pricing and segmentation itself. The phrase could be extended to include 'at the right price, with the right supply, etc.' This could go on and on, so it may be best to circle back with the realization that RM is indeed the systematic approach to applied microeconomics with regard to perishable products. The element of timing and spoilage is that which distinguishes this focused practice.

So what is the importance of this definition? It illustrates that any approach to revenue management should appreciate the intricacies of the market where supply meets demand and that there is a much larger temporal picture that cannot be separated. Tackling this reality with a scientific and systematic approach to an inventory allocation problem alone will, at best, capitalize on a mere piece of the puzzle. Although these efforts may result in slight improvements, the real power will come from understanding and engaging the entire supply and demand equation. Within the airline industry the supply is relatively fixed and the traditions of pricing have a history of being more structured, which may have led to the simple approach of the first generations of 'yield management' systems. This was likely the reason for the early-simplified approach to RM as it infiltrated other industries like car rental, hotels, etc. However, within many of these 'new' industries, the nuances of supply flexibility and dynamic pricing capabilities are more dominant and thus highlight the inherent problem of omitting these variables from the RM equation. So although RM came from the airline industry, challenges faced within other industries are fueling the expansion of this science well beyond that which was known as 'yield management'.

There are two primary areas within revenue management that will likely spawn fascinating discoveries within the next few years. These areas deal with the power of pricing and the ability to coordinate and capitalize on the flexibility of supply. With a more holistic approach, RM will become *the* science that integrates advanced mathematics with sophisticated business modeling and the utilization of the latest in information technology. The companies that embark upon the challenges of RM may not get it all right, but will likely enjoy a competitive advantage derived from the journey itself.

Montgomery Blair
Program Manager, PROS Revenue Management